795

Daughter of Shanghai

TSAI CHIN

Daughter of Shanghai

周
采
芹

St. Martin's Press
New York

The Epilogue first appeared in the *Guardian* (London), 13 June 1989, and
is reproduced by permission of the *Guardian* newspaper.

Photo credits:
"Playing Suzie Wong with Gary Raymond" © Alec Murray.
"China doll day" © Lord Lichfield.

Library of Congress Cataloging-in-Publication Data

Tsai Chin
 Daughter of Shanghai / Tsai Chin.
  p. cm.
 ISBN 0-312-11258-0
 1. Tsai Chin. 2. Actors—Great Britain—Biography.
 I. Title.
 PN2598.T75A3 1994
 792'.028'092—dc20   94-18495
 [B]   CIP

First published in Great Britain by Chatto & Windus Limited

First Paperback Edition: December 1994
10 9 8 7 6 5 4 3 2 1

For my son, Bruce

To Maple, my niece

Author's Note

₽

The spelling of Chinese words in this book is in the new romanisation system called Pinyin. I have made a few exceptions, when an old established name becomes unrecognisable under the new system, or when a term is more familiar to the reader in its old form, notably Peking Opera instead of Beijing Opera. My stage name, Tsai Chin (instead of Caiqin, as it would be according to Pinyin), remains unchanged. For readers unfamiliar with the Pinyin system, it might be helpful to know that 'Q', which appears in many of the Chinese names in this book, is pronounced 'Ch'.

Acknowledgments

I thank Carmen Callil for commissioning me to write my autobiography, and Alison Samuel of Chatto & Windus for her patience and efficiency. My special thanks go to my editor Jason Goodwin. I am also grateful to Kenneth Murphy who, for two years, sent me newspaper cuttings from the *Guardian* information archive.

My publishers and I are grateful to Kathleen Tynan for permission to reproduce the reading list (pp. 136–7) which her late husband wrote for me; to the estate of Ronald Duncan and to Faber and Faber for permission to include the poem (pp. 112–13) from his collection, *The Solitudes*; and to Pan Ling and Joint Publishing Company (Hong Kong) Ltd, for permission to include her translation of the poem on p. 219.

Contents

ℰ

Part 1

East

Father as the young stage idol, in
Military role.

Mother with her older sister,
considered a great beauty.

Mother in her 1920s' party dress.

Mother, the Convent girl.

Prologue

Lilin waited with her little bundle until the sun had set beyond the Huangpu river before tip-toeing to the door of her room and peeking out. The jewelry in her bundle clanked with reassuring heaviness. In the gloom she made out the figure of her maid, who seemed to be beckoning the all clear.

Did she hesitate then? Sometimes I see her pause, perhaps casting a last look around the room that had been her home for fifteen of her twenty years, feeling a tremor of fear, of excitement. With a few steps she would leave her home forever. Would she have thought of her friend, whose elopement had ended so tragically? For now she must step out, and disobey her mother as no Chinese child should. How would her mother understand?

The go-between had seen her mother several times, as was the decent custom amongst Chinese families. Lilin's mother had shown her the photographs, mounted on card, each stiffly portraying a young man posed seriously and carefully, one hand resting upon the back of a rosewood chair, perhaps. Each unsmiling face was proposed as a prospective rich husband. With tears streaming down her face, scarcely looking at the portraits, Lilin would reject each one in turn. How could she have told her mother? It would break her heart.

The truth was that Lilin, had long been in the habit of attending the theatre with girl friends. Like girls of her class, they usually sat in the box. Above all else, they came to see the idol of the day, Qi Lintong. They were all madly in love. Other women might hurl diamond rings on stage in adoration – women whose pasts bore little scrutiny – but Lilin and her friends sat demurely, if excitedly, nursing their crushes. They would have been surprised to learn how easily their parents had guessed these secret thoughts – and outraged to be told that this passion for an actor was a passing phase. Willy nilly, no daughter of a good family married an actor.

Lilin was strong willed. A Western education had put romantic notions into her head, and she was determined to marry the man of her choice. Qi Lintong was her man.

Lilin had an advantage over her friends because her brother was a 'ticket friend', an amateur actor, who dabbled in the arts on the look out for pretty girls and wild parties like so many playboys and dilettantes. So he moved in theatrical circles and, on less promising nights, he would take his sister along, and she, in turn, had found ways of meeting Qi Lintong.

Lilin stepped quickly out of the room and pulled the door shut behind her. With careful steps she reached the end of the corridor and turned into the courtyard. The maid melted into the darkness. Beyond the front gate lay the city of Shanghai, and there Qi Lintong would be waiting.

There was a peculiar surprise for her at the front gate. Scarcely had she opened it than her mother darted from the shadows clutching, of all things, a feather duster. As the blows rained down upon her, Lilin broke into a run, feeling delirium and a strange happiness well up inside her as she raced towards her waiting lover.

As she cleared the gate she looked back for the last time and saw her mother sprawled on the ground – unable to give chase on her tiny bound feet, she had tripped and fallen. This time Lilin certainly hesitated. Filial duty and love for her widowed mother were strong, but then she turned her head, and ran on.

What was Lilin doing that night in 1928? Now I think that she was acting for a new generation of Chinese who had grown out of the collapse of 4000 years of empire in 1911, when China became a republic, and that her own rebellion was part of the rebellion of that extraordinary age.

My mother could run fast because her feet were not bound like her own mother's. For centuries, Chinese girls had entered the excruciating period of binding and rebinding, deliberate crippling, to produce the tiny 'lily feet' that men admired. Nor had she run off with a respectable man, as old China understood respectability. Ten years older than she, Qi Lintong already had a wife. Under normal circumstances, of course, in those days that hardly prevented a man from taking a concubine if he so wished: but Lilin was a respectable girl from a privileged background with an expensive education behind her. Theirs was to be a twentieth-century romance.

Beyond all this there was that final blot, that inescapable evidence of her lover's character: fecklessness and degeneracy. Qi Lintong was an actor.

Since ancient times actors have been universally regarded with peculiar suspicion. The power of their magic to conjure up extreme emotions in their audience made people associate them with both the sacred and profane; they were worshipped as idols or treated as toys according to the whim of the authorities and the people.

The hierarchy that controlled old China was based upon Confucian notions of duty and responsibility. The Emperor, Son of Heaven, looked to the gods for his mandate to govern, as scholars and officials in imperial service looked to the court for their privileges. Society was divided into different grades, with proportionate responsibilities and privileges. Merchants and traders held a low place. And one group, whose duties and privileges were non existent, fell off the register altogether.

Ever since their patron saint, the Tang Emperor Ming Huang, had supported a company of entertainers, actors had been euphemistically known as 'Children of the Pear Garden'. In practice they were seen as members of the 'Amusement Population', '*le hu*', which included the very dregs of society. These people lived beyond the pale. Amongst them would be found the swarms of beggars that infested every city, ruffians, pimps and prostitutes, vagabonds all. Some made a living as pedlars or jugglers, maybe as acrobats or fire-eaters. Some, to be sure, had a talent for better things, and reached the stage. As in the West, these rogues and vagabonds could not be buried in sacred ground. So in China they were the only class of people barred from taking the civil service examination, which allowed successful candidates to attain the position of an official, the ladder to all honours and privileges. The greatest actor in the land had no illusions. For all the acclaim of his public, he was only a lucky vagabond, one who had worked his way to the top of the Amusement Folk.

Such a one was Qi Lintong. Such was the world that Lilin had chosen to join. It was a wildly improbable union.

1

Children of the Pear Garden

ළ

My father's real name was Zhou Xinfang. He was born near the city of Ningpo in Zhejiang province on the east coast of China in 1895, during the last days of the Dowager Empress Ci Xi's reign. A formidable woman who had risen from concubine to empress, she had controlled the destiny of her country for over fifty years, presiding over the most humiliating episodes for the Chinese in living memory. Xinfang was five when the Boxer Rebellion against foreigners was crushed. Eight foreign armies marched on Chinese soil. Once again, China was forced to pay indemnities, to forfeit more territory. The deep shame felt by a proud nation could not but impress itself upon the mind of an intelligent child: for within two years, Xinfang would become the family breadwinner.

Of all forms of entertainment available in nineteenth-century China, Peking Opera was the most popular, appreciated by all strata of society. The actors came mainly from two sorts of family. There were those whose parents were actors, and who passed down the traditions to their children. And there were many whose families were outside the profession, driven perhaps from the countryside through famine or war. Such families would walk for days to the city and for some bushels of rice, or a string of cash, hand over their children for training at a *ke-ban*, or drama school. The children, seldom more than seven years old, would be indentured to the institution until such time as they had earned enough to redeem their contract. Many, of course, were rejected.

The apprentice led a spartan life. Straw was put down in a long room for about eighty children to sleep on; meals were frugal. Their long hard day began at 5 a.m. every day of the week for seven years. Discipline was absolute. The teachers, veteran actors themselves, forced their students to endure extreme physical pain and to work beyond the point of exhaustion. Since female roles were played by men, boys destined to work as female impersonators would learn how to mimic walking on bound feet by standing on points on the top of an upended brick for the time it took a joss stick to burn away. Eyes are the most important feature of any actor, and Peking Opera demands that they project enormous energy and power. To train them to open wide at all times on stage required students to prop them open with half a matchstick. In class, if one student made a mistake, all would be punished.

At the same time they began learning plays off by heart, receiving them orally from the teachers, who were mostly illiterate. As if this were not enough to occupy their day, they would be required to help out backstage during the frequent public performances. Drama schools supported themselves by producing plays with well known professional actors.

Talent and dedication apart, an actor's survival depended on an iron constitution.

These children, when all is said and done, were the lucky ones. Slavery was common. What they lost in family warmth was compensated for by the camaraderie with their fellow students. For a child with the right aptitude, turning somersaults was surely more fun than back-breaking farm labour. Above all, they could take pride in what they did. Theirs was a profession that could yield untold artistic satisfaction for all and put fame and fortune within the reach of a few.

Jing Xi, or 'capital drama', known in the West as Peking Opera, was neither indigenous to Peking, nor had it ever been purely operatic in the Western sense. A relatively new genre compared with China's long theatrical history, it evolved out of the numerous regional music dramas about two hundred years ago. As its artistic prestige grew, it took the word 'capital' into its name and came to be considered China's national theatre.

While singing is of primary importance, other elements of the performing arts play a vital part in its presentation. Peking Opera uses arias, mime, dance, comic turns and gymnastics to enhance the plot, be it sad or funny. Chinese plays are divided not into comedy and tragedy, but civilian or military. Little scenery is used. It is a supreme form of total theatre where the burden and the glory of creating illusions on stage rest solely on the actors.

The actor trains in four basic crafts: singing, recitation, combat and stylised movement. Thereafter he specialises in one of the four role categories, *sheng, dan, jing* and *chou* – male, female, rough male and comic. Each role has its own set of conventions of voice, movement, make-up and costumes. These types are subdivided according to age, character and whether he is a civilian or a warrior.

Young Zhou Xinfang's career did not follow the ordinary pattern. He was a child prodigy. His ancestors had been respected literati, but the family had become impoverished by the time his father, Zhou Weitang, had reached his teens and decided to become an actor. Although he enjoyed moderate success he was nevertheless banished from his clan. When Xinfang was six years old, his father took him to a good teacher to learn *lao sheng* plays – 'old man', the leading man in Peking Opera, usually a refined civilian in the prime of his life or older, often noble and heroic in character. The child advanced quickly. Within a year he had mastered eight plays and in 1902 he was put on stage to play child parts in Hangzhou, the Lake City of Zhejiang, an important artistic centre. He was an instant success.

It was here that he earned his stage name, Qi Lintong, meaning 'seven-year-old wonder boy'. Later a poster mistook these characters for their homophone, and billed him as 'The Unicorn Boy'. Chinese unicorns are magnificent proud creatures, half lion, half dragon, plunging through Chinese myth to herald the coming of a sage. Qi Lintong was to be the unicorn.

Now, at only eleven, he began to play *lao sheng* roles with Tan Xinpei, the 'Great King of Theatre'. Tan taught him the secrets of his art because he was astounded by the boy's intuitive ability to play mature roles, and Qi Lintong's success was assured. At thirteen he became artist in residence at the country's highest *ke-ban*, in Beijing; there he mastered another type of role, that of the warrior.

When the Empress died, a nation cheered. The reign of China's last emperor, the child Pu Yi, was short. A republic was declared in 1911. But new forms and brave words were puny weapons with which to conquer China's many chronic problems. Xingfang, having trodden the boards for a decade, was a knowing youth of seventeen, fast making a name for himself in the provinces as well as in the capital, Beijing. The country was by now fragmented by powerful warlords who vied with one another to carve out fiefs with the backing of their huge armies, causing much suffering to the people caught in between. It was during his tours across the country that Xinfang began to write Peking Operas with a social content, a new development in traditional theatre – and one which would give him much trouble with the authorities later.

In 1913, he took Shanghai by storm, electrifying his audience with his forceful delivery. His stage presence was considered magnificent – even his back, they said, was expressive. They called him *hong*, red-hot. He had arrived.

Shanghai was not just another city. For an actor seeking national recognition it was the only place to be, the largest city in China, one of the biggest in the world. It contained the International Settlement, established after the Boxer Rebellion, which operated beyond the jurisdiction of whatever Chinese government held power at the time, and where foreign writ ran. The British were top dog. They deserved to be, for, backed by their gunboats, they had built Shanghai up from a fishing village on a mudbank by the Huangpu river to the greatest Asian entrepot. With them had come French and Americans, other Europeans, and also the Japanese, who had fought their way into the club of 'civilised nations' by defeating the Russians at sea in 1905.

At the bottom, but not till some years later, of course, came the White Russians with long titles and empty purses, and Jewish refugees from Nazi Germany. And always there were the descendants of the Portuguese traders who had once dominated the European trade in Asia, but the colonial aristocrats of the twentieth century looked down on these people because they were poor and had to work for the natives. The white man lost face. Collectively, though, they could all look down on the Chinese. And the Chinese merely despised them all, foreign devils and hairy barbarians!

For those who could afford it, Shanghai was an earthly paradise. Anything was available for money, any luxury, any vice. Here was the longest bar in the world, the most risqué nightclub. A boutique in Nanking Road sold only pink and blue baby bonnets. There were skyscrapers, grand hotels like the one where Noël Coward wrote *Private Lives* in just three days, and fabulous restaurants offering every cuisine, exclusive clubs along the Bund, the latest movies from Hollywood and classical concerts. Opium was plentiful, and girls or boys were cheap, from willowy native girls with flawless skins to voluptuous White Russians who claimed Romanov pedigrees and traded their bodies for a square meal. In the Avenue Edouard II in the French Concession, a sin palace called the Great World catered to the indigenous population. Here were theatres, restaurants and private rooms, gambling rooms for majong, massage parlours, ice-cream parlours, photographers, barbers – an amusement centre serving every male appetite. In its corridors of vice, teeming with pleasure seekers, gangsters paraded their sing-song girls and weedy pimps lured artless but eager monks into carnal knowledge.

This is how Shanghai was to be remembered in later years: as a sunburst of decadence and of dancing to a wild tune that was too fast to last. But there was more to Shanghai than this, something in its spirit that could never disappear and which made it the most exciting city in the world. It was a city of fabulous energy and endeavour. The Shanghainese were citywise like New Yorkers, chic as Parisians and had the lively humour of Cockneys. Their critics called them city slickers, snobs and cynics. But they were irrepressible, imaginative, quick on the uptake and willing to take risks. They provided China with her élite industrialists, scientists and artists, born out of the extraordinary ferment of the city. But at the same time Shanghai produced terrible forms of urban poverty, and became a seedbed for unrest, a sanctuary for revolutionaries.

For the next eight years Zhou Xinfang based himself in Shanghai as artistic director at the Dan Gui theatre, where he wrote, directed and performed in over sixty plays. He was one of the first actor-managers to employ actresses to play female roles. He made his first film. His records made the sort of impact in China in the twenties that the Beatles would make worldwide in the sixties. He had married his first wife and had three children.

On the face of it, his career looked like an actor's dream come true. In reality it was filled with the stuff of an actor's nightmare. Before he was twenty his voice fell. It was rumoured at the time, and it has entered the fabric of theatrical mythology, that a jealous actor was to blame. Xinfang, it was said, had been poisoned, and the poison worked upon his voice until he could no longer reach the high notes in which Peking Opera exults. But poison would have been unnecessary. Voices were not trained scientifically and, strained beyond endurance, they fell. It happened often enough, as it happened to actors in the neo-classical theatre straining to declaim Racine's alexandrines. But it spelled ruin for the *lao sheng*, who was judged on his voice above all else. Actors are universally dispensable, and Xinfang should have been reduced to eking out a living as a supernumery, to be heard no more.

Eventually he would regain his voice, but it was during this dangerous period that he survived by making the best use of his other attributes and experience. This would lead him to re-address the direction of his art altogether.

For Xinfang was not satisfied with his personal success as an actor. He had begun to feel that the theatre had a function to perform in shaping the country's future. It was the May Fourth movement that had really shaped Xinfang's political attitudes, as it shaped the attitude of progressive youth for generations to come.

During the First World War the Allies had pulled China into the war against Germany, and she contributed so much by way of labour and material that at its successful conclusion China hoped for an improvement in her world status. To their horror, the Chinese delegation at the Versailles Conference of 1919 learned that the Allies had secretly transferred confiscated German territories to the Westerner's ally, Japan: the northern border was left wide open to Japanese invasion.

When the news of this unequal treaty reached China, young Chinese found their voice and reacted with an unprecedented display of mass solidarity. Teaching at the time in China, the American philosopher John Dewey wrote: 'We are witnessing the birth of a nation.' On 4th May 1919 tens of thousands of teenage students demonstrated around the country; by June they had found support from striking factory workers and had shamed the merchants and shopkeepers into joining in. Citizens began a boycott of Japanese goods. Shanghai led the way: even prostitutes and beggars, criminals and godfathers, joined the strike – giving the victims of crime a much appreciated breathing space! Discipline was extraordinary: not a single incident of violence was reported as the crowds marched and demonstrated. This was the first time that women participated en masse. When they were up against authorities forbidding them to put up posters, they not only turned the other cheek but did so with a disarming sense of humour, best illustrated by this jingle from the period:

> Stripping and sticking
> You strip, I stick
> You do the stripping
> I do the sticking
> Just you strip
> I'll just stick
> If again you strip
> Then again I'll stick
> If you really must strip
> Then I really must stick
> You stick to your stripping
> And I'll stick to my sticking
> One bill, two bills, strip them off all
> Thousands and ten thousands I'll stick
> up on every wall.

This disillusionment with the West sowed the seeds for the Chinese to search for other solutions to save their country. Within two years a handful of men, Mao Zedong included, formed a secret society – the Communist Party. As for Zhou Xinfang, he began to reform Peking Opera.

Theatre had become part of the fabric of everyday Chinese life: it was there that for centuries the illiterate populace learned about their history and their heritage. And so it was there that Xinfang hoped to influence them to change their age-old feudal attitudes. The arts in general had dulled through repetition. Peking Opera, though still the most vital art form, was also in danger of falling victim to its own conventions. The plays extolled Confucian values, far removed from the urgent needs of the new China as it groped for a place in the world. All was passive; curiosity was suppressed. Actors paraded their virtuosity at the expense of dramatic content. To be *mei*, beautiful, was the criterion. And it was perfectly normal for them to approach their roles without having to understand the characters portrayed, in what was called *qian ren yi mian*, playing a thousand characters with one expression. Clearly form had overwhelmed content.

Xinfang set about overhauling the monolith of opera tradition, out-raging the purists in the conservative north. Those in Beijing who could not understand his work called it *hai pai*, Shanghai style, a derogatory term. For he was a fierce opponent of slavish imitation. Contrary to general practice, he believed that actors must communicate with each other on stage to breathe life into each performance. Technical brilliance, he insisted, must be charged with an emotional realism beneath the ritual grandeur, and this can only be achieved by observing real life. In the *Fisherman's Revenge*, an old play in the classical repertoire, he prepared for the title role by watching real fishermen casting their nets in the Huangpu river – a work procedure unheard of at the time. Whether or not he was aware of Stanislavski (about to be translated into Chinese by a close friend) he recognised the importance of each role in achieving unity of effect, and was not above taking a lesser part to illustrate his point.

In singing, perhaps because of the temporary handicap with his voice, he returned to the source of Peking Opera, the regional dramas and folklore traditions, finding music to suit his voice and discovering innovative possibilities for vocal expression. For that he needed his profound knowledge of Chinese music, from which he developed his own unique style of singing which connected stylisation with personal emotional truth, impossible to imitate – though many tried. The effect on his audience was not unlike that of Maria Callas' magnetism over her opera fans in the West. Before Xinfang, going to the opera was called *ting xi*, listening to a play; after him, the term changed to *kan xi*, watching a play.

He sought for more than just aesthetic appreciation from his audience. He used anti-heroes and his themes were relevant to his time, provoking the audience to feel and think. Women in his plays were sympathetically treated. With his rare ability to play warrior roles as well as civilian roles he would invest the warrior's quality of vitality into the normally passive *lao sheng*, and conversely borrow the latter's sensitivity in his portrayals of fighting men. This became the hallmark of his acting. By shifting the emphasis away from the archetypal towards more subtle and complex characterisation, while giving stature to men of modest proportions, he took the category of *lao sheng* roles beyond the limits prescribed.

Zhou Xinfang's willingness to challenge the status quo and to take risks was unique. Peking Opera actors were a feudal and conservative group. At first, perhaps, he innovated because he was literate where most of his colleagues were not, so that he was able to open himself to the new ideas erupting throughout the artistic world. For the early twenties were anarchistic and intoxicating years for Chinese artists, in parallel with what was taking place in Europe. The written language had been reformed, and for the first time it was possible to communicate in the vernacular, free from the rigidities of classical Chinese. This in itself released an explosion of creative energy. Women writers began to be published in profusion for the first time and translations of foreign works became readily available. A new form of theatre started to emerge, consisting solely of dialogue in the Western model, and known as the 'Spoken Drama'. It provided reformers with an ideal platform for social reform, addressing the audience directly. Ibsen was their inspiration. The flourishing Chinese film industry began to explore the position of women with dignity and sympathy.

So Xinfang found his work supported by many of those around him. Often they were students returning from abroad, more educated than himself. Socially conscious, they were a new breed in the theatre, and these young people would work closely with Xinfang – notably Ou Yang Yuqian, the father of 'Spoken Drama', and the brilliant Tian Han, a giant in the literary world.

That Xinfang succeeded in his reform despite fierce controversy was thanks largely to his popularity with his audience, which gave him the clout to have complete artistic control. But above all, the thorough grounding of his training had given him a profound knowledge of his art form that allowed him to experiment without destroying the aesthetic principles of traditional theatre.

In his early thirties, when he met Lilin, the woman who was to be my mother, the spirit of his reforms had begun to influence a whole era of film, theatre, novels and painting, now known as the Qi (Chi) School, after his stage name.

Lilin's story was quite different.

Of Lilin's grandfather I know little, except that he was not Chinese but a Scot by the name of Ross. At one time he may have worked in the customs office in Shanghai, which was controlled by the British. Or he might have been a merchant, dealing perhaps with tea or even opium. He apparently made himself a small fortune and to avoid the taxman he went into the interior beyond the reach of British jurisdiction. There he went shamelessly native and took a Chinese wife, presumably a common-law wife. They had a son, and then a daughter whose feet they bound according to the feudal custom of the time.

I imagine how traumatic it must have been for my grandmother, the little half-Chinese girl amongst a race so vain about the purity of their ancestral bloodlines. As her feet were tortured into tiny stumps her mother, suppressing her pity for her child, would chide her: 'Every little girl must go through this to get a husband,' adding, 'Especially you, you must be more Chinese, so endure.' Like her predecessors, the child endured, and in time she became betrothed. Because of her stigma, her parents were happy to settle for a suitor much older than she.

The evening after her marriage ceremony I picture my grandmother alone in the bedchamber with the man who was now her husband. He took off the red embroidered veil that had covered her head throughout the ritual, and they laid eyes upon one another for the first time. Her beauty undoubtedly impressed him and made it easier for him to love her. His kindness and good humour made her willing to respond. Each considered themselves fortunate and they warmed to each other 'like the cold water in the kettle coming to the boil', an apt saying to describe a successful and loving arranged marriage between strangers. Perhaps for the first time in her life, she felt accepted.

Her husband, Qiu Yangshan, was a wealthy tea merchant with a country seat in Shaoxing in the province of Zhejiang. They had three children, and they named the third Lilin, which means 'Beautiful Gem'.

When Lilin was five years old, her father died. The family moved to Shanghai, where the widow could be sure of company and chaperones, and where Lilin could attend a good school. Though my grandmother had been brought up in strictly traditional ways she wanted Lilin to have a good education. It was a shrewd recognition that the times were changing and the world would be different for the new generation. Particularly for the women, who entered the twentieth century in open rebellion for the first time in their history, joining anti-arranged marriage and anti-footbinding movements in their thousands. Their successful revolution had made it possible for girls like Lilin to receive an education equal to a boy's. Half-foreign herself, my grandmother sent her daughter to a convent school where she would learn to speak fluent English, a real advantage in cosmopolitan Shanghai.

Lilin grew up petted and wilful, permitted a degree of freedom unthinkable twenty years before. With her sophisticated brother she enjoyed some of the delights that Shanghai could offer – the theatre and the movies, the exotic Western restaurants and the parties thrown by the wealthy compradores and taipans of the city. Dressed in the latest fashion with her hair curled and her feet shod in high heels she would be off to the races during the day and tripping the light fantastic by night. She learned to be at ease anywhere, to switch between Chinese and English manners, food and language effortlessly. She was beautiful, enormously vivacious, very self-possessed, and eagerly pursued.

And one night she bundled up her jewelry and fled.

ᴓ

The family was profoundly shocked, though whether they were more concerned for Lilin or for their own reputation is hard to say. They made public gestures of fury and repugnance. Advertisements were placed in the papers announcing Lilin's disinheritance. She kept the cuttings all her life. An outraged brother made loud threats to take out a contract on Xinfang. The lovers fled to the provinces hoping that the family's hysteria would die down. It was the end of 1928.

Only a year before, Xinfang's eight-year tenure at the Dan Gui theatre ended abruptly when the theatre closed amidst political upheaval in Shanghai. Generalissimo Chiang Kai Chek took control of the city at the head of a broad political alliance, and immediately turned upon his left-wing allies, all but destroying the urban base of the young Communist Party. Thereafter, Mao Zedong was forced to redefine the Soviet model of proletarian revolution by concentrating upon the peasant masses instead. With Lilin, Xinfang was free to tour the provinces once more.

Those early days were hard for Lilin, a princess amongst the vagabonds, left alone in godforsaken hotel rooms waiting for her lover to return from his performance. She was not at all confident of her position in her lover's world. Xinfang, after all, had a certain reputation. He neither smoked nor drank, but he was no stranger to the amoral world of showbusiness where women were always available, particularly for a handsome and introverted popular idol. Lilin knew that he was a dark horse, and suspected that his friends considered her a clever catch who would not last long. But she had crossed her Rubicon and there was no turning back. Had the thought even entered her head, whom could she have turned to?

When they eventually returned to Shanghai, her relatives and old friends shunned her, and there was malicious gossip in the papers. But those who may have dismissed her as a fallen woman, permanently ruined, underestimated the love of Xinfang and Lilin for each other and her strength and determination to make the union work.

Lilin could not mope for long. She had a tough, practical streak in her. One evening she followed Xinfang to the theatre; soon it became a habit, and much later it became a necessity, after she had taken over his business affairs. She was shocked by the way thespians dealt with their financial problems. They seemed to live on pawn tickets. Xinfang was attracting more than capacity audiences, yet he had little to show for his success. Since actors owned their own costumes, Xinfang with other actors, would hock the costumes not needed for the day's performance. It made no sense to Lilin, given that he had to support his other family and his parents. She soon learned that despite an established guild, actors lived and worked in the shadow of powerful syndicates where physical intimidation and financial exploitation went hand in hand. Claques could always be organised to ruin a performance, should an actor refuse to toe the line. This was Shanghai, 'Sin City', and beneath the glamour and the nominal authority of the Western concessionaries, gangsters had the city sewn up.

Lilin had yet to learn how powerful the syndicates could be.

Like most artists Xinfang had no head for business, but Lilin did and she was determined. 'Tell them that you not only want a respectable salary, but you also want a percentage of the house receipts – otherwise you don't perform,' she instructed him. Her superior station in life had conditioned her to act with more than a touch of arrogance, if not foolhardiness. She reckoned that they could hardly kill their golden goose. But the answer was short. Xinfang was warned in no uncertain terms to keep his woman out of men's affairs, and to consider it unsafe for her to set foot in the theatre ever again. That evening, her heart pounding, she deliberately showed up at the theatre as usual. There were ugly faces, but no consequences. Xinfang's pay remained as before.

Lilin bore him two daughters, who were called Susan and Cecilia. Then Xinfang wrote a play that offended the syndicate. The play was banned and once again the couple had to flee from a contract out on Xinfang – not a threat now but a serious promise from the syndicates. This time there were the two girls to consider – and another child on the way. Lilin arranged for flight as best she could. Susan, a proud and serious four-year-old, was old enough not to be a problem, but little Cecilia was going to be a trial. A close friend offered to look after the toddler in Shanghai while they were gone.

Lilin hesitated for only a moment. The road ahead, after all, was uncertain, and life on tour meant constant travelling on weary journeys. The friend had no children of her own and could provide the little two-year-old with love and care. Besides, if Cecilia stayed, it meant, somehow, that the family would be coming back.

But it was a terrible decision. From that time on Cecilia's little mind grasped one thing: that her mother had abandoned her. From the day they were reunited, the two would never be at peace with one another.

They fled, as usual, to the north, where Xinfang was much in demand. Only this time there was a war on. The Japanese had occupied Manchuria in north east China in 1932; now they were beginning their encroachments towards the south. Lilin carried a pistol with her everywhere, an idea she took from the detective novels she constantly devoured. She carried, too, the casket of jewels she had taken with her on her elopement – for her children, in case anything befell their father. She had not used her only financial asset, despite their money problems, for she felt strongly the need to accord her man the dignity of providing for them.

And then Lilin took to childbed for a third time.

2

Born in a Trunk

I was born in a trunk, the offspring of an actor on tour like the girl in the Judy Garland song. Only I was born in Tianjin, a seaside resort about seventy miles south east of Beijing. Mother took one look and said to herself: Another girl? The third one! What will people think? – and henceforth decided to love me the most amongst all her children. She told me so later. Knowing Mother, she probably told all her children the same thing.

Before I was a few months old I had travelled in every imaginable conveyance – streetcar, train and boat, motorcar and rickshaw. Perhaps this would explain my wanderlust. Throughout my life I was to have an insatiable desire to rove, first through the close domains of childhood, later all over the world.

My earliest memory was of a separation. I recall the sense of being a part of someone gliding slowly away from a fixed point. Presumably I was being carried by Mother on board a boat slipping from the quay. And it seems that I was destined to repeat this first idea of separation by moving from the fixed point – the land from which I sprang.

Over my head, negotiations proceeded with the gentlemen of the underworld to smooth our return to Shanghai. With their newborn baby and the spreading war in the north, both Mother and Father were eager to return and the syndicate, as Mother had once predicted, did not really want to kill the goose that laid the golden eggs. Her manner, though, had changed from those early days. It was a shrewder, wiser woman who went to one of the Shanghai godfathers in private and kowtowed to him, knocking her forehead against the floor in a humiliating gesture of submission. She told Father only when the deed was done, so that face was saved; he, after all, had always refused to kowtow to them on principle, and he would have tried to dissuade his wife. The stratagem succeeded, and we returned to Shanghai.

Mother had been gone almost a year, and it was to be expected that Cecilia, who had been staying with friends of the family, would be a little shy at first. In fact, her reaction was strong. Mother's friend had become attached to the child, and refused to give her up; Cecilia was bewildered and unwilling to leave her 'home' to join a strange family, all the less recognisable and familiar for its new addition, me. Mother, as usual, succeeded in getting her way, but she had been shocked. The two friends never spoke to one another again, and between mother and daughter there would be an estrangement that widened with the years.

Father had regained his singing voice, but the theatrical revolution he had started made constant demands on his time, demands that would increase as China entered some of the most turbulent years of her history and his need to communicate through his art became more urgent. Mother had learned pragmatism since her early days, and she was well-placed now to take over the daily running of her husband's affairs. She went to work upon the godfathers more subtly than before and in time Xinfang did indeed receive his share of house receipts. Like Sarah Bernhardt, Father was paid in the only solid currency of the time: gold. By the time I was a little girl, they rented their own theatre, in which Father was actor-manager and Mother was in charge of front of house. Such steps were rare: an actor had become his own master, and fractured the ancient prejudice against his 'humble' trade. But the world of vagabonds began to be really respectable when Xinfang, the leader of his community, and Lilin, a woman of class and distinction, were finally married.

If Mother's elopement had been shocking, her marriage was at least unconventional. She scorned the idea of a hole-in-corner affair in favour of a public wedding with all the usual trimmings, flouting convention for the second time. One of her bridesmaids was a little friend of mine; I was not even invited! Indeed I was oblivious at the time of the fact that I had been born illegitimate. The event was held in one of Shanghai's most famous restaurants, and Mother coolly dressed in virginal white – a Western style, for red is the Chinese colour of marriage – with white wedding dress, white veil and white carnations. Father, as usual, was slightly ill at ease: he who so confidently played before thousands upon stage felt awkward at more intimate public gatherings, particularly amongst foreigners and their customs. The man whose grace and expressive sense of movement knew no rivals in the theatre remained forever clumsy with a knife and fork. On this day he wore a morning coat. 'As I was coming down the aisle,' Mother told me later, 'my eyes searched for your father but I couldn't see him. He was eating melon seeds pretending to be one of the guests.'

This wedding was her triumph. Xinfang's divorce from his first wife had taken years to come through; Mother had lived in sin and borne him several children already, weathering the malice of scandal sheets and the bitter silence of her family. Now, with blithe confidence, she received back all the people who had been unkind to her: the family who had disowned her and the friends who had snubbed her, and in a single stroke confounded her detractors. If Father was an actor, Mother had an intuitive understanding of grand gestures.

We already lived most fashionably in the elegant French Concession, which boasted Shanghai's most beautiful villas on the broad and leafy boulevards around Bubbling Well Road. These were the homes of taipans, wealthy Western merchants and businessmen, as well as their Chinese counterparts. Our house on Pushi Road (now Changle Road) was not so grand, though still comfortable by ordinary Chinese standards, part of a solid terraced row facing the road but back to back with an identical parallel terrace separated from us by narrow lanes. This type of estate, neither purely Western nor entirely Chinese, was quite typical of Shanghai.

In effect, our three-storey house was not so unlike a London town house. A double iron gate led from the street to a small roofless porch which gave directly onto the main, or 'guest' room, which was traditionally furnished, according to a pattern repeated in every Chinese 'guest' room. A high and narrow altar table faced the french windows and the front door, and sheltered a square table that seated eight at mealtimes. Four identical redwood chairs were backed against either side wall, separated by small square tables with marble tops. The impression was orderly, and formal. The french windows looked onto the skywell that separated ours from our neighbour's house.

At the foot of the stairs was a little boxroom called the tea room, where the servants prepared tea whenever guests called. Here, too, the male servants slept, but on the upper floors the space contained bathrooms for the family. There was a toilet under the staircase, and a kitchen beyond.

Facing the street above the guest room was a main room for the children, who also had the rooms above the kitchen on the first and second floor landing, looking onto the front of the terrace behind. We children slept with the women servants who looked after us and the rooms were filled with beds. When I pointed out how this made them look like hospital wards I was scolded for the inauspicious remark.

The third floor was my parents' domain, where they had a conventional Western bedroom suite in the dark wood that was fashionable then, ornately carved with fruits. Eventually the house sprouted a further floor to accommodate father's study beneath a flat concrete roof where we children often played. As we grew in prosperity and numbers, the decision was made to purchase the next door house, to give us a dining room connecting with the 'guest' room, and upstairs a luxury suite for my parents which could boast a private sitting room. The Western style of our furniture had become by then more pronounced. It was also rather more comfortable; Chinese redwood is the hardest wood there is. The only oddity of the doubled house was a great abundance of bathrooms, a particular luxury in China.

I dwell upon the arrangement of our house for this was our refuge and a whole childish universe, solid and understood. Beyond lay Shanghai itself, and the theatre – a dream-world, half sensed, half understood, that claimed our parents and made them fabulously exotic, made them over to a dream that still clings in images.

At the beginning of my life I saw my parents as two beautiful strangers, separated from me by their own mysterious existence. Working late and getting up at midday, they were never around at breakfast time. At night, long after I was asleep, they would return, and I might catch a glimpse, a few times, perhaps, between waking and dreaming, of them watching me, watching all their children sleep.

And earlier in the evening, when the servants had brought us to them to say goodnight before my parents left for work, my tactile experience of their proximity stimulated all my premature senses. Mother was soft and sparkling with her silk chiffon dresses, her jade in diamond jewel settings, and her scent. Father's face was hard, his kisses prickly. I was bothered but somewhat reassured.

Strangers when they projected themselves into our children's world, they seemed more familiar and comprehensible when I was with them in their 'natural' environment, where they worked. I was, after all, used to the theatre before I could walk. Backstage, tall actors with large painted faces passed me around like some live doll to receive their attention and affection. Father, concentrated and never talkative, was in his element, and somehow I understood this. At the front of house,

Mother dealt with Father's affairs with authority and precision. Young though I was, I got my first sense of what loving purpose meant.

Father gave everything to his work. Perhaps this was part of his tradition also, for the so-called 'Children of the Pear Garden', the actors, seemed to have a fierce pride all their own. Without social standing, their identity relied upon their profession alone. It was a near-fanatical article of faith. A veteran actor who once sat the wrong way on stage renounced his profession forever. The fact that he did it to cover up for another's mistake made no difference. The story of Gai Jiaotian, father's co-star, is legendary: audiences came to watch his breathtaking gymnastic feats, such as somersaulting from high up and landing perfectly balanced on one foot. One day he broke his leg. When he removed the plaster cast later he realised that the leg had been wrongly set, and his career was finished. 'What is to be done about it?' he demanded. He found a way. He broke his own leg again, deliberately, and had it reset. He was already in his forties, but he carried on an illustrious career until the Cultural Revolution when he died under torture, aged eighty-two.

When Father reappeared on stage he had metamorphosed into another being. When he played Kuan Yu, he was a god. Kuan Yu, a third-century hero who was deified as the god of war and peace, was every Chinese child's superhero. Father wore a spectacular embroidered costume suggesting a general in armour, with tall headgear and platform shoes. His face, painted red to denote a courageous but choleric temperament, made his eyes appear like two beams of penetrating light. Carrying a great operatic sword in one hand he entered the limelight shimmering with energy, awesome and magnificent. Along with his mastery of *lao sheng* roles, Father had become the greatest exponent of the Kuan Yu role, which possesses almost sacred significance in Chinese theatrical lore. The critics said he played the part like the god incarnate, with the same expression as Kuan Yu's effigies guarding many temple gates. For me, his child, it was also hard to see him as a mere mortal.

3

Christened Tombola Style

℘

So I recall those early years, when time and events fuse into memories of childhood. The house, the family and the seasons enveloped us. The Chinese pattern time in cycles of birth and death and the coming of each season, of rebirth and the coming of spring, when they celebrate the most important date on the Chinese calendar: New Year.

New Year occurs in February by the Western calendar, and it is the time when the rites of ancestor worship are performed. Tablets carved with the names of one's ancestors are stood on the altar table in the 'guest' room, and each member of the living family in turn kowtows to the watching spirits of the dead. Family lies at the heart of Chinese life, and is the basis of all Confucian relationships involving a hierarchy of duty and responsibility. The venerated spirits of the dead gather to watch over the progress of the family generation by generation, and their feelings must not be injured, nor their memories allowed to fade. Having said that, we skipped worship. Father was a progressive thinker and Mother was too Westernised.

But the celebration of family life still went ahead at New Year, and other parts of the ritual were observed. Preparations began at least a month before. The entire house was cleaned and swept to present a bright face to the coming year. As the shops would be closed for many days, meats were cured and chickens were slaughtered. Large crockery jars of marinated food of different subtle flavours would accumulate in the kitchen. Bad feelings had to be exorcised to avoid bad luck in the new year, so tradesmen's accounts were squared, and inauspicious words like 'death' or 'devil' were to be avoided in conversation. Naturally we children took it upon ourselves to dash into the kitchen and shout

out a sentence crammed with as many of these lethal words as possible, and then rush off again. The servants would shake their heads philosophically and mutter in their different country accents: what terrible children!

By now there were five children, and on New Year's Eve, the great family meal of the year would take place. A large round table was set in the 'guest' room, and two vases of pussywillows were placed on the altar table in place of the customary ancestral tablets. It was Father, oddly, who was responsible for the pussywillows: each year he and Cecilia would go out to buy them, and he would arrange them himself. Always, it seemed, just as we were about to begin our meal, everyone would notice that Father had forgotten to put up his paintings. Chinese only display their most treasured paintings on special occasions, in order not to take the appreciation of them for granted. As these paintings were in scrolls they had to be unrolled to be hung and Mother, who could not bear a speck of dust anywhere, particularly when the table was laid, would be most displeased. It was an odd ceremony, half traditionalised, half amusing: Father the absent-minded aesthete, Mother the house-proud organiser. Then the paintings would finally go up and the family would settle down happily to their meal.

Mother and Father sat together, surveying the little kingdom they had created and named. Father had chosen these names for us with careful thought.

Chinese names are not taken from a ready-made stock as they are in the West. They are usually made up of three characters, the first of which is invariably the surname. One other will often be a generation name and can be shared by all the children in a family or at least by those of the same sex. The third character is the personal name, and its choice can depend on the parents' fancy or aspirations: an ambitious merchant, for instance, might choose vulgar characters that symbolise wealth and good fortune.

Father chose his daughters' names from the Book of Poetry, China's most ancient book. Tsai, the generation name I share with my sisters, marries with my personal name, Chin, which means 'celery'. The two characters together form a literary allusion to school, and so to education, an ancient reference that has been obscured with time. At school I was nicknamed Celery, which I never minded, for celery is a nutritious plant with clear colours, neither masculine nor feminine.

My two brothers, both younger than I, were named on a different pattern. Ju-ao means 'proud chrysanthemum', the emperor of flowers –

never considered as feminine. Ying-hua means 'heroic and magnificent', and also 'Britain-China' – prophetic, as it turned out, for the
younger son would spend many years with me in England.

In the end we were not to use these names at home for in Shanghai at
that time it was considered smart to have Western names, as exotic as
any Lotus Blossom in the West. Mother was nothing if not fashionable.

One day, when I was still quite small, Mother excitedly summoned
her children. In her hand she held five little scrolls, one for each child.
We each had to pick one and, when we unrolled them, we found an
English word written on it which looked like a squiggle to us. And so,
tombola style, we were christened.

The little ritual did not end altogether happily, however. My eldest
sister picked Susan, which was fine. Nor did Mother quibble when her
elder son (Ju-ao) chose William and her baby (Ying-hua) became
Michael by default. But she was none too pleased that I had picked
Cecilia and that my second sister became Irene. She immediately told us
to switch names. I am not sure why she wanted me to be called Irene:
perhaps she knew the name meant Peace, and hoped I should one day
attain it. Perhaps she simply preferred it to Cecilia and wanted me, her
favourite child, to have it. Whatever her motives, my sister knew she
could not have got the better of the deal. Mother did not always play fair,
especially where her second daughter was concerned.

Father, of course, took no part in this. He had given us Chinese names
with carefully chosen significances, but he preferred to use a simpler
system himself. He addressed us by numbers, prefixed by 'Ah', which is
tacked on to the names of inconsequential people. I was Ah San to him,
Number Three. The Shanghai expression 'Any Ah San, Ah Si' means
'any Tom, Dick or Harry'. Even when we were older and considered
ourselves proper little ladies and gentlemen, Father would persist in this
embarrassing habit in front of our peers, but then, like many men whose
work is their life, and like the traditional absent-minded professor, he
lived in another world from which only Mother could retrieve him. It
was she, who understood him better than anyone, who gave us our ideal
of our father.

He was a man of simple needs. Unlike most Chinese, he cared little
about food and would eat his meals quickly, wolfing down just two
bowls of rice in a few minutes. He loathed vegetables yet he was
incredibly healthy and never became ill. However, to ensure that he had
his daily vitamin ration, Mother who never lifted a finger in housework
would sit and patiently peel fruit for him. Once the children watched

with greedy eyes as he finished off a plate of beautifully skinned tangerines. Cecilia ventured at length to ask, 'Are the tangerines good, Daddy?' He looked at her for a moment in genuine surprise. 'What tangerines?' he said. I doubt he ever bought himself a pair of socks, and Mother had to remind him when he needed new clothes. Once a year, a tailor would come to fit him out with new Western suits. But every afternoon, without prompting, he would put the money Mother gave him each day in his pockets and stroll to the Fuzhou Road bookshop district and return with at least one book. He read copiously, and his well-stocked library included translations of the Western classics as well as more modern works. *Don Quixote* was his favourite novel, the story of the idealist who bravely tilted at windmills.

Though he had taught himself to read, since he had never attended a normal school his grasp of mathematics was pathetic. Confusion with noughts was frequent, so that a $10 bill and a $100 note looked the same to him. Perhaps this was why Mother rationed his pocket money. He was so easily gulled.

Other wives envied my mother for having such a sweet and childlike husband. Her dark horse had been tamed in a few years – yet he could be surprisingly obstinate in matters he thought important. Once in a while, his placid nature would erupt like a volcano. He would be physically violent and his blind rage would send fear and panic through the house until we children screamed from the terror of it all.

A humble actor from the provinces was once asked to stay to lunch. The Chinese are by no means inhibited eaters and loud, juicy appreciative noises are socially perfectly acceptable. But this actor sounded like a one-man orchestra, sucking in his soup and spitting out his chicken bones with concentrated voracity. Tension began to mount around the table as each of us tried our hardest not to giggle. Father maintained a straight face throughout and this, somehow, heightened our urge to laugh. Mother, who could be most childish at times, was unable to contain herself for long. Naturally we children followed suit, until even the loose tabletop seemed to be laughing, shaking with our mirth, to the astonishment of our poor guest. When the actor left, Father, understandably, lost his temper.

Yet he was the most inconspicuous person in the house, lost in his world and remaining in his study. Sometimes even in public, perhaps in a crowded restaurant, quite oblivious to the whispers all about him – Qi Lintong is here! Qi Lintong is here! – he would retreat into his own thoughts until Mother nudged him back into reality.

The success of my parents' lives together must have been the attraction of opposites. While he was taciturn, and an altruist at heart, she was as talkative and materialistic as any Shanghainese. She never did fully appreciate his love for books and he was as much baffled by her need to accumulate so many material things. To go shopping with her was quite an experience; she never bought fabric by the yard but by the bolt.

Both, in fact, read avidly, and we children often saw them settled cosily in bed, Father with his Chinese journals to keep him abreast of current affairs, she with her detective stories and gothic novels in English. His screen heroes were Chaplin and Charles Laughton, while she adored Humphrey Bogart, in gangster movies for preference. She was always late. He was strictly punctual. They would arrive at functions separately.

Their relationship was based not only on love but on their regard for each other. They liked each other and were good friends, which enabled them to solve their differences – and in sixteen years I never saw them quarrel. We children would be really amused to see our mother flirt with Father, and him, the head of the household, trying to keep his dignity by pretending to be annoyed.

Mother, by contrast, was immersed in the minutiae of life, of hers and other people's, and, above all, her children's. She took every possible precaution to guard her children from disease in a country where infant mortality was high. Most people suffered from conjunctivitis, an eye infection spread through the careless use of communal towels. Ringworm and dysentery were common, though polio was almost unheard of. As in the West then, TB was the real killer. Raw foods were to be avoided and all the fruit was scrupulously washed under Mother's particular orders.

Over the years we children must have swallowed gallons of cod liver oil and other equally revolting mixtures in the name of preventative medicine. As a result, we grew up extremely healthy, though little Michael suffered from asthma at first and Susan was poorly until she had her tonsils out. The operation was such a success that we all followed. I could only pity the poor doctors who operated. Mother stood behind them each time to make sure the thing was done properly.

Her sense of hygiene bordered on the extreme at times. China's varied and delicious street food was out of bounds to us. Like royalty we went about without money, for she considered coins and bills the dirtiest things to handle. She herself went so far as to carry a little bottle of iodine to dinner parties with which she sterilised her chopsticks, much to the embarrassment of her hosts.

And so, each New Year's dinner, the business of the dusty scrolls flustered her entirely. Yet, looking around the table at her children, she regained her composure and saw each child with satisfaction as a unique and individual product of her rule. Her vision imposed an identity upon each of us very early on which we would struggle to cope with for the rest of our lives.

There was Susan, her 'good' daughter shouldering the responsibilities of being the eldest. How I envied her her gravity and dignity, qualities I entirely lacked when I was little. And there was Cecilia, the second-born and once-abandoned, whom Mother so often considered 'bad'. She had the courage to oppose Mother, and I submitted to her domination by moods that swung between fierce affection and unreasonable antagonism, depending on how she felt about our mother at the time. Matters improved as we grew up, for in many ways she became Father's favourite, and the imbalance was redressed.

William would be there, younger than I but the first son, though he took no special position because of it, and sat in order two seats away from Father. Because he was a boy he perhaps enjoyed a licence for naughtiness that Cecilia was never permitted. His carefree and easy-going disposition certainly worked in his favour. He was my childhood companion, only a year younger than I.

Michael was the baby of the family and was treated as such until his little sister, Vivian, was born much later. At the time I remember him as asthmatic, and consequently coddled by Mother.

And I was *huo po*, lively-explosive. My surplus energy would often get me into trouble with the grown-ups. Enraged and frustrated, I would break into terrible tantrums. I developed ways of redeeming my sins. Like a monkey on a penny-wagon, I would perform, singing and twirling at the drop of a hat. Anything to please and appease. Mother loved and encouraged these little entertainments. Father was simply embarrassed.

There would always be others around the table at New Year, some of our 'aunts', perhaps with their husbands and children. And always Big Big Sister, whom I loved the most. She was a cousin of ours on Mother's side, but already in her twenties she was considered an old maid; rather plain with it, which couldn't have helped. Although she was financially independent she could not be permitted to live alone without courting scandal. So she lived with us, and in return she kept house.

The day after our New Year's Eve dinner we began the brand new day of a brand new year, dressed in our brand new brocades, being served with delicacies that symbolised good things like wealth, health and harmony with our fellow men. Immediately after breakfast, which we children still ate separately from our parents, the family would sally forth to pay our respects to older relatives.

The first call, according to custom, was to my paternal grandparents. Although Grandfather was often to be seen at our house during the year, I saw my grandmother only at this time. Mother felt that at first she had acted the part of the perfect daughter-in-law, but gradually the petty dictatorship of the older woman, so different in background to my mother, drove her to rebel and now she was respectful, but kept her distance. Since my grandparents were financially dependent on my parents, this arrangement was feasible. Mothers-in-law, far from being the butt of comedy as in the West, were generally the scourge of their daughters-in-law, nothing to laugh about. The young women bided their time, and eventually became the oppressors themselves. Under Mother's influence I regarded my paternal grandmother as a rather unattractive person, who spent most of her time in her room with her prayer beads, chanting her way to Nirvana in a shrill voice. Sudden conversion to religion in old age was as common in China as elsewhere.

Grandfather was an actor himself, and we enjoyed his visits to our house. He was a good humoured old man and when the mood took him he would sing a little aria and do a turn for us. Afterwards he would produce some sweets from his pockets and give them only to his grandsons, which spoiled a happy time for me.

The next call would be to my maternal grandmother, whom I saw often as Mother was devoted to her. It was easy to see why Mother preferred daughters to sons, for her own history confirmed the saying, 'Marry a daughter and you gain a son; marry a son and you lose him.' Although the family fortune had dwindled by the time I appeared on the scene, Mother's family, unlike Father's, was still wealthy. My grandfather did well in his lucrative tea business, and left Grandmother a rich widow. In her heyday, it was rumoured that she owned one hundred slaves in her country estate in Shaoxing, and even now the jewelry in her coffers could excite envy. But I never saw her wear those jewels. Instead she wove cloth for the poor and frugally made wine from orange peel. In fact, she was a paragon of virtue: in former years, village gates would have been erected to honour virtue of her sort – just about the only female achievement that was recognised. 'How your grandmother mourned my father when he died,' Mother was fond of telling us. 'For years, tears would flow down her cheeks every time she picked up her chopsticks at mealtimes.' Looking at my grandmother, it seemed incredible that she was capable of passion. Permanently in black, her long gown reached to her tiny bound feet, and with her hair pulled back tightly into a bun, and her unadorned hands placed neatly on her lap, she sat upright and still like a statue carved from dark nephrite jade. Only her yapping Pekinese made the noise and commotion around her.

And yet there was something strange about her overall appearance which I took for granted until the day I stumbled upon the truth that I was of mixed blood. For if the skin of our family (including Father's oddly enough) was considered white, hers was translucent, and her aquiline nose on her unusually chiselled face was somewhat at odds with her bound feet which were the ideal 'three inches' in length, the pride and bane of all traditional Chinese women. As a child, just about the only glamorous aspect of my grandmother to me was her friendship with the mother of China's three fabulous Sung sisters: Eling, Mayling, and Chingling. They married China's richest financier, Generalissimo Chiang Kai Chek, and the father of the Republic, Dr Sun Yat Sen, respectively.

Mother, like myself, was the third child, and a petted and high-spirited girl from the outset. Her much older sister was quite different, another person who sat quiet and still, an iron beauty of aristocratic bearing. In youth, Mother told me, she never ventured out of doors without a jade pin in either hand to ward off plebeians who might come into physical contact with her. She married a proper suitor of her own class, a man who was privileged to have completed his studies in England, who was charming and urbane like gentlemen in Oscar Wilde's plays, and who did not have to work for a living. The Xis had two children, much older than I. Yao An, the elder son, followed in his father's footsteps but Xian An, the daughter, became an English teacher after studying in London.

My uncle, Grandmother's second child and only son, was a colourful fellow. There was a saying: it takes three generations to amass a fortune, one to squander it. My uncle did his best. He was a connoisseur of food, he frequented brothels, gambled at the races and dabbled expensively in amateur theatricals. This was the same brother who, out of moral pique, threatened to have my father killed when he eloped with Mother. But he can almost be forgiven because he had an incredible sense of humour. I was fond of sitting behind him when he played Russian poker in our house, for even when he was losing at high stakes he cracked jokes non-stop that made my belly ache with laughter. Of course he never did a day's work in his life. The sole hardship he endured was to be locked up in some cubby-hole for half a day when gangsters kidnapped him for ransom. Even that was not meant for him – they got the wrong man. People often used to confuse his family name with that of a jeweller of the same name. He also became a film extra for a day while he holidayed in Hollywood. That year he brought back many presents, and I especially admired the lipsticks which I now see were from Woolworth.

His arranged marriage was a loveless match. His wife was barren, so he took a concubine who gave him love and eight children. The two wives lived in next door rooms and malicious gossip had it that as time went by the deserted one started taking drugs and lovers. In the early days of their marriage, before the younger and fertile woman came into the house, a boy was adopted. At first he was coddled and pampered but later, when flesh and blood children were born, the novelty of his existence wore off. He was then completely ignored by the household. He stuttered severely, and my heart went out to this cousin of mine, even though he often cheated me out of my ice-creams. In the end he went quite peculiar. The last time I remember seeing him, he had made his habitat in a stair cupboard, and, in that cramped space, he collected old unwanted shoes.

These New Year visits, which were reciprocated on alternate days by every relation, lasted fifteen days. Each generation kowtowed to the generations above them, so we children had a busy time of it. We bowed and bowed, bobbing up and down like yo-yos, encouraged by the banknotes in auspicious red envelopes that were handed to us in return. I never liked to make my obeisance, having to kneel and touch my head upon the floor. What's more, I never saw the money: Mother had to recycle it amongst the children who kowtowed to her. It felt rather as if we children did all the work, and never got paid. But I was relieved that at least maiden aunts were not expected to give money. Otherwise they would soon be bankrupt.

With the fortnight of hard work involved, New Year never had quite the pleasure that Christmas meant to us. Although we were not Christians, we were Shanghainese, and we celebrated after the fashion with a huge Christmas tree. The emphasis was on the children and we were allowed to throw tea parties for friends, which was much more fun. Besides, we got to keep our presents, which was more than I could say for New Year, although, a few weeks before Christmas, we were obliged to write long, boring letters to Santa Claus promising to be good children for the coming year. Susan was of course the first to realise that Mother and Santa were one and the same person, and thereafter a little of the magic was gone – and the letter writing became more boring than ever.

In those days, before television and mass production, our toys were simple things bought from little shops around the corner, or perhaps handmade by ourselves. We became adept at folding beautiful shiny paper into boats, or creating a paper menagerie. We played games of patting paper balls, or kicking feathered shuttlecocks into the air. My real passion was hopscotch, a very complicated game in China. As in the West, girls liked skipping and boys played with marbles – but I fought to join in with the boys. Instead of rearing guinea pigs or rabbits, Chinese boys kept crickets in tiny bamboo cages, and we girls raised silk-worms in cardboard boxes.

Dolls were not really a part of a Chinese girl's life, perhaps because tradition regarded representations of the human form as idols to be treated with reverence. The only dolls my sisters and I played with had a Western influence, and we called them *yang wa wa*, 'foreign babies'. There was a black *yang wa wa*, but none of them were Chinese. The most wonderful of them all was a near life-size Shirley Temple doll, given to Susan by a family friend. But Grandmother would not allow anyone even to touch her, let alone play with her, for fear that she would be broken, which made her none too popular with me. So the doll was incarcerated in a glass case, to be admired like an idol after all. Throughout my childhood, I greedily coveted that Shirley Temple. Finally I did own her, when I was thirteen. It was too late. By then I was interested only in male film stars.

4

Bitter Strength

Reality for me was provided by the general atmosphere of living in a city like Shanghai. And the pattern of 'normal' life, away from the fantastical world of the theatre, was set by the servants who looked after me at home. Eventually, school would come between them all.

Once outside the haven of home, theatre and school, a child in Shanghai, no matter how protected, was a small worldly person inevitably exposed to the life of the city, mostly hostile and inhumane. Much that I saw at this time baffled me. In the crowded thoroughfare of the Bund in the British zone, for instance, I tried hard to be immune to the aggressive way the Sikh policemen directed the traffic, leaping from their rostrums to beat defenceless Chinese rickshaw-pullers whenever it suited them. These hated subjects of the British Raj had been imported from India, like opium, but as slaves to control slaves. Parks in the foreign concessions were forbidden to Chinese, although they were paid for from Chinese taxes. Outside one was a sign which has become infamous: 'Dogs And Chinese Not Allowed'.

As the city filled, the streets were lined with all manner of human misery and deformity. The fortunate were allowed to spill over into the foreign concessions where a day's begging or thieving was more lucrative. They were controlled by the syndicates. Once, walking down the streets with a woman servant, I noticed a man with a horrible face, with only a hole where his nose should have been. I asked my servant the reason for his deformity. She threw a quick glance at the man and quickly pulled me away. 'Never you mind. Disgusting!' she said scornfully. I was too young to have heard of syphilis. The beggar heard my servant's remark and shouted: 'Hey, your mother! don't begrudge me the only bit of fun I've got left!'

Servants in Shanghai were plentiful, as labour was cheap. The poor after all had always relied on their only capital, their bodies, to make a living. Men sold their *ku li*, or bitter strength, from which the word coolie derives. Women had various physical commodities to sell in different parts of their anatomy. Besides plain prostitution, a concubine's womb was used to perpetuate an otherwise extinct male line. And as wet-nurses, their babies' milk was sacrificed to nourish another mother's children. My sisters and brothers all had wet-nurses, but I was born on tour, and was consequently nursed on cow's milk.

Apart from wet-nurses brought in for the occasion, a well-to-do family in Shanghai normally had four or five servants, including a cook and several maids. A chauffeur was essential if the family could afford a motor car and wanted to be fashionable. Otherwise a private rickshaw puller was engaged to ferry the family about. In all this we were no exception. With Mother in charge of the purse strings, after all, we had prospered.

Father, with his impoverished background, found our prosperity and the attitudes it entailed difficult to accept. We children, being no fools, sided with Mother on the issue of our upbringing. On the only occasion I can recall an exchange of harsh words between our parents, Mother held her ground:

'In my childhood,' said Father, 'we had to make do with cold tea.'

'Cold tea still needs hot water to make it in the first place,' my mother retorted. 'These days, we buy a refrigerator to keep tea cold,' she added, making a face at me. Father gave up and left the room.

Mother saw to it that we were waited on hand and foot, in the way that she had been brought up. Her fastidiousness in our welfare could not have made her an easy mistress. We were not encouraged to do things for ourselves, and right up to the time I left home my baths were drawn for me, and the clothes I stepped out of were left on the floor for the servants to pick up.

Our bedtime was much more flexible than that of Western children. We were usually told a bedtime story, not by our parents but by the servants, but they were never read from a book for the oral storytelling tradition is strong in China. We preferred ghost stories, and the servants, being country folk well acquainted with nature and the supernatural, had them in abundance. Sisters and brothers would huddle together

wide eyed with terror and rapture, listening to tales of fantastic appar-
itions. When my elder sisters began to read, Cecilia in particular became
a fund of stories herself. And always any story that could be interpreted
as remotely sad would have the tears streaming down my face.

During the hot summer evenings the street would fill, as servants and
families from the houses up and down moved little stools onto their
porches, and spilled onto the pavement, to keep cool. We were sometimes allowed to join them. The atmosphere of these evenings was
wondrously friendly. Sitting on rattan stools or armchairs, constantly
plying their fans, the women gossiped amongst themselves. The men in
vests played cards, or maybe Chinese chess. My little brother Michael
excelled in this game, winning match after match all the way down the
street – a sign of things to come.

Under the night sky, the servants taught us to make friends with the
stars. They told us that the Milky Way was really a heavenly bridge for
the Celestial Weaving Girl to meet her cowherd husband on the seventh
day of the seventh moon. And it was very important to pray to the
Weaving Girl for a good husband. Since the subject of matrimony was
never broached by my parents, we did not take our servants seriously.
Considering that the two conjugal lovers could meet only once a year, I
personally didn't think their marriage that marvellous. So I never
prayed. That perhaps was an oversight.

Our servants usually remained with us for good, though every now
and again one would go off in a huff and return a little later, drawn by
the magnetism of my mother's personality. Fu Sheng, the chauffeur,
was king below stairs, having been with the family for as long as I could
remember. He became a driver through sheer determination and bra-
vado. As a young man from Pudong across the Huangpu river, he had
come to the city to look up a relative who was a chauffeur in the service
of an Englishman. One glance, and Fu Sheng fell in love with cars. Over
the next few weeks he secretly drove the car without the owner's
knowledge until he got the knack of it. It was a daring thing for a country
boy to attempt: had he damaged the car, or been caught driving, he
would have been accused of theft, and under the law of the foreign
concessions, prosecuted by the extra-territorial courts, native culprits
could expect heavy sentences.

Fu Sheng was illiterate, of course, but his intelligence commanded
respect. He was a born mechanic, which was just as well since the sort of
second-hand cars Mother bought from foreign brokers, after much
haggling, needed all the love and patience they could get to keep going.

Fu Sheng was also very fond of children and it was he who taught us many things that Father had no time for. We all learned to bicycle from him, and he would run along beside us all the way so that we had no fear of falling, and would only let go when we had learned to ride. William and I very nearly learned the secrets of anatomy from him, too, for we concealed ourselves to watch him take a bath, only to be discovered much too soon.

However, once a year, Fu Sheng would lose his temper over one problem or another, and would threaten to leave. Mother took it in her stride and waited for him to calm down. The issue was once the carelessness of women servants leaving sanitary paper in the toilet. Age-old superstition decreed that this would bring misfortune on the man who came upon it. So he complained to Mother – a woman! But then, who else could he have complained to?

In many ways, Fu Sheng represented the best in a Chinese. Of humble birth, he was patient and hardworking, but never servile. Like most servants, he saw little of his wife and children whom he left in the countryside to tend a little land. He accepted the situation with dignity, and looked forward to the future, having seen to it that his children got a proper education from his hard-earned wages.

Once he proudly showed me a school satchel he had bought for his daughter to take to school. I was so moved by this that I blurted out: 'Oh, Fu Sheng, you are my most favourite man in all the world!' Not quite the sentiment expected from the Third Miss of the house, even a little girl. He shifted from one foot to another, trying not to show his embarrassment.

Good natured Ah Zhu with a hare lip was the cook. Her satisfaction with life might have had something to do with her lucrative job in the household, for a cook was entitled to a percentage of all groceries purchased. This was in accordance with the 'squeeze' system prevalent in Chinese society at the time, which permeated practically all monetary transactions between employer and employee. Without any practical schooling she was – unlike Father – a whizz kid at arithmetic. Whenever she 'over-squeezed' Mother, and her accounts were questioned, she could always justify her figures by doing complicated multiplications in her head with a speed that never failed to impress Mother – and confound her, too. A cook had other advantages. Ah Zhu was treated with deference by the other servants, who relied on her for the quality of their daily meals. She obviously had a soft spot for Fu Sheng, since he was a man, and therefore as royalty downstairs, so he got the choicest morsels every time. But Ah Zhu was not mean, and she was amiable to everyone.

The maids were quite often young girls who stayed with us until they married. But many women servants stayed with us for years. I remember Ah Jing most distinctly, for she looked after me specifically and I grew very attached to her. Very thin and always slightly nervous, Ah Jing was as neat as a pin. She had long black hair shining like lacquer, which she pulled back into a tight bun. All through the years she was with us, she would massage her hair with a special comb for that purpose and once a year only she would permit herself to wash her hair – another superstition. Ah Jing was probably in her thirties, though whether she was an old maid, a married woman or a widow, I never discovered.

The servants' bêtes noires, literally, were our pets. We had two dogs and five cats (kittens picked up by Cecilia who identified with them because she felt unwanted by Mother). Ah Jing positively loathed the animals, and at best the other servants just about tolerated them. Each time the Alsatian bitch had puppies, it was surprisingly Father who took a great interest in feeding them meat and eggs. The women servants in particular resented this, perhaps understandably, since their children in the countryside were probably not half as well fed as our animals.

If the constant presence of servants gave a pattern to our early days, from the age of six, when we began formal education, studying would become our major occupation. Chinese schools expect a lot of homework from their students, no matter how young. From day one I began to practise calligraphy. With black ink and brush we wrote a page of large and a page of small characters to hand in every day. Upbringing and character were judged by one's handwriting.

On our street there were three affiliated schools. Directly opposite our front door was the Sacred Heart Primary School, a co-educational establishment with a Chinese curriculum. We all started there. Later, my two elder sisters graduated to the Aurora Middle School for Girls next door. And beyond that was the Convent of the Sacred Heart where the curriculum was in English for foreign students.

Although our primary school was only a stone's throw from our house, we were at first forbidden to cross the road to go to school without a servant to accompany us. Mother's protectiveness towards us astonished other people. Later, the same friends would marvel at her daring in sending such cosseted children across the seas on their own, and they were impressed that we could all cope with our new surroundings with unusual confidence.

Primary school was a bleak place. Not a tree or blade of grass was to be seen in the compound. This did not trouble me unduly at the time since the concrete playground was ideal for hopscotch. But the teaching methods, though considered advanced by the standards of the day, were positively Dickensian to the modern eye. Any stimulus to the joy of learning was totally lacking.

I enjoyed the artistic pursuit of daily calligraphy, but had problems catching up with the rest of the homework. Like Father, I was hopeless at arithmetic, and geography was dull. At that time, Chinese classics still formed an important part of the curriculum, and learning whole essays by rote without knowing their meaning, the custom since ancient times, was excruciatingly boring. The Dialects of Confucius, and Mencius' Ethics, were far beyond a little girl's comprehension or interest.

To make matters worse, the teachers were all mean-spirited individuals who meted out corporal punishment mercilessly. Boys from poorer families invariably got the worst of it. I felt so negative towards the teachers that I have since blotted their faces from my memory, and only their hands I remember well, because I was fascinated by the different ways they used to unfold their books.

Children who did well in this kind of educational system were either exceptionally bright or just unimaginative bookworms. Only Susan, who was exceptionally bright, fitted into the first category. Consequently our hearts were not in our studies and we would fail our end-of-term exams with monotonous regularity.

Cecilia was particularly obnoxious to her teachers and they were almost afraid of her. She had no interest in school books but would steal novels from Father's library – including some considered unsuitable for a girl her age. She thought at first that Father hadn't noticed. But as time went by, pages began to disappear from the books she thieved. Nothing was ever said, and it became a tacit game between the two of them.

One way or another I would usually manage to pass a few exams at the end of each term, scraping through by the skin of my teeth. William, on the other hand, went through all the best primary schools Shanghai could offer, though he only boasted that this gave him new schoolmates to play with every year. Michael had the best reasons for not attending school: he was always prone to asthmatic attacks in term time. As we began our holidays it would be Mother's turn to work hard. She would make the rounds of our various schools and charm, cajole or beg the head teachers to take us back for one more term.

Only history I found exciting, because it was so full of human drama. Yet that, too, caused anxieties: incapable of grasping China's historical time-span of many thousands of years, my little mind saw all the events condensed into a matter of recent years. The past seemed a horrible place to live in, with an endless succession of calamities – floods and famine, revolts and battles, men beheaded and women allowed to suffer. Yet I was beginning to learn that history could not always be relegated to a frightful past. History was in the making, all around us, as terrible and calamitous as ever, and it seeped in upon us despite Mother's precautions. Once, indeed, it burst upon us, and became transformed into a sort of comic opera, ludicrous and tragic at the same time.

One January, in Father's study at the top of the stairs, his copyist, Mr You Jingui, woke in his chair after a comfortable night's repose. He unfolded his arms from his generous sleeves and sat upright, feeling well disposed to life. He practised *qi gong*, a form of breathing callisthenics which rendered sleep all but unnecessary, and when he stayed to work in our house he ate with us but always declined a bed. This time he had been working in the study for a week and everyone had practically forgotten about him.

It was half past nine and the house was quiet. It was a cold morning and Mr You thought how nice it would be to pop down to the kitchen for a bowl of piping hot congee, and use the servants' toilet while he was there. Descending the stairs, he passed my parents' room, where they were still asleep after a late night's work. The sound of coughing on the floor below suggested that Auntie Four, our staying guest, was about to get up. He continued down and saw the wet-nurse feeding baby Michael on the first floor. When he reached the ground floor, Fu Sheng was snoring loudly in the alcove above the tea room, since he too slept late after driving my parents home. The other children, including myself, had already gone to school, and to Mr You's disappointment Ah Zhu, the cook, had gone to market, leaving the kitchen empty.

'Ah well,' thought Mr You philosophically, 'I'll just have a pee then.' At this moment there was a banging on the back door.

'Open the door please!' someone shouted outside.

Our house was guarded like a fortress, with two Alsatians keeping sentry duty at the front door, and double doors at the back to shut out interlopers. And the first house rule was: Never Open the Door to Strangers.

But poor Mr You was a bit of a stranger himself. He took a while to open the heavy wooden door, and through the iron bars of the gate he saw two men, each holding a chicken.

'Is this the Zhou residence?' they enquired.

'Most certainly,' replied Mr You with pride.

'Well sir, open the door. We are here to deliver these chickens to the Zhou family with Mr Yang's compliments.'

Mr You opened the gate and the two strangers stepped into the house.

'I have also a letter from my master,' said the other man, dropping a protesting chicken to the floor and pulling a large envelope from his pocket.

'Good, I will certainly see that it is handed in.' But before Mr You could rub his thick spectacles, he thought he saw the same man take out a gun from the red envelope.

'Hands up!' he shouted, adding softly, 'But don't be scared.'

The other man dropped his chicken, too, and Mr You's hands moved upwards. A pressure on his back turned his feet and he headed for the tea room. There he was told to stand facing the wall while one man stood guard and the other started up the stairs, just as the wet-nurse was coming down with some nappies.

'Hands up! But don't be scared and get into that room.' The good nanny was alarmed but she retorted: 'I've got a baby upstairs and I'm not leaving him all by himself.' So they agreed that they would both go and fetch Michael. So now the baby, wet-nurse and Mr You faced the tea room wall while the other man stood guard.

On the second floor Auntie Four was sitting in bed, contemplating getting a cup of tea, having a spit and then a cigarette. A knock on the door. 'Who is it?' A head popped in with a gun beneath it.

'Don't be scared, we . . . I . . . am searching for opium only, don't be scared.' With trembling hands Auntie Four automatically removed from her finger the only piece of jewelry she possessed and dropped it under the bedclothes.

'We want you to come downstairs, so please get dressed.' In order not to embarrass her, he waited outside until she was decent and escorted her to the tea room to join the others.

The man took a deep breath and started to mount the stairs once more, to the third and last floor where he must meet his Waterloo. On his way he picked up a maid coming out of nowhere and forced her to escort him to the master bedroom. Mother in her sleep distinctly heard three knocks on her bedroom door. She jumped up immediately for she knew that something was wrong. The second house rule: No Knocking on Doors. The Western custom made her nervous.

'Who is it?' cried Mother, with supreme caution.

'It's me, mistress,' whimpered the maid. 'Please open the door.' Mother gathered her wits. All the theories in her detective novels could now be put into practice.

'Is it Joe Bloggs?' she asked (using, of course, the Chinese equivalent).

'Yes.' Mother's suspicions were confirmed.

'No, I won't open the door,' she said.

A male voice said, 'Yes you will.'

'No I won't.'

'If you don't I'll kick it open!'

One, two, three! and the lower part of the door had a hole in the middle and a strange man squeezed into her bedroom like old clogged up toothpaste.

All this time, Father, who was never quite there except on stage, thought Mother was giving orders to her maid as usual. However, the noise of splintering wood roused him finally, and he opened his eyes to see a strange man raise himself to his full height, resume a menacing pose with the aid of his trembling gun, and stalk towards him. He was no John Wayne. Luckily he had married a Mary Pickford.

'Don't you dare touch him!' she cried, flinging herself in front of the gunman. 'I am the one you talk to!' At this point the robber froze.

'You've got a telephone?'

'Yes,' said Mother, thinking fast. 'I'm afraid that when I heard you coming up the stairs I called the police.'

At the mention of police, whatever confidence the man possessed visibly drained from him. Mother took her advantage and started talking even faster. 'Look, I know you want money. I'll give it to you, here in the wardrobe, you can see it's all there is. Now take it and go quickly because the police will be here any moment and we don't want any complications, do we . . . here . . . let me help you . . .'

Fortunately it was the servants' pay-day, so there were many packets of money which Mother urgently piled into his cupped hands, already half filled with his revolver. It must have appeared a fortune to the man's confused mind. Then Mother opened the shattered door and solicitously accompanied him all the way down the stairs. Outside the tea room she was introduced to his friend and again she expressed concern and stressed the urgency of their getaway. Finally she ushered them to the back door and politely bade them farewell.

With a great sigh of relief she walked back to the tea room and found everyone still standing there facing the wall. 'All right, you can put your hands down now,' she told them.

Above their heads, Fu Sheng stirred, stretched and climbed down from the alcove.

'Ah, mistress, what brought you down so early today?' he asked.

When the excitement had died down, a grand inquisition of course ensued. Who, Mother demanded to know, had opened the door to strangers? Poor Mr You had to step out and confess. Tucked away in the highest room in the house, he should have been the last person to hear the knocking, so no one had bothered to tell him the first house rule. But then, we had forgotten that although he might not sleep in a bed, Mr You still had to obey the call of nature.

Of course I was at school when the incident occurred, and perhaps there was a little too much colour in Mother's rendering of the story. But I believe that she was really brave, even considering the timidity of the robbers, and she deserved to tell the story her way. We ate the chickens that had been presented to us, and they were delicious. Only poor Mr You lost face and refused to work for Father ever again. He was, after all, not merely a copyist but a classical scholar in his own right.

The robbery was reported and a few months later two men were brought to our house for identification. Father said he had been too sleepy to remember their faces. There were good reasons not to identify the men. It was a time of great unrest. The law offered scant protection to the law-abiding and little justice for the lawless. Once in prison, a man could rot there forever, and no one wanted that on his conscience. Besides, organised gangs were everywhere and revenge was not unheard of. We had lived to tell the tale.

I hid behind the banister and watched: they had a wild look about them, with their shaven heads and their hands bound in chains. I felt sorry for them. One turned his head slightly and for the first time I looked into the eyes of true human misery. Fear and utter despair.

5

The Lesser Part of Mankind

ℯ

As the rumblings of the Japanese invasion drew nearer, Shanghai began to fill with the fugitives from the north. Japan's claims to Manchuria and Inner Mongolia had been recognised by the Kuomintang government in Nanjing, but the Japanese were busily exploiting Nanjing's weakness and ineffectiveness throughout northern China. 'Incidents' occurred to give Japan quasi-legal justifications for taking cities, punishing enemies and pushing her armies ever further south. Before her, Chinese authority and security crumbled. Neither Britain nor America was prepared to react to the threat.

On 7th July 1937, Japanese soldiers crossed the Marco Polo Bridge to the north of Beijing, and then refused to budge. Chiang Kai Chek's feeble government gave the Japanese the pretext they needed, and full scale invasion began. This move, so long delayed, allowed a powerful and well-equipped Japan to take on the ragged armies of China wherever and whenever she wanted. China fell so easily, weakened by the semi-colonial occupation by Western powers; no one interfered to help, and the Chinese people became casual victims of appalling Japanese brutality.

The Japanese were already well-established in Shanghai, like the other foreign concessionaries. They overran Chinese parts of the city after the Nationalist armies had tried to defend their positions. Bombing of civilians in urban areas began, before Guernica. In the densely populated industrial outskirts of Shanghai, where millions of poor people lived and worked, Japanese bombs laid flat factories and houses, killing countless defenceless men, women and children. The Nationalist government retreated when their capital, Nanjing, fell. The defenceless city was left at the mercy of the Japanese. Amidst scenes of indescribable horror, defeated Chinese soldiers who had surrendered their weapons and civilians alike were indiscriminately rounded up and tied together in batches of fifty or one hundred and machine-gunned, or worse still, used for bayonet practice. Anyone could be shot on sight at the whim of the drunken soldiers. Children were not spared after witnessing the repeated violation of their mothers. Within weeks, Nanjing was laid to waste. The generation older than I have found this episode in recent history hard to forget, and cannot forgive the Japanese to this day.

Another half a million refugees fled to Shanghai, a city already bulging with homeless people. The Shanghai Theatre Society to Save the Refugees was set up, and Father and his colleagues gave many benefit performances. Mother, as chairwoman of the Shanghai Women's Association, organised relief, and at home she hired a servant to sew padded clothes for the destitute. But these were drops in the ocean. As the bitterly cold winter set in, thousands died each night on the pavements. As the refugees poured into Shanghai, patriots young and old led an exodus, on foot, towards unoccupied China, either to Chongqing, where the Nationalists had finally settled, or to Yenan, where the Communists had built their stronghold.

The Japanese were hard masters of their new empire, but in the foreign concessions life continued very much as before as long as the Western nations remained neutral towards Japan. In the French concession, we were unmolested; Vichy France had no quarrel with Japan, and by the time war with Japan broke out in 1941, the French had already signed an armistice with Germany, Japan's ally.

Life for us all continued more or less as usual. Mother concentrated on her self-appointed task of breaking the traditional pattern that shaped the fortunes of most actors' children. She vigorously rejected the idea that we should follow our father's calling, as was the custom. She wanted to show the world that an actor's children could go on to better things. No expense was spared on our education, and the crowning glory of her grand scheme would be to send us abroad to study like the most privileged children in the country. Just as she insisted on payments in gold for her husband's work, she brought us up to expect no dowry, and to pursue a formal education as the only investment that could never be taken away. From the start she had said to me: 'Don't expect a dowry like other girls in other families. It will hang around your neck like a millstone. What you'll get is a bellyful of education. That way you'll travel light and go anywhere you please.' Her vision was of creating cosmopolitan supermen and women, ready for whatever life could offer. No wonder we would all fail her, each in our own way.

School was a burden to us all, but worse was yet to come. An army of private tutors would come to plague us after school and during the long summer holidays. Their job was called 'patching up': Chinese reverence for learning was such that private tutors could be much in demand.

They came in all nationalities, for we had to be able to speak foreign languages before they were taught at school. Chinese naturally taught Chinese and mathematics. English was taught by the British, and French either by French or by White Russians. These teachers never stayed very long. There was a tacit agreement between the children to sabotage Mother's grand scheme, and we made them as uncomfortable as possible. I personally got rid of one teacher who came to teach us English during the summer holidays. A large British matron with bright red rouge on her face, she gave herself terrible airs and considered it slightly demeaning to teach native children. She specifically insisted on having two Bath Olivers served to her at eleven o'clock sharp each morning with her English cuppa, which she 'partook of ever so genteelly'. Her students sensed her condescension.

One morning when she came to take charge of her 'class', I happened to be occupying her usual seat.

'Come along now,' she said to me, perhaps innocently but certainly without any charm. 'You must vacate that seat.' Her patronising tone was all too familiar and I responded in kind.

'Why?'

'Why?' she echoed, shocked that a Chinese, and a child at that, should dare answer back. 'Why? Because it is my seat.'

'But it is my house,' and before I realised what I had said, with a twirl of her loud patterned skirt she had gone to complain to Mother. I was punished, but it was worth it. She disappeared from our lives forever.

Other teachers I remember with more charity. One was a huge brooding woman from Siberia, another a plump and kindly Portuguese lady who instructed us at the piano. My only dread was that she was fond of her false teeth and would sometimes take them out to show to me. And there was one man I can never forget.

He was an old man in a long shabby gown whose duty was to 'patch up' our classics. In bygone days a teacher like him would have been in great demand, holding a respected position in the household, invariably an autocrat who would not spare the rod and spoil the child. But by now the vernacular Chinese was taking over, and a classics teacher was on the way to becoming an unwanted and eventually extinct species. Mr Li Tianhang was a very gentle man, and I doubt he would have been successful as a teacher in the old days, let alone in these changing times. He was so poor that even the servants declined his New Year tip out of compassion. I was touched by his dignity and by his love for his subject. In class, with his eyes closed and his head rotating, he would chant out the poems of the great Li Po and Tu Fu, Tang poetry masters. Often he would fall silent, touched by the beauty of the poems. My sisters learned a bellyful of classics from him, and when they left China they carried part of their literary heritage with them. But I remember only a few poems, all significantly dealing with a popular theme in Chinese poetry: memories of home.

Only Teacher Ding Yuzhu had staying power amongst our many tutors. Backed by Mother's authority, she became a part of the family. She came to us aged seventeen, and Mother took one look at her plain, good face and decided to delegate the overseeing of our education to her. I was her least favourite pupil, too hyperactive for her to handle. But she became a great influence on my sisters.

It was at that time that they began to teach the maids to read. I remember one in particular, a pretty girl with dancing eyes. She was not much interested, and in fact she became increasingly distracted as well as plump. When she left our service I heard that she was pregnant, which I understood was just about the most shameful thing that could happen to an unmarried woman. To this day I wonder what happened to her. The poor are not necessarily kinder than the rich to those less fortunate than themselves.

It was Teacher Ding, in fact, who first crystallised our sense of social injustice. Although she came from a classic feudal background, she was asserting her female independence by going out to work. She was fresh, young, intelligent, idealistic; she made learning a pleasure and flung open windows on stuffy areas of study because her views were never narrow. Soon, unknown to us, she would join the underground Communist Party.

From time to time, as if we did not have enough supervision already, a foreign governess would appear in our midst charged to make sure that we ate our spinach. Michael especially had to be given his daily dose of this abhorred vegetable, because Mother thought he needed it most.

Popeye's prescription for supermanhood had reached the four corners of the earth. The governesses usually spoke English with a Portuguese accent, for we were not, thank God, grand enough for a posh British spinster. The turnover of governesses was at least as high as tutors, but they had no real position in the household and so little authority that they made little impression on us.

My sense of a world outside the home, and beyond the fantasy world of the theatre, should have been reinforced by the death of my father's father, the charming old man who turned tricks for us. Father, I suppose, was grieved but I remember the funeral as a jolly and theatrical affair that lasted days. The Chinese are phlegmatic about death, and the important thing is to send the deceased merrily and noisily on his way.

A curtain divided the Temple's main hall. On one side, the tablet inscribed with my grandfather's name was placed on the altar, facing the entrance. On the other side, my grandfather himself lay in a thick lacquered coffin placed on a catafalque. Relatives stood around him in white mourning clothes, and my parents and we children wore loose garments made of rough hemp, in a filial show of humility before the spirit of the departed. Mother, whom I had not often seen in costume, looked a trifle ridiculous.

The Taoist priests lining the walls of the corridor beside us kept up a continuous chanting that was interrupted only by the blare of a horn announcing the arrival of mourners come to pay their respects by kowtowing to the inscribed tablet. The horn was the cue for people on my side of the curtain to set up a wailing cacophony, in their discordant keys. When the kowtowing was over, the wailing would abruptly stop until the next group of guests arrived. It must have been exhausting for the grown-ups. No wonder there existed professional wailers for hire.

One ceremony followed another, punctuated only by enormous vegetarian meals – since this was sacred ground where no meat was allowed – served at banqueting tables in the side halls. There was the Dressing of the Corpse. Each symbolic garment was put on as if the ceremony were a live stage show, synchronised to music and the clash of cymbals. As they are phlegmatic about death, so the Chinese are practical about religion. Anyone can choose to die a Buddhist, a Taoist or a Confucian. Taoism is commonly the religion of the simple and the poor. Grandfather was dressed in the ornate garb of a Taoist priest, for as such he wished to make his entrance into the other world.

Father performed a ceremony whose meaning I have yet to understand in which he dotted the tablet with a red brush. Father knelt in the centre of the hall, before the tablet. Behind him knelt rows of his disciples from the Peking Opera, and they followed his movements of obeisance with a grace and precision that came naturally to their craft.

Shortly afterwards these disciples were playing a noisy game of football in the temple grounds to while away the time. William and I stole out to join them.

I did not witness my grandfather's burial, for he was almost certainly taken to his ancestral plot in Ningpo, to be buried with his forefathers as every Chinese dreams. But in a procession following the coffin from one part of the temple to another we were told that my younger brothers took precedence in the procession, while we girls were obliged to walk deferentially in their wake. We protested in surprise, but even Mother had to bow to conformity and our protests were in vain. At that moment I discovered that I belonged to the lesser part of mankind.

After the funeral, I persisted in finding out the reason for the discrimination. An old-fashioned aunt, Father's cousin, finally lost her patience.

'A girl should know her place,' she said firmly.

'What place?' I echoed, in genuine ignorance.

'Don't you know that women are inferior?'

'No, but why?' I asked, even more surprised.

'Because we are unclean.'

I did not understand what she meant. It was before my puberty. But the message seeped through somehow. I wrote an essay in school entitled: 'To Fight For The Greatness of Womanhood'. I got nil for the assignment, since the content was no longer than the grandiose title. I hadn't the faintest notion how to go about it. I was eight years old.

Neither this death, nor the idea of my inferiority, could make me unhappy, yet I was not in every way a happy child. I was certainly privileged, and I was never lonely. Yet I lacked privacy, sharing a room with my siblings in a house always filled with people. Respect for privacy is not a Chinese characteristic. One would be hard put to find the word in a Chinese dictionary. As I grew older, I became increasingly introspective within an extrovert exterior. In the unnoticed corners of our house I began to live a secret life of my own. I watched grown-ups behave, and much of what I saw accepted as the norm disturbed me. I cried a lot. I was Cry Baby to my siblings.

According to tradition, when servants were dismissed they had to open their little bundles of possessions for inspection, to show that they had not stolen from the house. I felt their humiliation. At the window on

the first-floor landing, I would hear a scream of pain from the neighbour's house that kept me rooted to the spot. Cruelty has its fascination.
Though slavery was officially abolished, poverty and debt in fact maintained the institution, and the servant girl next door was frequently
mistreated by her keeper.

It was safest in the kitchen, our servants' common room. I was not
supposed to linger there, but if I sat very quietly they would all but forget
my presence and I could watch them going about their business. How I
loved to watch them eat their meals; they ate quickly and hungrily,
shovelling their rice into their mouths with their chopsticks. Their food
appeared so much more delicious than my own. Yet even in the kitchen
I ran the risk of being upset. A freshly killed chicken on the floor, for
instance, gave me a more vivid illustration of death than Grandfather's
funeral. While he lay so peacefully in his coffin, garbed in the splendour
of Taoist robes, the poor chicken was hopping alive with its head cut off.

During the hot and humid summer days in Shanghai, our wooden
backdoor would be left open in the hope of stirring a breeze inside the
kitchen. The second barred gate was kept locked for security reasons.
When the servants were off on various errands and the kitchen was
empty, I would draw up a little stool and sit with my face pressed against
the bars to stare into the narrow lane beyond. From inside the house, I
could smell the scent of a row of watermelons kept cool on the tiled floor
of the dining room. Outside, the stifling heat of the day had driven
everyone indoors. Sometimes the quiet was broken by the distant cry of
hawkers, calling their wares. Maybe I would hear them approach, and
see them flash by, a glimpse of sweaty men with bare feet, burdened
with heavy loads slung from a bamboo pole across their shoulder.
Perhaps it was the future actress within me that made me put myself in
their place; and I was touched by the hardships of other people's lives.

When my sisters and I moved into a bedroom which looked onto the
front of the house behind, there was a woman on the first floor opposite
who was to capture my attention most of all. She was a high-class
prostitute, who had obviously known better days and enjoyed some
notoriety, for even the servants had heard of her infamy. Now she was in
her late thirties, living in a single room with her maid – who was also her
apprentice. In the hot weather, when the windows were wide open, I
could hear her talking shop to her companion. Although too young to
understand her worldly transactions, I was riveted by her movements,
animated, vulgar, and fascinating. With the high collar of her *cheong sam*
loose, her slit skirt hitched up to her waist and with her hands on her

hips, she would strut about the room gesticulating and talking. And she would slap her thighs to make a point.

Alas, I never saw her with a man. Perhaps her working hours were confined to the nights, when I was asleep – even Chinese children went to bed sometimes. Perhaps she had closed her windows and drawn the curtains to receive her paying guests. So Father's anger was all the more unfair, when eventually I was caught watching her. She was only eating a melon, anyway. And how could you put three young girls in a room opposite a whore and not expect them to be curious? My sisters were equally fascinated by her, and I bet they saw and understood more than I did.

I wanted so much to get to know this woman, as I wanted to befriend the slave girl next door. But it was impossible, for the grown-ups never let the children out of their sight. She did, however, make a gesture towards the family, for as I found out later she had approached the servants to ask for one of our dress patterns. Did she, I wondered, have a child of her own? Inevitably the servants snubbed her, as servants do, and she flung abuse at them in return.

Years later, in London, when I was preparing for the role of a prostitute, Suzie Wong, I summoned this woman affectionately back into my memory. Her name, oddly enough, was Wong.

6

Christianity is Never Superstitious

ℓ

It was about this time that Banana (from the shape of his nose) joined Ah Zhu to cook Western food for the family, a great catch for Mother since he came straight from the French Consulate. The traditional redwood table in the dining room was replaced by a long mahogany table complete with high-backed Edwardian chairs that Mother picked up at auction. She began to brief us on the use of a knife and fork, which seemed to me a very clumsy way of eating with two hands rather than one.

Mao Sheng, also from the French Consulate, soon joined Banana, first as butler and later replacing him altogether as he picked up Banana's skills. He was very bright, and very much his own man. He liked to expound his theories on the state of the nation to a wholly uninterested kitchen. He was the only literate among them, and he kept up to date by reading Father's papers. He read anything he could lay hands on in an effort to improve his skill: we argued once over some schoolbooks he had borrowed, and I am glad to say he won the dispute.

Between school and tutors we had our weekends for leisure, when we went to the theatre and accompanied our parents to restaurants. The first translated Western play I saw, aged seven, was Gorky's *Lower Depths*, which dealt with the conditions of the proletariat; all these years later I still recall the wonderful acting of the late Shi Hui, one of China's greatest modern actors.

Mother spent a lot of money on the girls' clothes because she wanted everyone to admire us. We would all be dressed in identical Chinese or Western style dresses (see photographs), such as the black velvet number with a red satin trim that showed off our pale skin. On Sundays, in Sunday best, we did not go to church but to the cinema, usually accompanied by Teacher Ding. We saw Chinese films made by left-wing directors which tackled social problems and treated women with respect. And we saw solid commercial Western films, with Dorothy Lamour and Maria Montez playing exotic princesses. Later, alone before the mirror, I was always Maria Montez.

Returning, we would put on our own plays. Susan directed, Cecilia scripted, and I was of course the female lead. Since William was never allowed to join in because he would never take anything seriously, Cecilia was invariably the leading man, and small friends who came over were roped in, willing or not. Michael was still too small. Later we founded a society and produced our own money for a while. Michael would accumulate these pieces of paper which we all thought was pretty futile. Little did we know that he was practising to be the millionaire he would later become.

I was still far from bilingual when Mother removed me from primary school and sent me to the convent next door, where European children studied. Why I was singled out is still a puzzle to me. Perhaps Mother thought that as an extrovert I would be best equipped to deal with forward foreign children. And indeed, I was not in the least intimidated. I woke on the first morning of term feeling excited and cheerful in the face of a new adventure.

Alas, my first day at school proved disastrous. During play with other girls I was driven to fury by the constant bullying of my foreign classmates and jabbed a pen nib into a little girl's arm. She screamed loudly and the activity in the classroom came to a standstill. I was the centre of attention, and I rather wished I wasn't. Mother Robert wanted me to apologise to my victim, but I felt only a sense of injustice. Incapable of expressing this in a foreign language I merely refused to say sorry. The situation got out of hand and I found myself clinging to doorknobs for what felt like hours, resisting all attempts to send me home to face my mother's wrath. In the end Mother Superior Fitzgerald had to be called, and somehow she resolved the situation. But I never did apologise.

Despite the awkward start, my years at the convent were happy. I rapidly became bilingual and soon felt at home with my foreign schoolmates, who didn't dare bully me any more for fear of the pen nib. In time I even took a Eurasian girl under my protection. Half Chinese, half Scottish, she was prey to racial taunts on every front. Her brother was the first man I saw to wear a skirt. She herself eventually became, of all things, a well-known Spanish dancer in Europe, known as Margarita.

For a while I was fiercely defensive of anything Chinese, upset by a remark as innocuous as 'I don't like Chinese Blue'. But on the whole I was popular with teachers and pupils. It was an achievement for a native student to be cast as the lead, Cinderella, in the school play. I could reflect that I had conquered prejudice.

This was the first time I wore a school uniform: blue serge blazer, skirt, white shirt and dark blue tie. Special occasions called for a white uniform, set off by a dash of pale blue tie. I had nightmares about my white gloves which I continually lost, dreaming of walking naked wearing only a pair of white gloves. But while on the whole I found the uniform pretty, it was the white confirmation gowns of the Catholic girls that really dazzled me: they looked like Western child brides. Immediately I was converted to Catholicism, but Mother remained pragmatic. 'I'd rather you be a non-Catholic than a bad one. I think you'll forget the whole thing within a year.' Having attended a convent school herself, she spoke from experience. In the meantime I learned my catechism, diligently said my Hail Marys and kept up a barter system for exchanging holy pictures with my school friends. In the beautiful little chapel I knelt and fervently prayed for small miracles, like the removal of all grown-ups who annoyed me. Fortunately, my prayers went unanswered.

The nuns were addressed as 'Mother', and I loved them all but one, a British woman who looked like a cock in a nun's habit. I blame her for my fall from orthodoxy. I had returned to school after a minor illness, and her immediate reaction was to have me baptised in case I died. The very idea of leaving my parents so soon to go to that other place called heaven, no matter how wonderful it was supposed to be, was quite unacceptable to me. The crunch came when she stumbled upon my most treasured possession, a little book in which I pasted all my favourite cartoon figures, and in which I wrote down my declaration of love to God. I knew I loved Him as much as I loved Donald Duck, or Snow White and the Seven Dwarfs. She found me merely sacrilegious, a concept I had yet to grasp.

Serene Mother Robert, however, was a saint. It was her patience that solved the agonies of my first day, and her understanding that helped me find a way through the maze of information I was supposed to assimilate. Western symbolism would sometimes conflict with my own. Chinese history was bloodthirsty enough, without the wrath of the Old

Testament God and the peculiar antics of Greek heroes to compound my confusion.

'How can the Virgin Mary give birth to Jesus if she isn't properly married to Joseph?' I would ask.

'It was the Immaculate Conception,' Mother Robert replied.

'What's the Immaculate Conception?'

'Well, a kind of miracle.'

'What's the difference between a miracle and a superstition?' I asked in puzzlement.

Mother Robert stiffened slightly. 'Christianity is never superstitious, my child. Only pagan religions are superstitious.'

'Yes, Mother,' I said, not entirely convinced. And later I might say, 'Why are you a mother, and not married?'

'Because I am married to God,' she would reply.

'Are all the mothers in the convent married to God?'

'Yes, my child.'

'But I thought many Chinese people are sinners because they have more than one wife. So how can God have so many wives?'

Even Mother Robert got tired. 'God is God,' she concluded.

I sneaked into the nuns' quarters one day to have a look for myself. In a huge room, a row of beds lined either wall forming a central aisle that led the eye towards the unmistakable focus on the further wall, where a life-sized Christ hung upon the Cross, naked but for a loincloth, with a trickle of blood running down the side of his body. But I was too young to give a name to the sensation it aroused.

In many ways the convent was an invaluable training for me. Above all else, perhaps, it exposed me to Western religion. And religion – public, potent, ceremonial – is the source of drama.

But again, the drama was all around us in those years: the greater drama of nations, and the tragedy of war.

7

Japanese Occupation

℘

On Sunday 7th December 1941, when the Japanese unexpectedly attacked Pearl Harbor, events in Shanghai took a dramatic turn. Shanghai was waking to a Monday when the Imperial Navy of Japan began to shell the allied gunboats moored on the Huangpu river, and received their surrender. The Second World War, which had sounded only a faint rumble from the battlefields of Europe, broke upon the Pacific.

Though many foreign nationals had been repatriated after the Japanese invasion of China in 1937, thousands were now stranded in Shanghai. It seems in retrospect incredible that Japan's action came unexpectedly, that proper precautions had not been taken. For even the men who had stayed in Shanghai out of duty had been foolish, complacently condoning the Japanese aggression as a convenient buffer between the restless natives and themselves, arguing that the feckless Chinaman needed strong leadership. Although large numbers of European women and children had been repatriated, those wives who were stuck in the city had only themselves to blame, because they had been unable to forgo the luxurious life style provided by amahs and servant boys number one, two, three and more.

Their financial circumstances began to deteriorate as allied property was confiscated, and their social status began to diminish. At first they were only required to wear armbands to mark them out from other Westerners – the Germans, Austrians, Italians, and the Vichy French. Jews, including those who had escaped Nazi Germany, found themselves tormented once again by their uncertain fate, like the White Russians, who, under the nominal protection of the French, felt the anxieties of statelessness. These red armbands had an initial printed to indicate the wearer's nationality, and 'B' armbands were most conspicuous, the all-powerful British branded now like cattle, humiliated before the Chinese. The Japanese wanted to break the myth of the almighty whites, and they very nearly succeeded. In 1943 the internments began in camps set up in and around Shanghai.

We knew little about these camps, which only the neutral Swiss authorities could visit. They were terrible places, for sure, but grosser atrocities were being committed daily on wholly defenceless Chinese whose fate occupied Father most.

For some Chinese, fraternisation became a way of life. People like my father took the line of passive resistance. Japan's puppet government in Nanjing presented the invasion as a salvation, to unite the yellow races against white imperialism. Father led a campaign in Shanghai to move public opinion against this piece of fabrication. Its name was Yi Feng She, or Shift Wind Society: I like to think that this was a pun on the foul air that was passing through our land.

Father had grown up as the last imperial dynasty collapsed and the debate over foreign depradations grew intense. His work was Chinese, for Chinese: he had shown his faith in his native art and institutions when he had chosen to remould, rather than replace them. He had taken his art to the breaking point, but it had not broken. He had infused Peking Opera with ideas relevant to his time, and influenced others to do the same, in painting and writing and film-making. The theatre had become polemical in peacetime, and it was all the stronger now for its message of resistance to the foreign invader.

The theatre was a potent element in boosting the morale of the Chinese and persuading them to stand firm and united against the enemy. The law of Occupation prohibited public gatherings of more than five people, but the theatre drew huge crowds and could not be put down. In the peculiar ambience of the Peking Opera houses, the underground could meet with ease. Opera houses were never formal, like their Western counterparts. The audience would saunter in and out, like the British visiting a pub, and, what's more, they brought their children. The plays began at six without ceremony and continued without intermission until about midnight, with a programme that usually consisted of extracts from longer plays, unless a new play was to be performed. During the performance the children would play in the aisles, colliding with the vendors of tea, melon seeds and fruits. Hot towels were tossed with precision over the heads of the customers.

Adults gossiped amongst themselves, for they were familiar with the plots founded on myth, history and romances; only the climactic moments, or the arrival of the star, deserved their undivided attention. Then the audience would fall silent, the lights would dim for a second, and the auditorium would erupt with a thunderous intensity I have since heard only in Spanish bullrings or at English football matches. I proudly witnessed my father receiving this accolade innumerable times.

One of the men responsible for pushing the theatre as a means of resistance to the Japanese was Jiang Chunfang, who became a close friend of Father's. Born near Shanghai, Jiang had been educated in the northern Manchurian city of Harbin where, close to the Russian border, it was a matter of course that he trained as a Russian scholar. At the age of twenty he had joined the underground Communist Party, and was imprisoned for sabotage against the occupying Japanese forces. He escaped execution only by invoking the protection of the Methodist Church, which he had joined at the same time – later he married the Chinese parson's sister. His mother, illiterate but strong willed, had instilled in him a love of Peking Opera and as his interest in the theatre grew he began translating modern Russian plays. Finally, in 1938, he collaborated on the first Chinese translation of Stanislavski's *An Actor Prepares*.

The outbreak of the war with Japan saw him back in Shanghai, charged by the Party with uniting the urban population to resist the enemy. He was well-qualified to exploit the theatre as a vehicle for resistance. The purpose was not necessarily political: merely assembling large numbers of Chinese could act to boost morale. Jiang and his group were able to organise thousands of amateur dramatic societies across a wide social spectrum. One result of all this activity was to spread interest in modern drama on the Western model beyond the narrow social sphere of the Western educated élite to all ranks of society. Amateur dramatic groups were formed not only in schools, universities and factories, but also amongst white-collar staff of Chinese or foreign companies; clerks, pharmacists, post office workers and the like, as well as the dispossessed and destitute refugees who poured into the city. Lacking the technical expertise required for traditional Chinese drama, they concentrated on Spoken Drama instead, using translations and new Chinese plays written on the Western model. It was as if China's largest city gave itself over to an enormous and perpetual drama festival.

This drive to promote political consciousness through the new medium of Spoken Drama required the leadership of an actor of stature, inevitably someone who could command a national following. Father stood out from all the superstars in classical theatre, and Jiang approached him through Mr You Jingui (the man who had let in the robbers) to lend prestige and support to the project. He readily agreed to help.

Many of the Peking Operas Father wrote against the Japanese were banned. Among them were two giving the title roles to heroic figures in Chinese history whose names were synonymous with insubordination and resistance to the enemy: Wen Tianxiang and Shi Kefa. The ban did not prevent Father from advertising them. He had the characters painted on huge scrolls, hung on either side of the proscenium arch, and took space in the newspapers.

All his plays could not be banned. Just as Anouilh's *Antigone* played Paris during the German Occupation, meaning could be veiled in innocent historical tales, and the public was expert at retrieving it. Father's most popular play at the time was *The Bitter Legacy of the Ming*, which had a good run before it, too, was banned. Father played the last Ming Emperor who lost his kingdom to the Manchu barbarians and who hanged himself from a maple tree in Beijing (a tree marks the spot today). In one of the climactic scenes, the emperor slew his daughter to save her from the degradation of encountering their enemy. When asked why she deserved this fate, he replied: 'Because you are Chinese!' Every time they heard this line the audience's emotions were uncontrollable. From the rickshaw puller in the gallery to the dilettante in the stalls, they thundered together: '*You, you* . . . encore, encore!' Each time I saw this scene I felt as though Father were killing me, his own daughter.

But while Father threw himself into his war work, life at home remained much the same as ever, preserved within the perimeters of the French concession under the Vichy government. Change and chaos filtered through largely as a game provided by the grown-ups. Our old Ford turned completely black and sooty after Fu Sheng replaced the petrol tank with a charcoal burner. Soon the car disappeared altogether and Fu Sheng was reduced to a pedicab with a closed carriage, which required all his strength to pedal. Our windows were pasted with brown paper strips and hung with black-out curtains, first against Japanese bombing of the city and finally against Allied bombing of Japanese installations. After an Allied bomb missed its target and exploded in a city cinema we took more precautions. Thick bedrolls were piled on top of the heavy mahogany dining table and we children were told to hide beneath it. Mother was always there, and the sound of aeroplanes or explosions was just part of the fun.

One incident remains vividly in my mind, illustrating the precarious nature of our position. The Japanese organised a civil defence drill in which all males – meaning male servants, not masters – were obliged to participate. Fu Sheng and Mao Sheng went along with their empty buckets only to return with a Japanese corporal who ordered that every house must contribute water. Mother flatly refused. She felt that water was too scarce a resource to waste on a mere rehearsal. She sent word down to the corporal, 'Certainly not!' There was a pause, and then the sound of heavy kicking on the iron front door, booming through the house like a terrible foretaste of the Japanese's power. Mother quickly changed her mind, and water was immediately forthcoming.

The situation tensed as I got older. The Convent was closed down when the foreign children were interned, and I went to the Chinese school like my sisters. Mother was always security, and I asked for her each day when I got home. In one period I found her often in tears, discussing with Teacher Ding some plans to leave the house. I discovered the reason later. Father had refused repeatedly to perform privately for the Japanese and their collaborators. One evening, a huge car arrived outside our front door, sent by Wu Shibao, the Chinese second-in-command of the Secret Police. Father was requested to dine as guest of honour at Police Headquarters, the dreaded Number 76. After dinner, his hosts courteously gave him a tour of the torture chambers. Father got the message, and Mother was prepared. That night she took him straight into hiding in a foreigner's home. Father never performed for the enemy, and he returned unharmed so that, to my disappointment, we never had to leave the house. He must have been protected by his underworld benefactor, and by his profession, for the puppet government had to maintain the fiction of benevolence, and it could not afford to martyr China's most popular actor.

My bit in the war effort was to harass Japanese schoolchildren at every opportunity. William and I used to play with the concubine sons of Du Yuesheng, the most powerful secret society leader, who had followed the Nationalists to Chongqing. My two friends lived with their mother in the Eighteen Floors, now the Jing Jiang Hotel, one of the grand apartment blocks favoured by high-ranking Japanese officials. We threw stones at their children in the grounds, and then ran for our lives. Somehow our guerrilla tactics never got us into trouble, perhaps because the fathers were away working hard in their headquarters leaving only their docile and submissive wives at home. I sometimes saw these women bidding their husbands goodbye in their lobby, slim figures in kimonos bowing continuously towards the elevator doors until the men were well out of sight. How stupid they looked, I thought. At least Chinese women don't have to do that.

But only once did I come face to face with a Japanese in uniform. It was during one of our skirmishes, when I was trailing behind the boys, that an officer materialised apparently out of nowhere and shouted for me to stop. He looked refined, and spoke to me in English – our common language. I thought my number was up, but he only asked: 'Why aren't you in camp?' I hadn't the faintest idea what he was talking about.

'What nationality are you?' he asked finally. Couldn't he tell? I wondered. We were a few yards apart, and I stared at him across the gap racking my brains for the next move. 'I am Chinese!' I eventually cried in English, and ran as fast as I could, certain I could hear his footsteps gaining behind. But when I stopped, panting, and turned around, there was nobody there.

It was Mother who eventually cleared the mystery up, and revealed the secret of her background to me. Since it is a stigma to be of mixed blood in China, my parents had tried to avoid any mention of it. It was the first time I had heard that I was one eighth Scottish. Because of my brown, slightly curling hair, I did not look completely Chinese to the Asians – yet I had never been made aware of the difference before. Suddenly some lost incidents came back to me, and fitted into my discovery. It explained why Grandmother was so exotic looking – she had a Western nose in contrast to her bound feet. I saw why Mother was called 'Little Foreigner' in the gutter press, which I was not supposed to read. And it explained a curious incident when I had been eating Heinz alphabet soup, and Grandmother had uncharacteristically leaned forward to speak. She said: 'This is an H,' looking into the soup. 'And here is a T . . .' Her sudden revelation surprised us both. How could a conventional Chinese lady, I had wondered, be familiar with the Roman alphabet? I had asked then, but received no proper answer. Then it became clear.

I am touched by the thought of my grandmother now, so conventional and quiet, bearing the brunt of the mixed match. I was not troubled by the discovery, though it meant that I was a 'mongrel' myself, like the Eurasian girl I befriended. The little drop of foreign blood I bore could have compromised my sense of being Chinese, but in fact the opposite was true. For was I not truly linked to the cataclysm in China's history, by the blood of a foreigner, and born myself of the changes that were propelling China forward and away from her closed, feudal past? China's forced contact with foreign powers, which was to produce such changes, was echoed in my own family history. But the parallels were closer than I imagined, even then. I would learn that my destiny was bound into the destiny of my homeland, and that my life would be lived in the shadow of a changing China, a China that would spin into revolution, and beyond.

At the moment of writing, I see in my mind's eye my grandmother's slender face. I see no harshness in her eyes, no bitterness around her mouth. And yet, how much pain was buried in her stillness? How much emotion was concealed behind a wall of silence? I shall never know. I don't even know her personal name. But I realise now how much I love her.

Another surprise was in store for me. Admiring my parents' beautiful wedding photograph one day when I was still innocent and thirteen, I remarked to an adult that Mother's arms were nice and round. 'Yes,' the woman replied casually, 'that's because she already had you when the photo was taken.' It took a split second for the full meaning of her remark to penetrate – this woman meant to do me mischief. I gave her no satisfaction. I did not react. But the pain inside me was sharp, as though my heart was an apple that she had split in half. My moral standards were too limited for judgement and I despairingly relied upon my parents' infallibility. At the time, it took all the love I had to forgive them.

Gradually, over the next few years, my mother disclosed her past to me, which brought us close. The story she unfolded in her characteristic manner sounded like a romantic comedy, which in a way it was: the elopement, the little bundle of jewelry, the absurd moments during the wedding ceremony . . . In the attic I searched for evidence of her past. The white satin wedding dress had turned to creamy yellow and the newspaper cuttings broke in pieces in my hands. The more I understood, the more I was proud of her. As a young girl from a very respectable family, what risks did she take to follow the path of her heart? In the end she convinced me that I was the luckiest child of all. For, in her words, I am truly a child of love.

ℯ

With a break only when Father was forced into hiding, my parents managed to keep open house throughout the curfew. Dinner guests were usually selected by Mother, who held court afterwards over general gossip in the sitting room. My father's visitors seldom ate with us – Mother, I think, was slow to invite them – but talked with him in his study of more serious matters. They were often famous people in the arts world, but they came and went without attracting much attention. I well remember Gao Baisui, the most famous of Father's disciples, because he took the trouble to play with me. A sturdy man in his thirties, he obviously loved children and would walk on his hands to delight me – not a difficult feat for a Peking Opera actor. There was Tian Han, too, the distinguished writer who became a household name in China, a revolutionary in arts and politics, who often collaborated with Father in revitalising Peking Opera, hoping to attract a younger audience. The only person I would one day come to know well was Jiang Chunfang, the Russian scholar, because he survived the Cultural Revolution. Decades later, it was through him that I found out many things about Father. Both Tian and Jiang were leading organisers of the underground resistance, later to be regarded as dissidents when the Nationalists under Chiang Kai Chek resumed power, and destined to become important cadres in the Communist régime.

Mother's guests were relatives and old girl friends – some ardent fans of Father's who had become good family friends over the years. They were professionals not associated with the arts, usually men who visited the house without their wives. Being able to receive guests of both sexes was a mark of Mother's social independence, and her non intellectual 'salon' was frivolous and relaxed. Mother was always amusing.

My favourite guest was Billy Zhou, 'Big Brother', who at twenty stood six foot two inches tall, and was not only handsome and urbane but also had a lot of time for the children. He was the son of Mother's close friend, whose husband had become a Taoist, renouncing all that was impermanent in this materialist world. Their house was furnished with the minimum of possessions, but Billy was a sharp dresser and looked immaculate in beautifully tailored Western suits. He was a connoisseur of food and Mother could never spare him when we ate out in restaurants. But he was no dilettante, and he held down an unglamorous job. His desire to go to university was quashed when he bowed to tradition and entered into an arranged marriage; feeling strongly that a married man should not depend on his parents for support, he trained as an accountant. His beautiful wife, a Chinese Barbara Stanwyck, dressed in stylish suits and coats with broad shoulders and fur cuffs, and we were equally fond of her.

The younger sister of my spinster cousin Big Big Sister came occasionally. Sickly and tired looking at thirty, she gave her husband a child every year. Mother eventually took her to a German doctor who gave her an abortion and a hysterectomy. I remember Mother's instructions: wear shabby clothes so that the doctor does not charge too much. Mother was the first woman I knew who advocated contraception and approved of abortion.

But by far the most intriguing guests were a trio whom I respectfully addressed as Aunties Four, Five and Seven (I often wondered about the missing numbers). They were cousins, and childhood friends of Mother's. They always seemed to be in our house, where they would sit together on the sofa like a row of odd-sized crows. Auntie Seven was the only married woman among them, and so the most fortunate in the world's eyes. Yet she looked the thinnest and most miserable of the lot, weighed down by an unemployed husband and two young children. Auntie Four was the prettiest and the silliest, undone by those saucer eyes of hers. She had got involved with a married man and borne him a daughter – reputedly on Mother's advice. Perhaps that was why Mother felt most responsible for her, for Auntie Four might come with her daughter to stay for months on end, when she found it hard to make ends meet – it was on one of these extended visits that she hid her only ring from the robbers.

Auntie Five was the tallest and the ugliest and, from what I heard, quite sex-starved. Mother once felt her trembling in a cinema while a man groped her all over in the dark. Was it fear that preserved her silence then, or ecstasy? Her past served as a warning that Mother must have considered when she eloped with Father: Auntie Five had fallen in love with her impoverished cousin, who lived in the same house of three generations. One day, they were caught eloping, and before her eyes her lover was beaten to death. She was condemned to a life of spinsterhood and retirement.

If Mother was anxious not to allow us to follow the vagabond life, neither did she want us to grow up like these women, whose privilege cramped and repressed them. Women of lower class could find fulfilment in work, and independence with it. But girls of the Aunties' class and generation had only marriage to look forward to, and only one chance at it. Their happiness depended solely on whom they were married to, and if fate wronged them, as it had wronged these friends of

Mother's, their lives were blighted for good. In a feudal society in China, it was women who had to bear the brunt of moral hypocrisy, reinforced by the dictates of Confucius. And at a time when the country was finally undergoing radical social change, traditionally reared women were ill-equipped to meet the challenges. Their only security was their dowry, the very capital Mother had trained us never to expect. They had no education, and consequently no means to alter their assumptions about themselves and perhaps free themselves from their plight. Their puny efforts at self assertion had only bound Aunties Four and Five to a wasted life of semi-ostracism and shame.

The coming of Japan's defeat heightened the terror in Shanghai, as people contemplated the massacres in Nanjing and wondered how the soldiers would behave in defeat. The dreaded name of the Guan Dong army was on everybody's lips. The grown-ups discussed their plans for flight, suggesting that the girls should be disguised as boys by shaving their heads and blackening their faces. And they would be given weapons to carry. At first I imagined myself as Mu Lan, the Chinese Joan of Arc, brandishing my sword and terrorising the enemy, a daunting but dramatically irresistible prospect. But I soon realised that my weapon would be only a small knife, and that its purpose was not to kill my enemy but to do myself in, if necessary, to save myself from a fate worse than death.

I had a vague sense of the horrors of rape, but could not understand why it should bring such dishonour as to warrant self-destruction. The answer, of course, was that women must satisfy the male fetish of virginity and chastity. I was relieved not to have to put this ancient custom into effect, but the mystery and vulnerability of my sex remained unfathomable in my mind.

8

Mother's Finest Hour

t̸

'It's a long way to Tipperary,
  'It's a long way to go!'
I woke on the 14th August 1945, to hear my father singing this
unlikely First World War marching song. He spoke no English, so he
must have picked it up phonetically from British Tommies stationed in
China in his youth. I found him downstairs, radiant with joy, and asked
him the cause of all the excitement. As if I had not already guessed.

In eight long years of war, millions of Chinese had perished, and
untold numbers had suffered famine, looting and humiliation at the
hands of the Japanese. These implacable people, to whom surrender
meant utter dishonour, had surrendered at last! China would be free –
completely free, for Chiang Kai Chek and Roosevelt had negotiated the
reversion of all foreign concessions to China with the defeat of the Axis
powers. So, ironically, Japan's invasion did signal the destruction of
white colonialism in China. Only Hong Kong and Macao, colonies
rather than concessions, would remain in foreign hands. How differently the victors at Versailles had acted, ceding the lands of their Chinese
allies to the Japanese, and so precipitating the rape of China, and the
maelstrom of the Pacific War. Now the world's most powerful nation
imposed a just peace, and upheld the principles of national self-
determination. As the never-setting sun sank upon the British Empire, it
seemed to us that the Stars and Stripes unfurled in friendship.

All of a sudden, Shanghai was transformed. Americans were everywhere. The short, tense and robotic Japanese were replaced by long,
loose and gangling GIs from the land reputedly paved with gold, and I
had my first glimpse of a man with ebony skin. Prices rose immediately,

a bonanza for the shopkeepers, the prostitutes and the rickshaw pullers, but not so good for locals. It was not a time for complaints, though. Shanghainese were falling for everything the bright new world had to offer. Mass produced goods were an irresistible novelty, such as drinking glasses with laminated pin-ups on them, and anything plastic was in vogue with the modish Shanghainese. Coca-Cola culture was upon us.

Ladies of the waterfront took on a bizarre look in an attempt, I suppose, to wow their new overseas clientele with an image of the 'li'l girl next door': they bleached the hair on their head, and perhaps elsewhere, to different depths of blonde. Seeing them on their water-front beat, the Shanghainese coined a wicked name for them im-mediately: the Salty and Soured Beauties. Rickshaw pullers were experiencing the novelty of being pulled by their customers for a change, whose zany democratic gesture completely upset the balance of the vehicle, its owner's only asset. These GIs from Nebraska and Arkansas cavorted in the streets, having the time of their lives. Ya hooo! . . . Ya hooooo! they shouted, whooping it up with an uncouth vivacity that astounded the populace. Personally, I just loved it all!

Hollywood movies were back after a long absence. Our first film was *Union Pacific*, starring Barbara Stanwyck and Joel McCrea, which dealt with the Irish who built the Eastern half of the trans-American railway (the Chinese labourers who built the other, more difficult half never got into a Hollywood movie). Even Grandmother, who never went to movies, came along. Her eyesight was none too good and she sat like Mr Magoo, peering at the screen where white men with forked tongue were being attacked by galloping Red Indians on horseback along the fast-moving train. Grandmother's voice could be heard above the sound track loud and clear: 'Why are these idiots riding so fast on their bicycles?'

With the Shanghai Women's Association, Teacher Ding started organising housewives to present amateur dramas that soon became closet public meetings with political undertones. Putting ordinary 're-spectable' women on stage was an achievement. These women took their stands on a makeshift platform, clenched their hands in front of their abdomens, and began to recite in a voice as tremulous and dramatic as any Western opera singer in Wigmore Hall, 'During the eight terrible years of war, I endured . . .' They acted out their parts with tremendous sincerity and gusto, giving vent to otherwise unutterable pains and tribulations. The sincerity and the agony did not prevent the ever sardonic Shanghainese from dubbing their performances the 'Stomach Ache' school of acting.

I was selected to perform myself – and agreed with little inducement. In one of the larger Shanghai theatres I nonchalantly pranced on stage, my song prepared, and addressed myself to the vastness of the auditorium – and an ocean of small wonders like myself. I promptly forgot everything I was meant to do, and I cowardlily ran to the wings, only to be propelled on stage again by a fierce Teacher Ding. Eventually I finished my song, and even received applause. To this day, Susan can remember her embarrassment as she watched me making a fool of myself. This was my first public appearance in China and, to Susan's relief I am sure, my last.

One day, just as Teacher Ding herself was due to come on stage, a commotion at the entrance interrupted the performance. The Nationalist controlled police were making a raid to check on their political opponents. I took Teacher Ding's distraught expression as a sign of disappointment that her performance had been curtailed. Such a pity, to get all worked up for the stage and then have the whole thing collapse. But I did not know that tension was already rising amongst these women, between the wives of right-wing Nationalists who had fled to the Western provinces, and the left-wing women who had stayed in Shanghai to fight with the underground.

My mother heard at the time that Teacher Ding was indeed on the Nationalists' 'black list', marked for her Communist sympathies and, we supposed, her contacts with the Communist underground resistance during the Occupation. The black list was more than a bar to employment; it could mean arrest or even execution. Anyone on a black list was fair game, almost an outlaw. Mother, who loved Teacher Ding like one of the family, didn't hesitate. Just as she had once kowtowed to save her husband, she sought out the police official responsible and offered him two gold bars to remove Teacher Ding from the list. The Nationalist official looked up the name – and laughed. There was indeed a Communist Ding on the list, but it was another person, a man with the same surname. Mother's relief was overwhelming. But Mother paid the gold anyway, and saw to it that the name was erased. Mr Ding Jingtang is now the head of the Art and Literature Publishing Association.

The euphoria of peace did not last long. The Cold War set in, and the madcap GIs seemed less ebullient than before. The Beautiful Country – the Chinese word for the USA – was beginning to reveal blemishes: racism, isolationism. I overheard Father asking a returned traveller in disbelief: 'Do the black people still live in slums? Do they have any democratic rights?' And the war in the North resumed between Communists and Nationalists. Corruption fed upon bloated prices and inflation ruined the Nationalist currency, *fa-bi*, until a suitcase of notes bought a bar of soap. The instinctive response from the government was to tighten the screws.

It ordered that all 'special professions' should register with the police: 'special' meant actors, directors, writers – and prostitutes. It was the old Amusement Population again, once more to be treated as the dregs of society and lumped together beyond the pale. The aim was to keep tabs on the dissidents who were concentrated amongst the artistic community, but the ploy misfired. The intelligentsia were in uproar, and at a stroke the Nationalists alienated them all, regardless of their normal affiliations. Once again Father led a campaign, now against his own government, and he collected enough signatures to persuade the government to drop the matter.

Meanwhile Mother, just gone forty, celebrated the end of the Second World War by giving birth to a sixth child whom she promptly named after Vivien Leigh, China's favourite Western movie star. The spelling suffered a sea change, though. Vivian was a bouncing baby and became the most spoilt child of the family, since ageing parents tend to lose their grip on discipline. It was a difficult labour, but although Grandmother had come to stay, superstition prevented her from entering the 'blood room'. It was said that if a woman died in childbirth, she would go straight to the lowest pit in hell. Nonsense! I proclaimed; not only do we women have to risk our lives to perpetuate the human race, but we are delivered to purgatory should we fail to do so.

While Mother was recuperating, Father had to visit Hangzhou, the Lake City and site of his first public performance, with a male friend and a woman I suppose to have been the friend's mistress. I was never properly told the purpose of the trip, but I was chosen out of the five children as his companion, and we spent an enjoyably idle week there. Hangzhou is barely half a day's train ride from Shanghai. The city was dominated by the west lake, surrounded on three sides by high hills dotted with romantic monasteries and shrines. We whiled our time away in long rowing boats beneath flat awnings, meandering through pools of white and pink lotus blossoms. On the banks we strolled past tall willows bending gracefully to the spring breeze (is it any wonder that men have come to use this lovely image as a metaphor for ideal femininity, always so gently yielding, but never breaking?). Sometimes we came across elegant calligraphy carved on pillars, epigrams, I seem to remember, inscribed by long-dead poets to their courtesans.

This was old China. In ancient restaurants overhanging narrow lanes, we savoured masterpieces of local cuisine, a pastime which the Chinese, like the French, take most seriously. In the beautiful botanical garden we were served tea made with freshly-drawn spring water which rose above the lip of the tea-cups without spilling over. I discovered Father's knowledge of plants and trees, but, city born and city bred, I failed to share his interest. It was the first and only time in my life that I had Father all to myself, without brothers, sisters, or even Mother. But I did not take advantage of this rare opportunity to please.

On our last day, a frantic mother came running up to him, looking for her six-year-old son, an angelic-looking boy whom I had befriended over the week. Bored with the sedate company of adults I had taken the little boy climbing in the wilder parts of the high hills. It was easy enough going up; coming down was more of a problem. I had to carry him most of the way and although we got back safely it took up the whole afternoon. What a ticking off I had from Father on the train coming home! As far as I can remember, this thoughtless behaviour was the last of my childish escapades. Even I had to grow up. This incident marked the end of my childhood, and puberty began.

One bright January morning in 1947 Mother's finest hour had arrived. The first stage of her mission was accomplished. We watched Susan up the gangway of the liner that would take her to America. Until now, only the highest in the land had sent their children abroad to study, but for the first time a child of a vagabond claimed the privilege. A daughter, too! Everyone was so proud, the family, relatives, friends and the servants.

Immediately on her recovery after giving birth to Vivian, Mother and Susan left for Nanjing, the Nationalist capital, for Susan to apply for a passport to study at Columbia University, New York, New York, USA. Susan, after all, was academically brilliant, and the only one amongst us who had not changed schools. She had wanted to study in Paris, because she was best at French, but Mother would not hear of her innocent daughter risking exposure to the notorious wickedness of Gay Paree (stereotyping of other countries is not an exclusive Western prerogative). So Susan was packed off to clean-living New York instead.

Mother overlooked nothing. Tailors ran to and fro filling trunks with Western and Chinese clothes for every season. Then there were shoes, handbags, lingerie, toiletries and even Chinese medicines to see to, plus furs and jewelry. It was as if Susan was being exiled to Hick City rather than the consumer capital of the world. Susan, who shared her father's simple tastes, would scarcely touch her vast wardrobe, a veritable trousseau in the name of education, not matrimony. America was far away, and the fare was astronomical. Mother had no idea when she would see her first-born again.

They were destined to meet only one more time.

The following New Year our dining table was laid with an empty place, and Susan's presence was symbolised by a plate with her zodiac sign upon it. Over the years there would be more empty plates, fewer children. Twice a year we heard her voice on expensive long-distance phone calls. The lines were generally bad but it made little difference since Mother spent most of the time sobbing into the receiver. One year, the family went to Father's recording studio to cut a record for the absent sister. Father was meant to speak first, but as the record went round and round no sound came out of him. At the time I thought it was odd that he should have stage fright after having made so many records in his time, but at this moment of writing it dawns on me with a wrench that he who was so disciplined was actually struggling to control his emotions. Finally he blurted out, at random: 'Today is Sunday.' The tension snapped and we all fell about laughing. By now half the recording time had been spent; Mother used the remainder by sobbing into the microphone. So my sister received an avant garde production in the style of John Cage, three minutes of silence, laughter and tears all orchestrated by chance.

With Susan's departure I was promoted over Cecilia to be Mother's confidante. I was the ideal candidate, pliable where Susan was objective, and full of admiration and adoration where Cecilia would have been at loggerheads. And so began the inseparable bond between my mother and myself which was to colour my future relationships with others. It was love without boundaries, intense but unthreatening, tactile but innocent and, above all, trusting without fear of rejection or betrayal. Mother was infinitely wise in my eyes. I followed her everywhere, even to the bathroom to watch her brush her teeth. Like Queen Victoria lovingly watching Albert shave, I felt that everything she did was beautiful.

'Where there's a will there's a way,' was her favourite motto, and I would almost kill myself trying to live up to it. I kept no secret from her, for that was her wish. She wanted me to understand that it was for my own protection. My innocence and gullibility erected no defences against the dark forces of the opposite sex who might do me harm. The antics of the birds and the bees were as mysterious to a child in the East as in the West. As children we were told that we came from our mother's armpits, suitably distant from the genitals. To Mother I reported change in my pubescent body immediately. 'Never let anyone touch your breasts,' she advised, meaning before marriage, presumably, 'or they'll drop.' Drop? Drop where? I wondered. 'And never accept any present from a man, even if it's a handkerchief,' she added. Had she read *Othello* to know of Desdemona's blameless imprudence? I was being confused by her powerful injunctions. A wall of caution was built in me. I was to learn later that the first command was impractical, and the second downright uneconomical.

But I took it all in, and obeyed.

Cecilia meanwhile plotted her revenge, and when the time was right she took it. As though she had learned the art of witchcraft overnight, she was transformed from an ordinary duckling into a swan. 'Throughout my childhood,' she explained to me later, 'I tried my best to win Mother's love. I failed. So I prayed to God for beauty instead – and I got it.' Which god? I should like to know. From that day, the balance of power in the house shifted, for Cecilia got all the attention and our open house began to fill with young male guests on any excuse to catch a glimpse of her. Poor William was unable to understand why it now took so long to get rid of his male tutors, who were hanging on by the skin of their teeth, going berserk with adoration. Cecilia took to it like a swan to water, floating haughtily past her admirers and appearing not to notice the devastation around her. Mother was put out, for she wanted me to be the centre of attention – ignoring the fact that I was still a tomboy in pigtails and no one's vision of a femme fatale.

I was not particularly jealous of Cecilia myself. After all, I had always looked up to my older sisters, and considered them intelligent and well-read for their age. Cecilia had a mind before she had beauty. Furthermore, her classical beauty commanded unqualified esteem. She had a Madonna-like face, what the Chinese approvingly call 'melon-seed' in shape, with a high forehead, wide-set eyes, Grandmother's aristocratic nose and a generous mouth. She was the kind of woman who could merely pull back her hair in a bun to look stunning: that I do envy! Taller than the average Shanghai girl at five foot three inches, she

was not too tall to intimidate the opposite sex, and she bore herself with
dignity, carrying off the Chinese high-collared dress that showed off her
hourglass figure and graceful neck to perfection. Later, at St John's
University, they called her the Alabaster Beauty, and years later her
peers recalled her with wonderment in their eyes.

When I cut and permed my hair in the June Allyson pageboy style, I
turned into – well, no swan, but a bright-eyed hoyden. My favourite
outfit was a spotless white Western dress with white socks to match, and
my most treasured possession, a big bright red shoulder bag made from
the chicest material, genuine plastic. As the epitome of a Chinese
bobbysoxer I found a few admirers of my own, and had no need to envy
my sister. Cecilia now replaced William as my constant companion,
since he was still a mere boy, and when we moved to a larger house we
young ladies shared a suite of rooms where we lounged about planning
our new social life. Our camaraderie was based on the strict assumption
that I took second place to her, the belle of the ball.

Our new house stood in the same street but in a swankier part of
town. Using some pieces from her collection of jewelry, Mother had
actually purchased it as an investment some time before, and shrewdly
leased it to the neutral Portuguese Consulate during the war. The rules
of *feng shui* had been observed in its construction, for it had been built at
a strange angle to take advantage of certain auspicious astronomical
features. It was a rather ugly arrangement whereby the square house
was plonked down diagonally in a square lot, dividing the garden into
four little triangles and setting the front gates at an angle to the house,
which deprived it of dignity. It was beautiful all the same, with arched
doorways and louvred shutters, and a closed verandah fronting the
house – the warmest place on winter days in a house that had no central
heating, for the sun poured in cheerfully. There was a stove in the
drawing room adjoining the large dining room where guests enjoyed
themselves as before, and where Cecilia and I threw our frequent dance
parties. Beyond, the hallway was dominated by a heavy oak stairway
down which I glided in my first Western ball dress – apple green taffeta
silk – to receive my guests, pretending to be Scarlett O'Hara throwing a
ball at Tara.

Our suite on the third floor was out of bounds to male visitors,
naturally, and I would later work hard there, trying to effect a change in
the success of my studies. By now all the furniture was Western, either
custom made or bought at auction, and I preened myself for hours
before the oval mirrors of our white wardrobe, scattering piles of clothes

on the floor for the maid to pick up. William's opinion here was never to be solicited. He pronounced every effect 'terrible'.

In the attic, Father's rare collection of costumes, all exquisitely hand-embroidered, lay neatly folded and labelled, but Mother's accumulated fabrics, the result of buying by the bolt and not the yard, lay in thorough disorder. I had taken up dressmaking, and was a confident cutter since if I made a mistake I could just return to the attic for more. At first my family approved of this quiet diligence, so unlike my wilder and noisier pursuits, but soon Mother begged me to stop sewing and to put away the needles. Her guests were leaping from chairs like scalded cats.

The kitchen and servants' quarters were in a separate building behind the house. Above them, connected to the house by a small bridge, was Father's study, a large room that was now perfectly tidy, in contrast to his old room which had become quite overrun with books and piles of manuscripts. It was furnished according to his simple tastes without curtains or carpets, and apart from the two-way desk, a comfortable armchair on either side, and bookshelves, there was only a scroll portrait of himself by a famous artist, a gift that Father treasured. In this house I spent the happiest three years of my life.

The young and altogether green gallants my sister and I attracted did not burst in upon our lives but had to be coaxed through careful planning, so that the first male friend would go out and spread the word that ours was a house of liberty, equality and fraternity. A hapless Stephen Chang was chosen to be our torch bearer when he accompanied his mother on a visit. The mother was *hua qiao*, an American-born Chinese, which meant he belonged to a broadminded family. As they were leaving, Cecilia hit on the brilliant ruse of lending him a book. After all, we could see he was keen, but he was clearly shy, as boys of his age tended to be. Now he had a pretext to return.

If our parents were precocious in permitting their teenage daughters to associate with boys, it was not before a certain amount of struggling and negotiation, particularly with Father. He was more old-fashioned than Mother, who was basically agreeable, and she had to point out to him that all his talk of female emancipation appeared to stop short at home. 'Give them limited freedom,' she contended, 'and they won't do silly things behind our backs. We can keep an eye on them.' Hawk's eyes, as it turned out, scrutinising our observance of all the rules: no single dates, safety in numbers. Sometimes a young man escorted Cecilia to a party, but Mother always checked first with the hosts. On these occasions Venus always kept her Apollo waiting for hours while she dillied and dallied to make herself fascinating. This delighted Michael, who found a captive partner at pingpong.

Dancing cheek to cheek was out at parties, and necking or smooching was unheard of. Girls were either good, or they were bad. Only Billy Zhou was trusted, and he took me to my first nightclub when I was thirteen, to Didi's which was small and fashionable. What a glamorous evening it was for me, gliding past Eurasian women with Mona Lisa smiles in the arms of suave Englishmen. I thought their smiles were meant for me, so I returned them like an idiot and they stared past me haughtily. Ah, I realised, that was how to bewitch men. After a night out we would find our parents still awake, and tell them about the evening. It was a good feeling.

Despite all precautions we were considered fast by more traditional families. Our friends were mainly from Westernised families whose parents were as broadminded as our own. Some school friends cut me dead: boy friends meant one was a scarlet woman. Sour grapes. Our girl friends from old-fashioned families generally had no problems about visiting us, but the boys had to keep quiet. If we ran into them in public places with their parents, we would pretend not to recognise them, suppressing our giggles.

Mother loved having young people around, basking in her daughters' popularity like a Cheshire cat. Our friends were always welcome to stay for dinner and Ah Zhu knew how to make the food go round, particularly with the aid of that classic standby, fried rice – not the soy sauce sodden dish sometimes served in the West but a fluffy dish with eggs, ham, peas and leftovers, always delicious. Father was less impressed by our choice of male friends, whippersnappers calling themselves Alfred, Henry or Raymond, without a single idea on art or literature. When William began to be interested in girls and to be meticulous about his appearance, Father was amazed to discover that his son's haircut could cost four times as much as his own. But he never complained, secluding himself as usual in his study.

Even there he could not quite escape the loud noises coming from the wireless, for the sound of Western popular music filled the house. Every song seemed to include the word 'heart' in the title – 'My Foolish Heart', 'You Belong to my Heart', 'You are always in My Heart', which sounded like the Shanghainese for 'On my stomach there's a crab, how it itches when I move', which we thought hilarious.

The dance parties we threw lasted all night, but they were innocent affairs. There was no alcohol to inebriate us, only the intoxication of gregarious sociability involving the whole family. Father betrayed his enthusiasm by helping Fu Sheng move furniture for the dance floor, and even Grandmother would take up a position in the wings. Little Michael and Vivian would dart amongst the dancing feet until they grew tired and were put to bed. Congee, not kedgeree, was served for breakfast, hot and soothing, and once all the guests had gone we would tumble between clean sheets and, snug under the covers, lull ourselves into delicious slumber to the song of birds outside the window.

New Year's Eve, the last day of 1948: the last picture I have of the family together. Cecilia and I had not yet changed into our party clothes, but we gathered by the Christmas tree for a photograph. None of us are smiling. Could we know that we would never be together again? In the distant years that lay ahead, most of the children would be scattered, unable to return; the aged would remain in the empty house where all the precautions of the geomancers could not protect them from the evil that would befall them. Who could have envisaged that the four walls of Father's peaceful study would become his prison? And, had we seen these things, how could we have prevented their coming? For ill and, as I would learn, for good, all things must change.

Remember you are Chinese

'I send you to school to study, not to act!' my father thundered, in a rare outburst of fury. Once again I had failed my end of term exams after too much socialising and too much acting.

I had entered middle school. I had begun at McTyeire High School, the élitist girls' establishment in Shanghai. Although it was a Chinese school, it was funded by American Presbyterian wealth, with lovely green lawns fringed with apple trees that blossomed in the spring, and a collection of handsome and imposing buildings. There lay the temple of my heart, a well-equipped theatre. I was moderately good at sport and played basketball well, and on occasion I tried my hand at baseball – my first taste of the American way of life. I had three best friends, and of course we went around as the Four Musketeers, with me playing D'Artagnan. Like most girls of that age, I had my fair share of crushes on older girls, writing ardent letters of admiration. These senior students were from rich and therefore right-wing families, but they nevertheless belonged to the school's left-wing faction. I was not at all influenced by their politics, for I had other things on my mind. While they rallied and argued with their right-wing teachers about the merits of Communism and Capitalism, I was fully absorbed not, as one might expect, in my studies, but in writing, directing and even acting in my own plays. Naturally I always took the lead. Within two years I failed my grades yet again.

Once again I had to change schools, arriving at the Shanghai British School determined to pull my socks up. Father's anger jolted me out of my irresponsibility. I had been jumped up to a higher class, and here the curriculum was in English – very British English, with hockey sticks and

British uniforms – so I would have to keep my wits about me. I had no choice. I began to study in earnest. A stove was put into my freezing sitting room, and night after night I pored over the course books until my leather-bound English dictionary was dog-eared but sensuously soft to touch. Where my education revealed holes – mostly in science – I crammed pages of facts and figures, drawing on my early training in learning incomprehensible Chinese classics by heart. As Mother said, where there's a will, there's a way.

At the year's end I passed my exams. Miss W. Penfold, headmistress, was quite dazzled by my grades and my real character completely eluded her. She described me in her reference as an excellent worker hoping for a university career. 'Irene Chow (the old form of romanisation for Zhou) is decidedly of the student type, quiet, with good manners . . . I am glad to recommend her as a pupil to any school.' I would need that recommendation only too soon.

But that first taste of self-discipline taught me important lessons. I realised that books could satisfy much of my curiosity, and I have read avidly ever since. Scattiness and vanity took a holiday while I discovered a serenity within me I had never recognised before. I could not forever banish the frivolous and scatterbrained side of my nature, though; my Jekyll and Hyde personality was to play havoc with my life.

℘

Discipline conquered idle luxury in my behaviour just as a new dis- cipline was banishing wealth and corruption in my country. It was a still night in May, when the guns that had been pounding beyond the city perimeters were silenced, and an unprecedented calm fell upon the wild city itself, and an expectant hush surrounded our house.

Mother got a phone call from her brother, who was in another part of the city, to say that Shanghai had fallen to the Communists with little resistance.

The family immediately went up to the attic and waited. After an hour or so, we could make out a row of crouched figures in the twilight, moving along the pavement opposite, closely hugging the base of houses. These soldiers, with pack and rifle on their backs, cloth shoes and bands upon their legs, were spreading into the city without making a sound. The following morning, Shanghai was 'liberated'. It was an impressive take-over, almost without bloodshed, and without looting or indiscipline of any kind. This was a new kind of army, an army of believers, of firm faith and good purpose, whose motto, 'borrow a needle, return a needle', so rigorously upheld, marked them out from the common run of armies in Chinese history who behaved like bandits and fought for plunder. The unrivalled discipline and politeness of the Communists allayed the fears of the Shanghai populace.

But we had one worry. A few months earlier, like other households, we had been obliged to accommodate officers of the vanquished Nationalist army, and they were still in our dining and sitting rooms with their dependants while the Communists took control of the city. It was like the comedy, *Hotel Sahara*, in which Peter Ustinov and Yvonne de Carlo as the hoteliers cope with the same dilemma, caught between opposing armies. As usual Mother thought out a plan. She sent Ah Zhu out of the house to telephone her, and when the phone rang she picked it up within earshot of the Nationalist officers. *'Wei, na-non ah?'* Hello, what's up? she bawled into the receiver. 'You don't say? . . . Really . . . Oh my God . . . You mean . . . really . . . every house? Oh dear, the People's Army are searching every house?' Within half an hour the officers, already in civilian clothes, had hastily decamped with their entourage.

In the first year, while I was still in Shanghai, life continued much as before, really as if no bloody revolution had occurred. The Shanghainese dropped the jitterbug like a hot potato, and swept up the peasant dance tread as the latest fad. Little Vivian was kitted out with a miniature People's Army uniform, in which she looked especially cute. Michael discovered Mao Sheng, the avid reader and kitchen politician, demonstrating his impatience for a classless society by trying on his master's hat and coat for size, scandalising Ah Zhu. Out in the countryside, though, a relation of Mother's whom I remembered as a jolly fellow bringing me sweets, was shot as a landlord.

Father, for all this, was pleased. The struggle of actors and actresses to be recognised as responsible members of society had been won, for they were no longer perceived as vagabonds and whores. Real whores, after all, were being 'rehabilitated' and taught a new trade in a general clean-up of 'bourgeois pollution' and the filth of Shanghai, when child slave-workers were freed from the factories and sent to school, and the vicious secret society gangs were apprehended and broken up. The Godfathers, alas, had already got away. Now many a Chinese Mrs Worthington nursed ambitions to put her daughters on the stage.

Generally, the morale of the intelligentsia was high. For idealists of Father's generation, who had witnessed the end of empire, the ravages of civil and foreign war, and the awakening of a people to a sense of their own dignity, it had been a long haul in quest of their country's place in the modern world. Many times their hopes and aspirations had foundered amidst corruption and stupidity. Now they looked forward to a new régime which would apply new solutions, and make China strong and respected once again.

Within a year, the 'China hands' were told to leave: businessmen, missionaries, and schoolteachers. They left a country they had called home without bothering to learn the language, but they would find it hard to readjust to life in their own countries, denied the special privileges they had extorted as colonial masters. The Communists now declared all religion superstitious, and the foreign missionaries had to pack up and go, broken hearted, feeling betrayed by their native flock. Some of these evangelists were latter day saints, but the rest were regarded by the Chinese as imperialist propaganda mongers.

The British School closed, and once again I was faced with a change in curriculum, perhaps in language. But Mother's plans were laid.

The Shanghai School had a sister establishment in Hong Kong, the King George V, where I could continue to study for my Cambridge School Certificate in preparation for the achievement of Mother's goal, that I should go abroad. Cecilia, once again, was overlooked, on the feeble pretext that her English was not up to scratch – and on the stronger ground that her command of Chinese literature, and her facility in her own language, already showed signs of developing into a literary talent. By staying in China a while longer – she, too, eventually came abroad – she was able to develop her closeness to Father, to become his companion, to browse with him for books in Fuzhou Road, to discuss literature and history with him in his study, and most enviably, to accompany him on his travels. For now he not only toured, performing to peasants in remote villages and hidden hamlets, but also used the first opportunity to travel freely around a peaceful country to where he might explore the roots of folk drama, and where the Grand Master of Peking Opera was received with reverence for his talent and with love for his humility.

@

I, who was about to leave, packed and ready, my farewells made, promises given and forgotten, faced my father alone in his study, that quiet sanctuary. Our leavetaking was brief, although the silences were long. He handed me a copy of Wen Tianxiang, brush written and my parting present, a play about a patriot which the Japanese had censored when I was a child. I took it from him in silence. We did not touch. Very Chinese. Over the years, my impressions of my father and my country would merge into one, increasingly remote, ever more romantic. I took him to stand for all that is good in a man.

I stood there looking at him, looking at a man so mild in temperament yet so passionate in his beliefs, who stood for all that was best in drama and in China. I had come to know him through the eyes of others, first through my mother's loving eyes; later through the books written about him while he lived; and finally, after his death, he would come alive for me in the affection I received from the men and women who had known and worked with him.

At last he spoke, gently and simply. 'You must always remember you are Chinese.' Those were his last words to me.

I never saw my father again.

10

Hong Kong

ℓ

The small snapshot has faded after all these years, though the exuberant figure it portrays was always blurred. My short hair is permed, and I lean half out of the train window. A huge camera dangles from my neck. One outflung arm holds a sandalwood fan, the other is waving frantically, and I am laughing as the train begins to move, unable to contain my joy at these first steps towards seeing the world.

Who took the picture? I left Father and Cecelia at home. Maybe William, Michael and little Vivian were there, with Fu Sheng who must have driven us to the station. Now I study the photo and I cannot remember these things. I see only an excited girl, and a train window, and know that this was the moment I faced West, turning my back upon my roots.

Mother came with me, bringing our servant Ah Jing to look after us. The train was crammed with families on their way out, excited people on their first great journey like myself, others about to rejoin relatives in the south, or abroad, or maybe with the Nationalists in Taiwan. Like Chinese everywhere, formalities were cast aside in the hubbub of excitement: we were like an audience at the Peking Opera, joking and eating and watching the entertainment roll by, mile after mile of the flat paddy of the south. There was none of that funereal reticence I was to encounter on British trains. It was a journey of two days and two nights. We were crammed together, families, and friends, and amiable strangers.

Mothers fed their babies while the men cracked melon seeds and played cards, or dived into their mountainous luggage to retrieve some choice morsel for the journey. Our belongings were numerous and untidy, hard suitcases and soft bundles, an assortment of string bags and pretty baskets. Mother was surrounded by baskets of fruit herself, and everyone was buying from the hawkers at every station, sampling the local cuisine with relish and enthusiastically arguing their merits. The Chinese not only eat to live, but live to eat. In a land where the threat of famine is never far away, the race puts food top. Even today, the first words of greeting are not 'How are you?', but 'Have you eaten?'

Paul Cao was on the train with us, a very rich capitalist whose family owned factories in and around Shanghai; we knew him well, and I took this opportunity to nurse a crush on him. He was escaping the new régime. Like many others who missed Shanghai he eventually returned a few years later to find himself in the middle of a particularly virulent anti-capitalist campaign, during which, to facilitate his re-education, he was obliged to pull manure carts in Shanghai for a couple of years. The 'night soil' is a precious fertiliser in China, so in some ways his job was not unimportant. One day, in a congested street, he lugged his wheeled barrel past a car driven by Fu Sheng with Mother in the back. Mother saw him, but said nothing. Instead she dropped an enormous wink, and Paul winked slowly back, and passed on.

Paul told me this story himself after he managed to return to Hong Kong in the sixties. How we laughed about it! Calamity is close to Chinese life. As the threat of famine gives every Chinese a heightened appreciation of food, so the Chinese, or more particularly Shanghainese, sense of humour is a survival kit that treats ordeals with philosophical nonchalance. Foreigners interpret this often as callous indifference. On the contrary, our laughter was in celebration of catastrophe overcome, from a comprehension of its horror. Later in England, I would be asked constantly whether the Chinese had a sense of humour. Think of the largest nation on earth, with one of the oldest civilised histories, not managing to find their funny bone, and the mind boggles.

Hong Kong, which means Fragrant Harbour, was as beautiful as the picture postcards promised – provided you looked at it from the same point, at the same time. By night, standing on the Peak, the harbour glittered with the brilliance of a thousand neon lights, sparkling like a brooch of diamonds, emeralds and rubies upon a dark velvet cushion. This is how Hong Kong wanted to be seen, but the dawn revealed the cushion to include shanty towns of makeshift shacks, without running water, without proper sanitation, and without electricity to let them twinkle in the night. They mushroomed across the colony with an unstoppable speed as more and more refugees poured across the border in Kowloon, the peninsula leased by the British to add size to their tiny island colony.

The fierce and stubborn southerners had been surprised by the British guns a hundred years before, and now they were suffering another invasion from the north, as countrymen from different provinces descended upon them with their different dialects. The most insufferable of all, needless to say, were the Shanghainese, whose ingrained sense of superiority was not going to budge in the face of a few provincial southerners. The feelings between hosts and guests were mutual, and it would take time for them to integrate. All the Shanghainese stuck together, and the well-to-do were very merry, squandering their money in their usual manner as if they were not refugees but pampered visitors. Perhaps the showiness paid off, for they inspired confidence. Many would soon be insolvent, but within decades some of these canny and versatile people would be millionaires again, contributing to the economic miracle in Hong Kong.

Mother and I were not exactly splashing it about, and although we took tea frequently at the Peninsula we stayed in a small hotel on the Kowloon side. It was at least comfortable and clean; it is hard to imagine now, when every inch of Hong Kong seems to be at a premium, but we had a front room with a large verandah to alleviate the humid climate. Ah Jing was with us, always nervous, always skinny; she slept on the floor between our two beds and then faded away into Hong Kong, faded from my memory for years. I wonder what became of her. In the meantime we roared around the city with our Shanghai crowd, doing the tourist things, eating seafood and shopping and bargaining in the bustling markets; we took the ferry across to Hong Kong Island, and then watched it silently beetle back and forth from the commanding heights of the Peak. We swam at Repulse Bay, and dined afterwards on the terraces of the grand hotel that overlooked the little resort. We went to nightclubs, and compared them with what we knew from home. What we had known: for the nightclubs of Shanghai were dark now.

Mother left me settled at the King George V School, lodging with a Cantonese family, and she returned home. Over the next two years while I was staying in Hong Kong she could come and go, taking me to hotels or renting flats. But in general I was alone, I had some money, and I was all of seventeen years old.

It was only to be expected that I would turn my attention to the opposite sex – most cautiously, and in a proper spirit of enquiry only.

Mother's injunctions and Chinese tradition certainly put anything else out of court. Where previously I had always played second fiddle to Cecilia, I found that men were now devoting their attentions to me. Among my circle of male friends, a few were slightly older Brits and Americans, and I soon found that my animated facial expressions, which could never pass for beauty in China, appealed to Westerners. I gave them no encouragement. No respectable Chinese girl would be seen dead with a Westerner on her own, if she valued her reputation.

Women are universally jealously guarded from foreigners by their menfolk. In China in former times they were kept out of foreigners' sight, and their dress was selected to cover them from the neck down. Even their hands must not show. In popular nineteenth-century literature, if a maiden chasing a butterfly in her secluded garden were even to be glimpsed by a gardener she would have to marry him immediately. Her lily white hands were tantamount to complete nudity.

Foreigners seeking to meet a Chinese girl in Hong Kong would not have found it easy. An entrée to a respectable Chinese family was a near impossibility, and as for courting their daughters, such a thing was unthinkable. The foreigner would be thrown upon a narrow section of women of the lower orders – and thereby remove himself beyond the pale altogether. So the cycle of prejudice fed upon itself. The foreigner's intentions, though, were usually not good. As I was to learn, Western fantasies conjured up the image of a submissive virgin Lotus Blossom; I wondered where all these demure little Oriental damsels came from, never having encountered the type myself. But the fantasy was strong. Later as an Asian actress working in the West, I would invariably be cast in plays with Far Eastern locations, and I would portray women whose characters were pure stereotype: oriental dolls, oriental tarts – or both at once.

In fact I fell for a shy and gentle boy of my own race and age, sweet seventeen and incredibly innocent. But this first love ended abruptly after six months when I met a dashing young man in a dark crested blazer, fresh from an English university where he had acquired perfect English manners. My fickleness in love was beginning to show already. This apparition of urbanity so impressed me that I remained oblivious to his atrocious temper until it was too late. Because when we met again in England, I married him.

Matrimony was not on the horizon when I set out to prepare myself to be the superwoman Mother demanded. I took evening classes after school in typing, tailoring and English. On my slender resources I thought it wise to tolerate my British tutor's intolerance towards my race, and at school I kept to myself. This was not the informal meeting point of Shanghai, but a proper white colony; my school friends and I were amicable, but the sense of apartheid was more complete. On the bus, pretty blond English children with their crisply dressed Chinese amahs regarded me sideways with contempt. Their mothers indoctrinated them early. The British passion for exclusion seemed partly at fault: 'Keep off the grass', 'Out of Bounds', 'Trespassers will be prosecuted' dogged my steps, and obscurely I felt them aimed at me. At the time I did not feel especially humiliated. I was only vaguely aware of the subterranean racial tensions that are unavoidable in a colony, and these buried impressions have only surfaced at a safe retrospective distance.

Mother was in Hong Kong to arrange my going abroad when I passed my School Certificate. Originally she had planned for me to join Susan in America, intending that I should follow my sister in an academic career. I had been obliged to disabuse her.

My background, my childhood games, my temperament and now my opportunity pointed in one direction. I would be an actress. The prospectus from the Royal Academy of Dramatic Art, in London, had arrived, and I had studied it until I knew almost every word by heart. Nothing would stop me from going to England. Mother's fears were realised, but her objections were unavailing. I had set my heart on my course.

In the meantime, while the forms came through, I took a job. Women in those days were not encouraged to work, unless it was to pass a few months while looking for a husband, but I was in earnest and could hardly wait to begin my first job, as a receptionist at Butterfield and Swire, one of the great eastern shipping companies. I saw it as my first step towards independence. For three months I worked happily amongst passenger lists that whispered exotic places in my ear and made me itch with wanderlust. Yet one day I overheard one of my English workmates being ticked off for having addressed the Chinese clerk by the simple courtesy title of 'Mister'. I was shocked to learn that as a second-class citizen he was forbidden such respect. That was the colonial mentality in a nutshell.

After about two months, Sir John Kinlock, my department head, called me in to offer me promotion. My papers had come through, so I declined gratefully. I explained I was leaving to study drama.

'Good luck to you,' he said warmly, and added half jokingly, 'perhaps one day I'll see your name in lights.' I smiled at him with every certainty that this would, indeed, come to pass. Seven years later he came to see me in my dressing room at the Prince of Wales in London, where my name flashed in neon out front. Not every tale can be so satisfactory.

Mother brought Michael to Hong Kong. Her other two grown-up children were not keen to leave China, for Cecilia was at university and William had begun courting the girl he would eventually marry. Sweet and gentle Michael had grown since I last saw him, now twelve years old – and a keen young photographer! I willingly adopted movie star poses, well on the way to becoming an actress, I thought. (One of these photos is on the jacket of this book.) Michael was now the right age to attend an English public school, Mother's new plan.

Time for the three of us together in Hong Kong was short. Very soon, we children would have to leave our mother for Great Britain. My contact with the British people had so far been in the strained atmosphere of colonial rule. From now on, I would be living amongst them, destined to spend most of my adult life on their home ground.

I cannot remember a parting. How, and where, we left each other, is once again blotted from my memory. Yet I so clearly remember the expression on Mother's face in one flash of an instant a week or so before my departure for England.

Looking back, it was as if the two of us were taking part in a contrived shot from a Mizoguchi film, a wistful scene enacted without dialogue. I had just woken up in the double bed we shared in our hotel room. From my pillow, I saw my mother framed in the mirror of the nearby dressing table. Her hair was uncombed, her dressing gown was wrapped untidily about her, and she was looking down.

The object of her attention was a diamond ring which she had given me from her large jewelry collection when I was fourteen. Although jewelry was not permitted to be carried across the border, without Mother knowing I had innocently brought it with me as a memento. As I see it now, the ring represented all that was gay in her life. She was performing a silent ritual of farewell to that way of life she enjoyed before the revolution, and to a past where she was surrounded by her children. Taking this ring I would be leaving her. Nor would she wear any such luxurious gems when she returned to the puritanical atmosphere of her home city.

It was a private moment, caught by chance, and I came upon the reverse image of my mother reflected in the looking glass. For that instant, I saw for the first time a tired old woman, profoundly sad. Although I did not understand my feelings fully, I burst into tears. She turned, and looked surprised.

Part 2

West

China doll days.

Cockney Tsai singing 'Any Old Iron'
on T V.

11

Codes of Conduct

ө

As our P&O liner approached Southampton, Michael and I stretched eagerly over the bow rail to catch a first glimpse of the land we would call home. It was a lovely October morning, and if for a moment the cranes and derricks of the great port reminded me strongly of my hometown, I sensed also something in the smell of the air and in the chill blue sky that had nothing whatever to do with China. We had been a month at sea, and at last our feet touched English soil.

A stranger from the education agency was at the quay to meet us, a handsome but stiff man called Mr Llewellyn who helped us through customs and immigration. Mother had given me an Omega watch as a graduation present and the customs official charged me duty. The shocking sum of £10 has stayed in my mind ever since.

Brother and sister were separated as soon as entry formalities were completed. Michael was promptly dispatched to a public school in Shropshire. It must have been a traumatic experience for a sensitive twelve-year-old Chinese boy who spoke no English. From China and the warmth of familiar and protective people around him, he suddenly found himself alone in an alien world of British education and British discipline. Could he avoid the humiliation of corporal punishment and the constant threat from small-minded bullies that balanced the privilege of a British public school education?

As for me, I felt no qualms in facing my new life. I was young, and considered myself sophisticated enough. The cost of uprooting would become apparent later. For the moment, I was happy to be dispatched to board with a couple of elderly spinsters on the Isle of Wight until my RADA audition came up. The spinsters, of whom one was weak and the other strong, ran a village school, as well as taking in foreign students: here I made my first black friend. Here, too, I could not help noticing that the old ladies treated the children quite badly, petted the dog and fell over backwards to please the cat. I waited for three months, and in early January of 1953 I made my way to London. Such was the confidence and belief in myself that Mother had instilled in me, that it never crossed my mind during audition that I would fail to get in.

London wore a garb of drabness where the scars of the Second World War still lingered. Only when the sun filtered through the dense black fog did she manage to smile a little. It would take another decade for her to laugh – and even to swing on the chandeliers. In London streets I passed grimy shells that had once been cosy homes, and which gaped at me now like open wounds. In the grocery shops women practised the acquired virtue of queuing clutching ration books. London looked grubby.

On my first day at R A D A I saw my fellow students as glamorous and sophisticated creatures. I was rather surprised to find some of the girls wearing make-up to school, and I was mildly shocked by the tactile ways they greeted their male friends, quite unlike the reserved behaviour of the Chinese. But, as I later learned, they in turn assumed I was some sort of oriental princess, for although I wore no make-up I had a dark brown Kilinsky fur coat around my shoulders and wore a diamond ring. Over the coming months I appeared in at least fifty entirely different outfits, not as an exercise in ostentation but purely to save on dry cleaning bills: the dozens of especially tailored silk dresses Mother had packed into my trunk stayed cleaner if I wore them in rotation. As for the diamond ring, I assumed every girl had one. One girl finally asked whether I'd bought it at Woolworth. I wasn't in the least put out, since I had never heard of the place.

It was not strange that my fellow students should treat me as something apart and rare, like a princess, for few English youngsters at that time could have encountered a Chinese outside a laundry. Unlike America, Britain could only boast a tiny Chinese community concentrated in the ports of London and Liverpool, where old merchant seamen retired into the laundry business. A few Chinese professors might be found in universities, but Soho had less than half a dozen Chinese restaurants. The Chinese conquest of English eating habits still lay in the future, when Chinese take-aways would vie neck and neck with fish'n'chips. Mrs Lucy Chan, who ran the South China Restaurant on Rupert Street, and was the widowed mother of a friend of Cecilia's, fed Michael and me for nothing; otherwise Michael and I had no one to feel at home with. The other restaurateurs, such as they were, catered to a Western palate, and dished up a curious hybrid called chop suey which took a while to get used to. They came from another level of society and they spoke Cantonese. They tended to clan together, unable to speak English and struggling to survive in an alien environment. Between them and us there was no natural acceptance.

Whereas most foreigners can use their embassy to introduce them into a familiar social circuit, Michael and I were exceptional in that we had no embassy to go to. In order to preserve Commonwealth unity, Britain followed the lead established by India as one of the first countries to recognise the new régime in China, but at the time of our arrival the People's Republic had not yet organised its diplomatic corps. Socially, China was still represented by the emissaries of Chiang Kai Chek's Nationalist government in Taiwan. They attempted to woo me on account of my famous father – but for the same reason I shunned them. My father was on the mainland, not in Taiwan.

I toyed from time to time with the idea of contacting our long lost English relatives, the Rosses – but after a while the desire faded. Though Michael and I were thus entirely cut off from our native culture, I was not aware of culture shock. I spoke good English, and I was determined to assimilate with the British.

To my relief I found the natives quite unlike their compatriots in the colony of Hong Kong, extremely courteous and considerate people, kindly and fair-minded. They were wary towards foreigners, but that did not trouble me unduly for the same distrust was shared by my race, and both sides defended themselves with the same weapon: good manners, reserve and inscrutability.

The weather was indeed unpredictable and the food unimaginative, but these were minor irritations. I couldn't help noticing that the capriciousness of the island climate made the English as obsessive about weather as the Chinese about food. Where the Chinese would say 'Have you eaten?' the English would begin every greeting with a 'Chilly today, isn't it?' or 'There's a nip in the air'. In fact I arrived in London in the year of the Great Fog. Darkness fell in the early afternoons, and grew deeper and deeper as the day dragged on, in what looked like clusters of pitch-black wool smelling curiously of sulphur. If I stretched out my arms I could barely see my hands. Mother, I knew, would have been delighted: for her sake I would stand in this eerie atmosphere outside the lit stairwell of the Tube, expecting Jack the Ripper to appear at any moment, hotly pursued by Sherlock Holmes. London was just like its portrait in the detective novels.

And there was a fascination about it. An added fascination, perhaps, because for the first time in my life, although I could not have named it then, I was experiencing loneliness.

By no stretch of the imagination could I have romanticised about English food. It would have been wrong to label the English as entirely philistine, for a tour round Fortnum's quickly suggested otherwise, but a nation's culinary sense must surely be judged by the standards kept by the ordinary people. Compared to a Chinese, or even a Frenchman's home, an Englishman's home was indeed his castle, neat and clean with flying ducks on the wall and a village of gnomes at the bottom of the garden. But what did the average Englishman put in his mouth? Bread, jam and exhausted cabbage leaves! A Chinese would lay hands on anything, of course, even tree bark when he was starving, but whenever he could he cooked himself quick-fried vegetables. As for the duck, he dreamed of it settling cosily in his belly, not in ceramic replica on the wall.

Still, potatoes and puddings were only the equivalent of boiled rice, and healthy and hungry that I was, I lapped them up much to the joy of whoever cooked. I did draw the line, though, at rice pudding, sweet and sodden with milk, which seemed a horrible prank to play on the Chinese staple. My first and last spoonful made me want to throw up, and I only controlled myself for fear of offending the cook. (Oddly, for all my distaste, when I revisited China years later, I occasionally missed bacon and eggs, bangers and mash, and Welsh rarebit – not to mention smoked salmon and caviar.)

The business of assimilation was only rarely hampered by overt racial prejudice, which I seldom encountered. Only once, but much later, was I refused a flat on account of my race. I had never been slapped in the face before but this incident made up for it good and proper. I can still remember how my cheeks burned with shame for something that was not of my doing, and it gave me a painful insight into the feelings of those addressed by the signs blatantly glued to the windows of bedsit land in those days, which read: 'Irish and coloureds need not apply.'

If there was little obvious prejudice towards me, I was still the object of curiosity. City gents on the tube, all looking the same and inscrutable in their pin-striped suits and bowler hats, would peep at me from behind their papers. The man at Lyon's Corner House was bolder:

'Excuse me,' he said, 'I hope you don't mind . . .' Oh dear. I thought, I'm sure it will be something I do mind. 'I don't want to be personal, but may I ask if your breasts are real?'

He was doing a survey, I was to understand, because rumour had it that the erogenous zones of a Chinese woman were different from his own kind, and he had to find out . . . 'I mean, you know . . .' he was getting a little flustered by this time since the look on my face was far from inscrutable, 'you people are supposed to be flat-chested, aren't you?'

I looked him straight in the eye and snapped: 'Everything about me is real!' And left.

Perhaps the most dreaded were the women missionaries who seemed to have followed me all the way back from China. Nostalgic for their glorious preaching days, they accosted me in department stores where I was enjoying a bit of window shopping. 'Do-you-speak-English?' They would enunciate really slowly and clearly as if I were hard of hearing. 'Je-sus-Christ-Our-Saviour-die . . .' I soon found a way of putting a stop to that. 'I'm most frightfully sorry,' I would return in my poshest accent, lying: 'But I happen to be a devout Buddhist.'

I began to learn all manner of unpleasant things about my own race. We ate dogs, for example. How shocking! China being so vast, it was impossible to know the customs of every province. My defence mechanism came to the fore: I pointed out that the British eat rabbit, but the Chinese don't; the French eat horse, but neither the British nor the Chinese would dream of doing so. So Chinese eat dog: carnivores eat meat, period.

I learned that we are a cruel people. My hosts would point to the Boxer Rebellion, when many Westerners in China died at the hands of the insurgents. I realised that I had learned from different history books. Each nation writes its own history, and a hero to one can be a bandit to another. In well-to-do homes I came across exquisite little watercolours arranged on the walls, each depicting a different form of Chinese torture. These paintings had a Western flavour to them, obviously made to order for some Westerner resident in China. And I wondered why this fascination with the cruelties of other countries?

Years later, when I had grown accustomed to the small talk of polite society, I deflected sallies less bluntly. When confronted with a remark like: Don't you people have water tortures and the thousand cuts ho ho ho . . . I would smile beautifully and reply in an equally amused tone: Quite so, and don't you draw and quarter? he he he . . . By then, though,

I was beginning to look at my native country through foreign eyes, and my life as an outsider was undergoing a sea change.

I had little problem identifying the English class structure by accents and manners. The upper classes, when I encountered them, spoke very loudly as if no one existed. the quiet middle classes, on the other hand, never complained. If I protested about the quality of food or its presentation in an inexpensive restaurant (the only kind I could afford) the other diners were so embarrassed they pretended not to notice. Where were the Brits who snapped their fingers so impudently at Chinese waiters back home?

Tea seemed to be the nation's panacea. The meek lower middle classes drank their 'cuppa' with careful concentration, their little fingers poised genteelly in mid-air. Only the working class seemed to behave with ease, especially in pubs, bubbling with Cockney humour and energy. The news-vendors addressed me as 'luv' or 'darlin''. This familiarity from a perfect stranger, and a male at that, took some getting used to, before their friendly warmth became for me a hallmark of a city I would come to love.

My fellow students at R A D A might have laughed if they saw the way their 'princess' coped with the mundane chores of daily life. Cosseted by servants all my life, I had to learn the simplest tasks from scratch. I literally didn't know how to boil an egg, and forgot to fill the kettle before putting it on the stove. The ceiling of one hostel I lived in bulged with the water from my overflowing bath. Susan advised me to move to a women-only hostel where matron stood over me with folded arms to ensure I made my bed properly. I shudder now to think of the first time I took my clothes to a laundrette. There were no driers in those days and I hadn't the faintest idea what to do with the wet bundle I brought home. So I shoved it into a cupboard out of sight and left it to mildew.

My desire to assimilate had its limits. 'Never forget you are Chinese,' my father had said, and I thought of myself as an ambassador for my race. I gave myself three stringent rules to follow.

Firstly, I had to make a good impression, especially with ordinary people. If, for example, I were to be undercharged by a shopkeeper, I must make good his loss on discovery, even if I had to walk back a distance to do so. His next Chinese customer, I hoped, would then be well-received. Secondly, I must stand up to bullies. Chinese have a reputation for not hitting back – which is why 'yellow' means cowardly in cowboy movies. Since all bullies are cowards themselves, I hoped that they would think twice before picking on a Chinese again. Lastly, I must claim the country I lived in by immersing myself in their cultural interests. In the past, Chinese studying abroad had been notoriously aloof, and had little social contact with Westerners. The fault lay not only with the colossus called Western racial prejudice but also with my own people's ingrained insularity. Mutual discrimination, as I had noticed in Hong Kong, feeds upon itself, and I was determined to be a minuscule brake on the system. These self-imposed and perhaps rather self-important codes of behaviour were not always simple to live up to. In time, they would put me under exhausting pressures, and expose me to unexpected internal conflicts.

12

High Heels and Blue Stockings

In my twenties, as I saw it, there were two distinct types of women. Men gravitated towards the pretty girls on the understanding that they left their brains on the shelf and wore smiles on their faces. Woe to those who should rebel, for they would be accused of all sorts of things. Penis envy was only one of them. Then there were the academic types. They all wore glasses, were flat-chested, had big feet, and answered to the name of Blue Stockings. The two species had little opportunity or inclination to meet, for they regarded one another with distrust and scorn.

I was left in no doubt as to which category I belonged to. And yet, without realising it then, I was hungry for what women on the other side of the fence enjoyed. In my circle I met few who were interested in the larger issues of life. So like a stray dog panting for a bone, I turned myself into an intellectual snob instead.

Whatever input of intelligence I managed to scrape together came from the men who gravitated towards me. I am grateful to them for that. I've had to learn to hand pick them carefully over the years, as though I were selecting courses at university. Contrary to general impression I was not much interested in them as lovers (with some notable exceptions) but as mentors to be recycled into permanent and valuable friends. Partly it derived from a longing to establish roots. It was nevertheless a mercenary kind of seduction and I became quite expert at it.

So I have to admit that men have always been important to me in my life, as father, son, friends, lovers and husbands in that precise order. But never as providers.

Husbands foot the list for I never quite managed to take marriage seriously. Oh, I do believe in marriage – idealise it, in fact, because of my parents. In the old days marriage was the means to a woman's survival and a guarantee of her respectability, and motherhood was her raison d'être. Love barely came into it. My mother, defying convention, married for love, and her success converted detractors and gratified romantics. It was almost too successful, too exceptional: I knew I would not be so blessed. The Chinese also say that marriages are made in heaven; but what I had seen of most marriages suggested, on the face of it at least, that hell might well be other people.

There was another factor. In a foreign country, at a young age, I was struggling to establish an identity for myself; between two cultures I carried the additional burden of finding out if I belonged at all. Marriage would not assist me, because I feared that it would swallow me up. A woman lost her surname and her independence in marriage. Until recently in China a woman was referred to by her husband as *nei ren*, an 'inner person' who did not exist outside her husband. In her domain, the Family, her identity was fixed purely by her relation to other members of the group. By the time she became a matriarch like my grandmother, her given name would have become a memory, almost her secret. Times have changed, of course, and women are more independent, but in the 1950s I was jealous of those glimpses of my identity that I received, and was wary of diluting myself in marriage.

But if I did not take my marriages seriously, I have never regarded them as mistakes but rather as necessary stages in my development. Of course I have experienced pangs of remorse, and sometimes reflect on how my feelings had cooled before I reached the registry office, for reasons that I won't go into and for which I no longer apportion blame. I wonder how many women, in all honesty, have felt the same? I married partly because I was lonely, I suppose, and partly, as I recognise in retrospect, because I was emotionally lazy. There was a wildness in me which I did not understand then and which I feared. Without believing it, I hoped that marriage would help me curb a reckless need to be free.

Perhaps this explained why both marriage ceremonies had a farcical air about them. While exchanging marriage vows with my first husband, instead of the line: 'To be my lawful wedded wife,' he blurted out prophetically: 'To be my awful wedded life,' which reduced me to giggles. It was not trouble with his English, but nerves. Both of us were hopelessly inexperienced virgins, but that condition could be remedied.

The terrible recognition that we had nothing in common besides our nationality dawned more slowly, and was immutable. Our very interests were worlds apart. His technocratic training encouraged him to dismiss artistic endeavours as superfluous. Traditional male pride determined that no wife of his should ever work, and he was traditional enough to regard the theatre as the worst sort of work, although he knew quite well that it was the reason for my coming to England. In the year we were together the more autocratic he became the more I frustrated him with a growing display of self-assertiveness. Indeed, I made his life the purgatory he had involuntarily predicted. It was mercifully short. Later he was gallant enough to describe that time as having 'never a dull moment'. I can well believe it. For that, I will only say that his name is Chang. He is now a millionaire somewhere in the East, and I would never intrude upon his privacy and respectability.

The best we have between us came within a year of our marriage. I was a mother before I was twenty, biologically more than ready, psychologically unprepared. I went into labour just before a Saturday midnight, and only the scarcity of Sunday traffic stopped Bruce from being born in a taxi. When the waters broke my husband had to telephone for instructions from the landlady (who thought at first that it was something to do with her plumbing), only to discover that I should have been in hospital long before.

As my labour reached a crisis in Westminster Hospital, I pinched the poor nurse and shrieked for my mother, but I remember only a sweet pain when the child was put into my arms and I held his tiny body close. Only two months later, however, I left my husband, as I had already had to leave RADA, and took Bruce to live with me in a grotty bedsit off the Bayswater Road. As a token of independence, it was unforgivable in a Chinese wife.

Mother and child were inseparable for a year. My baby was chubby, round and soft, and I held him close to me as if we were one, as if he had not ceased to be part of me now that I carried him outside my body. A happy baby who seldom cried, he lived according to my rhythms, and if I woke late he would have waited patiently until I fed him. When I took a French correspondence course – God knows why – I would read him whole acts of *Andromaque* and he would listen in rapt attention. We were in a world of our own.

Only once I went out without him, when the woman downstairs offered to babysit. She was middle aged and over painted and appeared to be living with a rather shady man. Thinking back, I suppose she must have been a prostitute from the Bayswater beat. The next thing I knew, my diamond ring and some gold bracelets had disappeared, but I was too shy to confront her; the jewelry was uninsured and I saw no point in calling the police.

When Bruce took his first steps to explore his new world, I felt that the umbilical cord had been finally severed. I became less self-sufficient and the world outside started to beckon, rekindling my former ambitions. Throughout my marriage I had felt guilty for not fulfilling my purpose in being sent to England: so I re-applied to RADA.

On my return to the Academy, I put Bruce in the care of a nursery far away from London, the most I could manage financially. Every Sunday, accompanied by my new friend Elizabeth Rees-Williams, I would take the train to see him. Bruce was well looked after, but saying goodbye to him each time, and leaving him in the hands of strangers was a wrench I could hardly bear. Finally I agreed to let his father, who had since left university, take him back East, where he would be cosseted by his grandmother as her first grandchild, and a boy.

Brushing my own selfish motives aside, I told myself that I was doing the right thing in letting my son go. He would be brought up in his own culture, enabling him to grow up confident and complete. Too often I have met Asian men suspended in an alien and sometimes hostile environment abroad. All these years ago, before a Race Relations Board and a policy of equal opportunities was thought necessary, Westerners had more licence to show blatant prejudice towards what are now called people from the Third World. My own brother, Michael, would take years to overcome such obstacles before achieving success through sheer determination. A woman had less difficulty in being accepted, especially if she was easy on the eye. And yet, despite my rationale, I have found it hard to extinguish the secret guilt I felt for giving up my son.

When I became more prosperous, and considered myself more mature, I toyed with the modern notion of having another child, and raising it alone. This impractical idea amounted to wishful thinking, a fantasy to compensate for what I had lost through my own fault. At least by then I had gained enough sense to know that it would be one more irresponsible act, considering the itinerant life I was leading. After Bruce left – another important moment which my mind refuses to recall – I began to have recurring dreams about him. In my dreams I felt the sensuous pleasure and comfort of a plump baby on my lap, held close to my breasts, only to realise on waking that my arms were empty.

That dream vanished when I saw my son again more than a decade later.

So now I returned to the Academy, where earlier I had studied under the Principal, Sir Kenneth Barnes; I now found John Fernald in charge. In many ways this second period was more rewarding. Earlier I had been remarkable as the first Chinese to study at RADA (indeed, the only other Chinese actor to have studied in Britain previously was the veteran director Huang Zuolin, who came under the tutelage of Michel Saint-Denis in the thirties). As a result, the teachers tended to make a fuss of me, and I suspect allowances were made. I was given too much inducement to rest on unearned laurels. Now that I was older, and more accustomed to English ways, I could make more sense of what I learned. Rumour had it that Sian Phillips and I were Fernald's favourite students. Certainly he made me feel very talented and this gave me enormous confidence, for which I am eternally grateful.

In many ways I was more at home on stage than many of my fellow students – I had known my way around a theatre before I could walk, after all. But while my instinct was apparent and my movements – to my great surprise – were considered graceful, I was to have 'problems' with my voice that would dog me for years to come. In those days, students were obliged to conform to a standard pattern of voice production known as the Royal Academy's Voice Beautiful. This was particularly difficult for a foreigner to achieve, and it was not until later, under the guidance of the late Iris Warren, that I could shake off the strain of reaching for Voice Beautiful and begin to trust and develop the particular qualities of my own voice, making the kind of rebellion against tired forms to which my father had devoted his life.

Nowadays the benefits of drama school to the aspiring actor are unquestionable, for the days are gone when novices could choose to cut their teeth on the boards of repertory theatre instead. Although 'rep' was already in decline in the fifties, and the openings for actors in theatre companies around the country were beginning to diminish, 'rep' still offered an alternative entrée and the value for most people of learning an actor's craft at drama school was questionable. As a foreigner, though, the debate simply did not apply. Drama school was an indispensable passport to entering a seemingly impenetrable and cliquey world, a haven where it was possible to enjoy complete security while savouring the illusion of 'belonging' to the theatre. Outside, we would take the dangerous plunge that led to success or failure, where survival depended on talent, hard work, luck and above all, stamina.

The ability to hold on despite everything meant not only coping with the grind of endless disappointment, but also possessing the wisdom to deal with success, should fortune deign to smile.

Most students would never even make it onto the first rung of the ladder, but simply disappear irrespective of their success at school. It was often they who cast me pitying looks, implying that I would never find a job when I left, since I was a foreigner. And I gritted my teeth and became all the more determined to prove them wrong. Years later, I felt enormous pride at being made an Associate Member of the Academy. At least my name was listed now with Laurence Olivier and John Gielgud!

School gave me an opportunity to rub shoulders with the potential greats of the coming generation. Some students seemed to have a definite stamp of future eminence upon them, like Albert Finney and Peter O'Toole, while others like Sian Phillips, Richard Briers and Peter Bowles would have to wait longer for the recognition they deserved. The rest were working actors who would be the backbone of British theatre. And one, barely noticed at the time, would be acclaimed as the world's finest actress: Glenda Jackson.

I made many friends at the Academy. Angela Crow, with her huge eyes and flaming hair; James Booth, the Cockney actor who would later star with the tiny luscious Barbara Windsor in many British films; and Jack Hedley, who had been a sub-Lieutenant in the Royal Navy before he came to R A D A. One day he surprised me by revealing that while he was stationed in Hong Kong a few years previously, he had tried to make my acquaintance at some function and I had shied away from him. By the time I returned to school, Michael had left his and come to London to study art. We saw each other frequently, and since he did a really suave cha cha cha we often went out to the Hammersmith Palais for dances, with my friends the Diamond sisters, Marion the actress and Gillian, who became a casting director of some clout at the National Theatre. The Honourable Elizabeth Rees-Williams, who accompanied me on my visits to Bruce, became a friend for life – very important to an exile without family. She gave up a career in acting when she started marrying film stars – Richard Harris and Rex Harrison, in that order.

The great French actor Jean-Louis Barrault handed me my diploma when I finally left R A D A, and from there I took the usual avenues towards finding work, arguing that although specialised roles would be hard to come by, once found there would be little competition. Thus I worked out that the chances of landing roles were about equal between my British colleagues and myself. My first professional work was to present a BBC radio series called 'A Visitor In London', in which I traipsed over interesting institutions and interviewed their custodians. I remember holding a long conversation with the Director of the Victoria and Albert Museum on the gripping theme of paperweights, a subject I naturally knew nothing about. Ignorance, fortunately, is bliss to the young. I compensated for my enormous ignorance with boundless enthusiasm. The possibility of failure, or dying a death, never entered my head. I got a few plays and three times played the role of princess in Christmas pantos, thanks to a very British theatrical tradition, once, much later, sharing the bill with Al Read, the northern comic.

Between jobs I regularly wrote to hundreds of producers – letters that doubtless landed straight in the bin – and took modelling jobs to support myself. Elizabeth and I at one time decided to fall back on the actress's standby, waitressing, but her over-protective father, Lord Ogmore, didn't approve of the idea and we let it drop. As an alternative I put my sewing skills to good use by making copies of lampshades I saw in Peter Jones, and selling them to anyone willing to buy them.

Soon I was getting film roles, good parts for a beginner. Perhaps the most interesting was in *The Inn Of The Sixth Happiness*, in which I played Ingrid Bergman's fourteen-year-old adopted daughter. This Chinese epic seems to appear on British TV every Christmas, and I often think how wonderful it would be if Burt Kwouk, who was so good in the film, and I received royalties on each showing!

As for television itself, my first appearance was an interview programme called 'Sunday Afternoon', in which I was interviewed by Mr Anthony Wedgwood Benn. I was a foreigner battling alongside native actors, and all things considered, I had not done too badly for myself in the few years since leaving drama school.

13

First Exposure

I attracted notice in the British press for the first time when I appeared on stage at London's West End Drury Lane Theatre. It was an unexpected privilege, for in many ways Drury Lane is synonymous with the British theatrical tradition I wanted so much to experience. Charles II met his Nell Gwynne here; it has been burned down and rebuilt a few times since then, but it remains the country's oldest theatrical institution, founded in 1662. I might be forgiven for dreaming that my life as a performer had been launched from the pinnacle of my profession.

Drury Lane gave me my first glimpse of what Western stage success could mean. I occupied the star dressing room, and found it staggeringly luxurious compared to the dingy backstage areas I knew from China. All the status symbols were there: en suite bathroom, plush wall-to-wall carpet in powder blue, matching velvet curtains. There was even a private telephone. Not that I knew any important people to ring, or even expected to receive any calls from unimportant people either, but there it was – my very own personal telephone. For a month I mimicked Cinderella, revelling in my luxurious apartment before I returned to my bedsit with broken linoleum peeling from the floor and a shared toilet at the far end of a dark corridor, and where the telephone was just a temperamental pay-phone at the foot of the stairs.

The incomparable impresario, Peter Daubeny, was responsible for bringing international theatre to Britain on a grand scale in the fifties, and for his 1957 Season he had invited a Peking Opera Company to his theatre. I auditioned for the job of the compère who would explain the unfamiliar theatrical traditions to the Western audience. At the start of each performance and again after the interval, I proudly stepped on stage to recite my piece, conveying to a vast audience the unique and intricate symbolism of my own theatre.

The excitement I felt at this experience was dampened by hidden anxieties I entertained about appearing at all. My decision to take the job was entirely dictated by financial need and, more importantly, by the need to gain professional experience. It was not stage fright that prompted this reluctance, but another problem altogether. The troupe I compèred came not from mainland Communist China, where my father worked, but from the exiled Nationalist government on Taiwan. I had no way of knowing how the Communists might react to the news that Zhou Xinfang's daughter was appearing in the West with the theatrical ambassadors of an outlawed régime, but I had no reason to think they would be pleased.

Under the circumstances I considered it wise to maintain a low profile. As long as the Chinese company did not catch on to my real identity, the Taiwan papers would not report it and the thing would never be picked up on the mainland. Since I had discarded my surname, using Tsai Chin as a stage name, I uneasily supposed I stood no chance of being detected.

The charade teetered on the edge of the absurd. There I was, trying to remain invisible to the cast backstage, talking to no one if I could help it, and hiding in my gorgeous dressing room whenever I was not required for rehearsal, when the very next day a few actors came up to me and greeted me with great warmth. The property manager began to reminisce about his days working with the Grand Master of Peking Opera. Like St Peter denying his master thrice, I muttered: Who? I don't know who you're talking about.

The deception could hardly be maintained for long, and the cast were able to put two and two together fast enough. There were millions of Chinese around the world, but so very few in Britain at the time. Few Westernised Chinese of my generation would know so much about their traditional theatre, interested as they were in Western movies and fashion. My nose and eyes are my father's, and it was not impossible that some of the cast had seen me backstage in the old days. The cat was soon out of the bag, and I was presented with the ironic problem of finding publicity just when I wanted it least. And the less I wanted, the more I seemed to get. The *Daily Express* made me a front page story on September 10th, the second day of performance. Not, as it happened, on account of my father, who was unknown in the West, but under the headline: 'Tsai Chin Is Too Good To Lose!' I had been denied an extension of my work permit, and Peter Daubeny was creating a stir in order to keep me (his efforts met with success, I might gratefully add).

All of a sudden I was good copy, for there wasn't much competition from the Taiwanese troupe who were not very good themselves. Their poor standard was understandable. Since most of the good actors had remained on the mainland in 1949, the newly formed Taiwanese company had been obliged to rope in amateurs for supporting cast on this first foreign tour before a proper troupe could be trained. Watching them from the wings (I had given up my cloak of invisibility) I sometimes had to put my hand over my mouth to suppress giggles as I watched some amateur in the 'chorus line' doing his best to copy the movements of his more proficient neighbour, and lagging forever one step behind. To my utter surprise, the critics showered me with attention and waxed ecstatic over my looks. The *Star* said that 'to explain the intricacies of each item in the repertoire is a charming Audrey Hepburn-like beauty.' *Plays and Players* took it about as far as possible: 'delightfully performed by a young lady whose charm far surpasses that of Misses Dors, Monroe and Lollobrigida put together'! For someone who could not pass for a beauty in China, this unrestrained praise for my appearance was heady stuff.

But to a potential serious actress, these compliments were ominous, the beginning of a pattern that would persist. In time this so-called beauty, regarded almost as a talent in its own right, would seem almost a curse. Throughout my career, I would have to accept looking like a Chinese version of someone else – Hepburn, Eartha Kitt, Zsa Zsa Gabor, even Bette Davis (the comparisons became increasingly prestigious as time progressed, I suppose). And even years later, when I returned to China as a star director in my own right, I was primarily seen as my father's daughter – something to be proud of, naturally. Fighting for my own identity on every level, professional and personal, would be a fierce, continuing struggle. At that time, though, I supposed I had better be grateful for the compliments and say nothing.

As I feared, the Nationalist propaganda machine seized on the story, and the news reached Beijing. My father was criticised for my work, but it was only a mild reprimand for he was in high standing with the régime. Only later, in 1966, when the Cultural Revolution loosed hell throughout the country, the forgotten incident would be recalled, and join the list of accusations against him.

For the moment, my family was happy and well in Shanghai. Letters from home frequently included newspaper cuttings lauding Father's achievements. In 1955 China held great celebrations to mark the fiftieth anniversary of stage performance by the two greatest classical actors: my father, Zhou Xinfang, and Mei Lanfang, the internationally recognised master of female roles. Their crowning glory was to be both designated 'National Treasures'. There were only eight such Treasures in all China.

It was akin to the new pride felt by Chinese all over the world. After decades of foreign dominion and civil war, China was again her own mistress and her people looked forward at last to a period of unparalleled social stability with a sense of purpose and a patriotic mission. Chairman Mao's prestige was high as the miracle-worker who had freed a quarter of humanity from colonial oppression and their feudal mentality, and thereby demonstrated that human nature could be changed. Liberal idealists and militant revolutionaries around the world rallied in hope. China had become a world power to be reckoned with, and where only twenty years ago she had been the sick man of Asia she now inspired awe, and the grudging admiration of capitalist countries. We overseas Chinese, regardless of political sympathies, basked in reflected glory.

We were all delighted with Father's honour. Who would have thought the day would come when members of the 'Amusement Population' would enjoy official respect? The change was comparable to the transformation of the position of England's 'rogues and vagabonds' when Henry Irving became the first actor to receive a knighthood from Queen Victoria in 1895. Like other distinguished artists and scientists whom the state chose to recognise for their achievements in creating the new China, Father was garlanded with official titles. Many, like that of National Treasure, were courtesy titles but a few entailed positions of genuine responsibility. For a man of his profession and temperament such accolades were not without paradox.

In 1956, all institutions in China were undergoing direct nationalisation. Henceforth, every worker would receive his salary from the state in accordance with the Communist principle: 'From each according to his ability, to each according to his need.' Father gave up his lucrative earnings as a self-employed actor and received his regular salary from the 'Iron Rice Bowl', the sum of China's national wealth. Because he was a star, with a position to maintain in the public eye, both Father and Mei Lanfang drew incomes of well over 1000 *yuan*, higher than any state leader including Mao Zedong himself. With the creation of the Theatrical Association, to which everyone connected with the performing arts had to belong, Father became the Vice-Chairman nationally, and the Chairman of the leading branch, Shanghai. Needless to say, he was

President of the Shanghai Peking Opera Company, an umbrella organisation for the merging of all local opera troupes.

The life of actors improved dramatically. Unemployment was abolished. Indentured apprenticeships were replaced by normal studentship, and cruel malpractice was stamped out. Theatre moreover escaped from the grip of underworld entrepreneurs, who were apprehended or forced into exile.

Peace brought a chance to begin long overdue research into China's rich theatrical history on a national scale. The Communists had successfully exploited theatre in their propaganda campaigns through villages in the civil war, and they held the art in high esteem. Countless ancient manuscripts surfaced from old archives and private collections; near extinct performing traditions were rescued in remote areas; and everywhere there was a revival of fading theatrical genres. For the modern theatre, new translations from the West were encouraged, especially from the Soviet Union. The same country also provided valuable advice on Western acting and production methods from the world-famous Moscow Arts Theatre.

Although Chairman Mao's strictures on Literature and Art laid down in 1942 had to be observed, and numerous plays were vetted and remodelled to serve the cause of socialism, the cultural climate in those early days of revolution was temperate and experimental, providing a congenial and inspirational atmosphere for the work of the artists involved.

Father reaped the fruits of his early successes, and continued to explore new or rediscovered dramatic sources. Vivian was still at school, but Cecilia had become very *qian jin*, politically progressive, and she volunteered with her contemporaries to go out into the countryside to help eradicate illiteracy amongst the peasants. William, now married to Jane, decided like me to tread the boards – another blow to Mother's initial efforts to prevent us from following in our father's footsteps. It's in the blood, as they say. In fact, Mother could see that times had changed, and she did not object to William's decision. Father approved once he had decided that his son had talent. At twenty, however, even with the best instruction, William would need superlative discipline and hard work to begin training as a classical actor. He adopted the stage name Zhou Shaolin, the Young Unicorn.

Mother was proud of me, too. When I began to make records, I was told that they were played incessantly in the house – though what Father could have made of them I don't know. I was too afraid to ask.

Photos winged their way between three continents. From England I sent pictures of me with my baby, and of Michael, who had now left art school and was struggling to survive as an artist in London. Susan (now Susan Cha), a French teacher in America, looked happy with her firstborn and her physicist husband. And from China I regularly received group portraits recording each birthday, wedding or addition to the family. They celebrated the marriages of their absent daughters (my first one only), and the births of unseen grandchildren were lovingly fêted. In these photos I saw relatives, friends and servants – all those I grew up with and had been close to back home. I could see that life was good for them in China and I did not give it much further thought.

My energies were concentrated on surviving in the West – on more than surviving, in fact, for I intended to be spiritually as well as materially rewarded. These two conflicting aspirations would rend me for years to come.

14

The World of Suzie Wong

Mr Penn was the uncle of a friend of mine, Dahlia Penn, the actress. He was, by all accounts, an influential man, and he very kindly offered to approach the Immigration Office regarding my application for a work permit. As a Chinese citizen I had no rights whatever to remain in England, and I was plagued by uncertainty: one could hardly rely forever on the good offices of impresarios and publicity experts like Peter Daubeny. When, on that beautiful spring afternoon, I went to visit Mr Penn to consider the strategies we might adopt, I had no idea that I was also about to meet the man who would solve my problem for good.

I caught sight of the other guest immediately as I entered the sitting room, a very tall and imposing man with a striking ascetic face, leaning slightly stiffly against the mantelpiece. He had deep set eyes, brown and intense, an aquiline nose, a good head of brown hair and a small beard. My mind went back to the holy pictures of my convent days. He looked like Jesus Christ in a duffel coat. In time I was to discover that he had a self-righteous streak, and I would call him 'JC' when he became overbearing. The nickname clung in the theatrical circles to which we both belonged.

Peter Coe was a coming young director from a fashionably working-class background. Working class was in vogue during the late fifties, when the Angry Young Men found room at the top to express their disgust with what was beginning to be called 'The Establishment'. Peter and I got on very well, and were soon seeing each other regularly.

It was inevitable that Peter, the intellectual, attracted me where actors, even stars, did not. Father had been a famous actor himself, and I was sufficiently accustomed to the trappings of fame to avoid being dazzled. Writers, and to a lesser extent directors, were a different kettle of fish. Not that they made light loads of their egos either, but their vanities were less raw and extroverted, and expressed themselves in intellectual games rather than flamboyance. Intellectuals had the capacity to take pleasure in a female presence, and to defer to her wish to contribute, where macho types wanted women as children, to be seen and seldom heard. Intellectuals and I complemented each other. I was always impressed by their mental powers while they were often mesmerised by my physical vitality. Of course, in time I came to think that their attractiveness was a carrying-over of my feelings towards Father, as though I might find through them the cerebral part of him that had forever eluded me.

The first great Western writer I encountered was E. M. Forster, at the house of Lord Harewood. For some reason Mr Forster and I were left alone in the drawing room that evening. He was old and I was green and it was a panicky moment for me. I felt so utterly insignificant in his presence that it certainly was beyond me to be so trite as to compliment him on his work. So we just stood there in an embarrassing silence until, to our relief, he was rescued from me.

It was Ronald Duncan who took me to Lord Harewood's that evening, a friend I had made when I attended his lecture at the British Theatre Association a few months earlier. He was a small man with a magnificent head, whose natural integrity was wholly uncompromising. Apart from Peter, Ronald was one of the earliest catalysts of my desire to improve myself intellectually. Visting his idyllic Devon farm where he lived with his wife, Rosemary, I had my first glimpse of the world of the Western intelligentsia, where creativity develops from the business of sorting out their complicated personal relationships. As a benighted outsider, on the lookout for fresh seams of knowledge, how effortlessly I took it all in, and looking back now, how blasé I was about the effect I had on them in the careless privilege of youth. In 1982, when I heard of Ronnie's death, I leafed through his book of poetry, *The Solitudes*, published in 1960. I found his signature with this dedication, which I had long forgotten: 'Tsai, for whom I write some of these.'

Damn and blast you!
You behave like a pickpocket,
    or an absent minded thief,
Raiding my sleep, when you don't even need my peace,
Stealing my heart, when you certainly don't want my love.

And all this done so bloody gracefully,
Done out of perversity, done out of sheer caprice,
Till I am undone, utterly besotted.

True, it's not your fault, you're not to blame:
Your sleight of hand's so practised, you don't even know you do it
And can't even think who it is
     who now complains bitterly —
     because of his anonymity.

I tell you beauty like yours should be punishable.
What right have your eyes to run up and down the street,
     creating this disturbance?
Your breasts are urchins; your lips, ragamuffins;
Everything about you is delinquent,
The whole of you gangs up
     to chuck pebbles through my fragile maturity.

But one day, madam, I'll read the Riot Act to your thighs,
And claim back all my property, bit by bit, till I am whole
     again.
Till then, do not reform,
Treat me as an unguarded barrow loaded high with grapes,
     or an unstaffed stocking store,
Snaffle my peace of mind, knock off my capacity to work,
As for my reputation, I value nothing which you do not take;
     Nor want these rags, the remnants which you leave.

When I moved in with Peter the following year I was still married to
my first husband, and our cohabitation was considered rather chic by
our theatrical friends. Society at large still frowned on such permissive
behaviour — but the trend was in our favour. Ten years later the thing
wouldn't have raised an eyebrow. In the end, after my divorce came
through, we married and contemplated having children. The second
marriage ceremony was as farcical as the first, for the registrar chose to
deliver a trite little homily on the sanctity of matrimony, and his voice
vibrated thunderously like Charlton Heston playing Moses in the
wilderness. Unfortunately we were only cooped up in the Chelsea
Register Office, and the effect of his booming biblical cautions, delivered
in a pronounced Cockney accent, reduced me to again uncontrollable
giggles.

Peter and I set up house in a flat in Cygnet House on the King's Road in

Chelsea. I was delighted to have a real home of my own at last, and overnight I transformed myself from a hopeless ignoramus to an avid DIY handywoman. To be sure, we were poor and had to struggle to make ends meet, but we were also young and our future looked bright. We were two struggling artists, a budding director and a promising actress, and youth with hope can tolerate poverty without much loss of dignity. We believed in each other's talent and knew how to give one another the right kind of support. Peter's belief in me was, I felt, rivalled only by my mother's.

Peter was very romantic about the Chinese. He thought us perfect, which was a heavy responsibility to deal with. Surely there existed some shading in the characters of a people who represented a quarter of mankind? I was beginning to realise that the Left could be as stubborn in their prejudices as the Right, and that the conscience of left-wing intellectuals over the problems of the Third World gave them a rose-tinted view of Third World people that could act as a barrier to real understanding.

In the beginning, our love was self-sufficient. We were tremendously excited about each other's professional or financial achievements, without the jadedness that would blight our marriage. Later, anxieties and disappointments over conflicting expectations for each other would drive a wedge between us. Peter was a bit of a hypochondriac. When we first lived together he had a few medicine bottles at his bedside. By the time we parted three years later, the bottles had moved to my side. In retrospect, however, the bond between us, making allowances for time which smooths away rough edges, was unique in my life. He was a close friend right up to his untimely death in a motor accident in 1987.

For now, there was not only triumph for us both. There was also a triumph in which we both shared.

The World of Suzie Wong, which opened in November 1959 at the Prince of Wales Theatre, came as my first big break. The play, adapted by Paul Osborn from Richard Mason's bestseller, told the story of a love affair between a young Englishman and a Chinese prostitute who is nonetheless innocent at heart. Frances Nuyan, perhaps the most beautiful woman I have ever laid eyes on, starred in the original Broadway production, and had this moody actress been available for London I would never have had the chance to play the title role. However, I was summoned one Saturday afternoon in September to Donald Albery's headquarters (now the Albery Theatre) to meet one of London's most powerful producers. I was buoyant. Though the drama is set in Hong

Kong, Suzie Wong happens to be Shanghainese, and I felt that the part was tailor-made for me. Most actors feel the same way whenever a particularly juicy role comes up for audition. I did not really need the role. Jerome Whyte, the American producer of *Flower Drum Song*, a Rodgers and Hammerstein musical that portrayed San Francisco's respectable Chinese community, had already cast me as the London lead. Both plays were smash Broadway hits that year, and consequently anyone who looked Chinese was in great demand, a rare situation for minority actors.

Donald Albery was clearly anxious to get his play on first. Only the day before he had been negotiating over the phone with the American producer, David Merrick, in New York, and they had agreed that if Donald could find the right actress and the right director within twenty-four hours the deal could go ahead. This explained the unorthodox Saturday meeting.

After I had read for Donald I knew without his saying so the part was mine if I wanted it. As we talked, I happened to mention that I had met him with my husband at the opening of the Mermaid, where Peter directed a wonderful production of *Lock Up Your Daughters*. Donald's reaction was so quick and unexpected that I had to ask him to repeat himself before I could take in what he had said. When I got home that evening and Peter asked me how I had got on with the audition, I replied: 'Donald Albery asked if I would like my husband to direct me in *The World of Suzie Wong* and I said *Yes!*'

The look on Peter's face justified my decision. All of a sudden I found myself going from famine to feast, with two starring roles going begging in the West End and the exciting but agonising decision to be made between them. I think today that Suzie Wong was the right choice, and not only for my sake. It was that show which launched Peter as a stage director on an international level. Within a week Peter flew to the States to review the New York production. He and Donald worked together later on and he masterminded a number of commercial hits on both sides of the Atlantic, including the musical *Oliver!*

The World of Suzie Wong, set in Hong Kong's redlight district, was to be the last successful 'exoticus eroticus' to titillate a Western audience. A bevy of Oriental girls, wearing the Chinese *cheong sam* slit up their thighs, was a deliciously shocking sight in the late fifties. Alan Brien in the *Daily Mail* asked, 'Are We Being Corrupted By Suzie Wong?' I doubt it. The miniskirts in the streets and the almost obligatory stage and screen nudity of the following decade made the antics of Suzie Wong and her consorts look like a kindergarten romp. The show was really more of a spectacular than a play and the critics hated it.

Bernard Levin, who was later to become a good friend, called it 'a lot of Chinese junk' in the *Daily Express*. In *The New York Times* review the glamorous critic Kenneth Tynan, who was later to be rather more than a good friend, with one stroke of the pen insulted both *Flower Drum Song* and *Suzie Wong* by dubbing the former 'A World Of Woozy Song'.

But the audiences loved it. Donald Albery made sure that the play got as much pre-publicity as *My Fair Lady*. I had the lion's share of the media hype. Ignorant of any higher standards I believed in the play whole-heartedly, and gave it everything I'd got. Perhaps that was why I was spared in the general savaging of the show. Harold Conway of *The Sketch* called me 'five feet and a bit of dynamism'. Milton Shulman wrote 'if only her role had matched her ability'. Caryl Brahms suggested that in future, plays should be written for me especially. My favourite review, from Anthony Cookman in *The Tatler*, said I was direct, unsentimental and enormously vivacious. After all the doubts and moral anguish, the *Mail* found Cecil Wilson to be kind to the play itself. He began: 'If you knew Suzie like Tsai Chin plays Suzie, oh, oh, oh what a girl!'

The show gave the audience their money's worth. I was lucky to have Peter directing me, for he was not only a good director but as my husband he knew me well and believed in me. I was fortunate, too, in my handsome partner, Gary Raymond, fresh from his success in the film version of *Look Back In Anger*. Richard Coleman provided the comic touches as my long-term, as opposed to distinctly short-term client, and Mary Steal played my Western rival with sympathy in an unrewarding part. There was beautiful support from ten delicious girls as my colleagues in the brothel – not to mention all the lovely sailors. Not for the first time I got my brother Michael small roles to play – such as the barman, pulling my rickshaw. With the sudden shortage of Chinese actors, many in the cast naturally had to be amateurs. At least two of the girls took their careers seriously: Barbara Lee Yuling, who would later marry and divorce our boss's son, Ian Albery, and Jacqui Chan – my understudy as well as having an important part of her own who was a great friend of Tony Armstrong-Jones, the man who would later marry Princess Margaret. Before the play completed its two year run in London, Jacqui would tour Australia with it in the title role.

One night I did something I had never done before, and was convinced I'd be sacked on the spot. There was a drunk out front, disturbing the performance. I stopped in mid sentence and told him severely but with icy politeness to leave – while the rest of the audience clapped delightedly. I wasn't fired, and I heard afterwards that Donald Albery had merely commented that only Gielgud had ever done that before. I think I started a trend, because Albert Finney did the same thing a few months later.

For a pretty flimsy play it was incredible how much of a stir *Suzie Wong* created. The name Suzie Wong became synonymous with the oriental tart with a heart. Real London tarts adopted the name when advertising their charms in newsagents' windows. In Hong Kong tourists were trekking down to Wan Chai in the hope of catching a glimpse of the real person, who, according to the author, never existed.

More excitingly, the show started a fashion craze. Women abandoned the blonde Brigitte Bardot look and grew their hair long and sleek. Some even dyed their hair jet black and pencilled their eyes to be more almond shaped. Unfortunately for some, for it is not an easy dress to carry off, the *cheong sam* became the thing to wear. Walking and sitting in a slit skirt requires grace of movement, and the high buttoned collar needs correct posture. On the gentle curves of a Chinese girl the dress looked sexy but still demure; on Western women with rather more voluptuous proportions the effect was cruder. The dress was so popular at Christmas parties in 1959 that Lee in the *Evening News* drew a cartoon of a woman commenting on her friend's *cheong sam*: 'Dammit Myrtle, I've told you a thousand times you can't wear too-clinging frocks. Look what you've done to that one: split it.'

The play ran for two years and I was the sole permanent fixture, contracted for the duration to Donald Albery. Gary Raymond, my leading man, left after a year to be replaced by Graham Limes, which proved a happy partnership. He was followed by Derek Waring, an extraordinarily untemperamental actor with a roving eye, who eventually settled down with the incomparable actress Dorothy Tutin.

Peter still viewed the Chinese as near-saints so he was shocked and hurt when a five-foot tall Chinese waiter hit him on the head with a plate in a restaurant. Peter had refused to pay for a dish he found unsatisfactory and the waiter had felt the need to express himself across the language barrier. Peter had to have stitches, and to everyone's embarrassment the incident ended in court with Peter suing for damages. The judge fined the waiter £7 and said: 'I have always wondered why waiters bring the bill on a plate. Perhaps it is to hit the customer over the head if he doesn't pay.' The story ran headlines in the *Daily Mirror*: Mr Wong and Cold Noodles. Had I been present at the altercation, I could have stopped the thing going so far; but by then Peter and I were splitting up.

Suzie Wong wasn't a musical, but it sort of gave the impression that it should have been; I was eager to sing a song in the play by way of compensation for not being able to appear in *Flower Drum Song*. Director and producer agreed readily and I chose a Chinese song from the twenties about a woman awakening to her second spring, which was also the title. Donald thought it was a little too long in Chinese, and that day Lionel Bart – who later wrote Peter's *Oliver!* and was Britain's leading musical writer – dropped by at the theatre. He was promptly asked to put in the English words, which he did on the spot in ten minutes flat!

Lionel delighted me by quite unexpectedly asking me to record the song for Decca. The English lyrics were short, repetitive and silly, and it was renamed the 'Ding Dong Song'. Lionel told me to sing it very high pitched in a cutesy oriental manner, and I obliged. He was no fool. The record, Chinese on one side and English on the other, backed by Harry Robertson's lively arrangement, not only did well in England but became the biggest hit in the Far East for a couple of years. I could have become a millionairess on the royalties – except that all the Eastern sales were on pirate labels. It didn't upset me too much, because in those days I was naively idealistic and thought that an artist's sole concern should be to perfect her art to the best of her ability. Would that I had shared my father's luck in finding a manager like my mother!

I would say that *The World of Suzie Wong* was my only real break, reviewing my career as a whole. Though it was difficult to shed the label of being Suzie Wong in the years to come, playing the title role in one of the resounding successes of the late fifties and early sixties gave me a foothold, no matter how insecure, in British theatre.

⊘

A few years after the Taiwan troupe toured England and just before I played Suzie Wong, my father's Shanghai Peking Opera Company came to London. At the reception it was an emotional encounter for Michael and me to see the beautiful Li Yuru again, the leading lady of the company, whom we had known since childhood. A few days later we went backstage to ask her out, but we gathered that she was not permitted by the company officials to accept our invitation. Father did not come, and the reason could only be guessed. Though I was

TOKYO-MELODY

VOCAL VERSION

GOOD MORNING TOKYO

Original Text & Music by
HEINZ HELLMER & HELMUT ZACHARIAS
English Lyric by LIONEL BART

Recorded
by
TSAI CHIN
on
DECCA
F 12039

2/6

FRANCIS, DAY & HUNTER, LTD.,
138-140 Charing Cross Road, London, W.C.2.

disappointed I was by no means inconsolable. I had a falsely secure feeling that time was infinite and that life was forever. Another time, another place to see my father would suit just as well.

I had claimed the country of my exile, and I assimilated with the English as I had set out to do. In the eyes of the casual world, I was a success. Yet everything has a price. The more I joined in the lives of my hosts, the further China receded. I even had very few Asian friends, apart from Lucille Soong, the Chinese actress and model, and Sama, the RSC manager, who is Indian. They were a great consolation, but gradually a sense of deprivation began to take hold of me, and this sense, this longing for the comfort of my own culture, increased imperceptibly. Recurrent dreams of guilt and longing invaded my subconscious. My baby visited me in dreams to sit on my lap, and I walked through endless strange and empty houses, some entirely different from each other, others revisited again and again, and always the voices of my parents were never far beyond my footsteps.

In one horrifying dawn, I woke up drenched in fear. I dreamed that my mother died. The world collapsed. The power of the sensation stayed with me, more powerful and terrible than anything I have felt before or since in all my waking hours.

Unknown to me, at the same time my mother was in a Shanghai hospital, where her left breast was removed because of cancer. A telepathic message, as I saw it, was transmitted through an invisible but unsevered umbilical cord between us. There was, as it transpired, no cause for alarm. My dream of her untimely death was but an omen, like many dreams of foreboding that since antiquity have foreshadowed a coming tragedy.

15

Last Encounter

When *Suzie Wong*'s West End run came to an end in the winter of 1961, I flew to New York to appear in a special Christmas edition of *The Defenders*, starring E. G. Marshall, a fine actor and wonderful man. There were five other actresses besides me: Julie Newmar, Gloria De Haven, Shirl Conway, Zhora Lampert and last – but certainly not least – Eva Gabor. It was the first of many trips to the States, and I loved the buzz and excitement of the city, the colour and energy of crowds in the street against the grey of the city in December. I was also unexpectedly overwhelmed by the friendliness of Eva Gabor, which went to prove that beautiful women, when they are confident, are capable of camaraderie among themselves. I can still hear her denying a journalist's charge that I sounded like her less amiable sister, Zsa Zsa – not at all what I wanted to be told. 'Darling,' said Eva, 'I do not hear it, I just do not hear it at all.'

I had just been cast in another television series which took me to work in Hollywood, but I had to relinquish the part before I had even begun costume fittings. American Chinese actors had complained about my not being a U S A resident.

After living in London for so many years, I found L A a tough, strange city. I felt alienated and uncomfortable during my short stay. I was interviewed by a succession of film executives, who looked rather small behind huge desks, and whose heads seemed to be glued to the centre edge of the desk across from where I was sitting. They looked like giant tortoises in oblong shells, strange creatures from another planet. We did not seem to speak the same language.

The only meeting I remember was with the brilliant and gentle director Fred Zinnemann. He had seen me act in *Suzie Wong*, and liked my performance, so now he was considering me for the Chinese lead in James Mitchener's *Hawaii*. In the event, Zinnemann never made the film. I lost my second chance to work with Zinnemann when plans for an MGM production of *La Condition Humaine*, to be called *Man's Fate*, were shelved a few days into rehearsal: MGM crashed, the first of the big studios to collapse. That film, dealing with Chiang Kai Chek's purge of the Communists in Shanghai in 1927 (the year my father left the Dan Gui theatre and one year before he eloped with my mother), was to star David Niven and Peter Finch and Eiji Okada, the leading man in the famous film *Hiroshima Mon Amour*. The crucial ingredient of my business, luck, was not on my side.

Coming to New York, however, gave me the opportunity to dip once more into the associations of my past. As soon as the shooting ended I rushed to see my two sisters again.

Susan lived with her family half an hour's drive from Washington DC in a charming town called Silver Spring. We were now comparative strangers to each other, but in a sense the distance allowed us to start our relationship afresh, and she treated me quite as an equal, and not as the capricious younger sister she had known. I found her serious and wise, her serenity and affection not only comforting but also therapeutic. During my subsequent trips to Washington, I came to value her strength of character which would eventually nourish and sustain me through the hard times to come.

Cecilia, now living in San Francisco with her accountant husband, Joseph Chung, had had to start a new life as an exile much later than the rest of us, and she bore the constant regret of one whose natural development had been arrested. In China she might have been a successful writer, and although she had been published in Hong Kong under the pen name of Zhou Yi, the market for her work in Chinese was extremely limited in the West. Her beautiful face had taken on a troubled look. Nothing, however, had changed in her attitude towards me. Her moods were as unpredictable as ever, and she was easily provoked into uncontrollable explosions of anger. Equally easily she would be happy and lighthearted. She seemed to be intent on reliving the past, when she had vied unsuccessfully for Mother's love; when she had dominated me by unpredictable turns of temper. Childhood relationships are established very deep, and only conscious efforts from both people can change a well-established pattern of that kind. Cecilia did not seem interested in breaking with the past, and as an adult I was no longer prepared to indulge her. The closeness we had once enjoyed together, the memory of which had made my heart pound with excitement as I prepared to meet her again for the first time, was not to be revived.

ℓ

Mother herself came to England in 1961, for what I could not have known was to be our last meeting. All her children, except William, had left home to live abroad, since that had always been Mother's self-denying plan. Contrary to popular belief, it was possible to leave China until 1966. Vivian was now in Hong Kong. Back in London, Michael and I met Mother at the airport. Michael, who had left home at twelve, was never one to wallow in sentiment. But as we drove back into London in my car he covered his face with his hands and murmured: 'Mother, why did I have to leave your side so early?'

On her way to England Mother had visited Vivian in Hong Kong, where she would eventually become a civil servant in the British colony – the family's first and only bureaucrat – and settle down with her Cantonese actor husband Wong Hoyi, so Cecilia and Susan, with her little daughter, Serena, flew from America to see her. I was then about to divorce Peter, and I was living alone in the two-room flat we had shared in Chelsea. The six of us, and sometimes Michael, who was living in Chiswick, slept on the floor or in makeshift beds. The arrangement was very Chinese: the warmth and closeness of family life crammed together in a small space was easily revived. It was very cosy, and sometimes rather too lively.

Mother had barely changed. She was plump as I last saw her, and looked healthy. She was not apparently self-conscious about her recent operation, though later when I took her to a doctor for a check-up she was reluctant to undress in front of me. I did not insist, for I dreaded to look on the healed wound. The shame of my squeamishness still haunts me now.

On arrival she went into a twenty-four hour hibernation to sleep off the effects of the journey, and on waking she decided to relinquish maternal authority in favour of ruling her six-year-old grandchild, Serena. In this way she staved off the disappointment of her expectations. In some way she had hoped to recapture the past when her brood was under her charge and utterly dependent on her. We, her children, had all gone separate ways; our common cultural roots had been overlaid with different professional and national values – East Coast, West Coast, London. Years before, Mother had given us our labels. Now the messages were confused for her, and she could only laughingly concede that we had become perfect products of her eccentric upbringing, independent achievers – and egotists.

Susan put Serena into a private school near Chelsea. Michael worked as a waiter to support himself as an artist. Susan calmly took over the management of the household, volunteering to do most of the cooking and to pay for some of the food. Cecilia decided to paint London red, for she still needed to prove before her mother that she was the centre of attention. I was the mug responsible yet again for promoting her as the belle of the ball, but it was not so hard to arrange as I had quite a few spare men around who were only too happy to act as gallant escorts for an evening's entertainment.

When Serena was asleep, Michael at work and Cecilia out on the town, Susan and Mother and I spent wonderful evenings on our own chatting about all things under the sun. Men and sex, I was amazed to find, were not taboo. Mother and Susan were convinced monogamists and I was surprised to find them so knowing. We could be wickedly irreverent on the subject, telling tales until our stomachs ached with laughing. Mother was a little sad about my pending divorce, but not so much on moral grounds as from her feelings towards Peter. When they met they took an instant liking for one another, and she regretted the end of the marriage. She was hoping I would settle for an easier life and worried that I might end up living permanently alone.

The only subject Mother avoided discussing was China. Mother had always yearned to go abroad. Her disappointment was intense when in 1956 Father made a triumphant tour of Russia: spouses were not allowed to travel with the troupe. On the last of eighteen performances in Moscow, the audience went wild with enthusiasm, practically carrying him from his dressing room to his hotel and dancing in the street. Mother was upset to have missed the fanfare. As compensation the government allowed her a visit to England instead, to visit her children; it was a great favour accorded her out of their esteem for Father.

She was instructed not to talk about what was happening in China. The country had changed since the early years of optimism when everyone was prepared to shoulder the enterprise of building the country anew. The Dictatorship of the Proletariat was increasingly becoming the dictatorship of those who claimed to speak for the proletariat: there was an internal struggle for power as differences of opinion within the Party began to emerge. Mao had called for a blossoming of ideas, the famous 'Let a hundred flowers bloom' movement in 1957, but he was hurt and surprised by the force of the criticisms that were expressed by the intelligentsia. He ordered a purge of 'rightist' intellectuals, further alienating and disappointing the creative and academic élite. Plays were censored with greater ferocity, and artistic creativity struggled against a host of political directives aimed at popularising the Party line. But the Party line itself was open to sudden changes and reversals.

The conflict of the leadership was aggravated by a series of natural and political disasters. Bureaucratic bungling, combined with a succession of harvests ruined by flood and drought, had caused the failure of the second Five Year Plan, the so-called Great Leap Forward, begun in 1959. There were now serious food shortages. Along with America's implacable enmity after the Korean War, which continued to deny mainland China a seat in the United Nations, China's isolation seemed complete, with the rift in Sino-Soviet relations, which came to a head when the USSR withdrew her technical advisers. An ideological battle of words began between the two Communist superpowers. China was thrown increasingly upon her own resources, and grew introspective, isolated, and suspicious of the outside world. It was in this mood that the Cultural Revolution would erupt five years later.

These things Mother avoided relating. Perhaps she did not quite dare face up to the direction events were taking. And how would we, her half-foreign children, take in the complexities of the kaleidoscope that China seemed to have become? Our country had become enigmatic, a place confusingly glimpsed in contradictory press reports, a land of endless political and ideological reverses. We, like Mother, hoped that the twists of politics could be kept separate from the daily lives of ordinary citizens. China had known turbulence before. We could not have known how Mao had determined that turbulence at the top of the political world would invade each life, and blow a whirlwind through the entire nation.

Mother and I enjoyed a few months alone, behaving almost like sisters, when my real sisters returned to the States. I presented her proudly to my friends. Her good English served her well and she was much admired by those who met her. Cary Grant, whom I knew slightly, rang her personally to invite her to a preview of his latest film, *A Touch of Mink*, in which he starred with Doris Day. Mother, who had seen so many of his movies in the days before Liberation, was thrilled.

Just as I had adored her in childhood, so she continued to impress me. It was a joy to see her carrying herself off so elegantly in London's smart society, with serene dignity and humour, like royalty. She was indeed a queen in her own right.

Her visa ran for six months, but before its expiry Mother was beginning to miss Father and China, too. She who had so loved the West, both in her mind's eye all those years in Shanghai and now in reality, yearned for her own country. Everything was 'better in China'. When I took her to Torquay for a play I was touring, I booked her into a good hotel with views across the bay. Torquay may be no St Tropez, but the seafront views are stirring. She took one look and decided that even the sea 'was better in China'.

Her decision to return to China, a China troubled and unpredictable, when she might so easily have stayed amongst the familiar pleasures of the West, proved that her love for Father was stronger than her fears for the future. At times she betrayed her anxieties unconsciously. She talked of her death, and of her wish to be buried rather than cremated. Burials were feudal, and wasted good land that could more profitably be used for cultivation, as the Communists correctly maintained. This fear for what might happen to her after her death was a mirror to her intuitive fears about what might happen to her before. All her fears were realised; and in the end she was cremated, after all. Nothing could be done about it then. For this reason, I want to be cremated when I die – not before my time I hope – in the expectation of joining her.

In England, Mother worried a great deal about Michael, who was struggling to be a painter, working to support himself by waiting on tables, and reduced to living in someone's garage. She was never to know that before long her son would find fame and fortune as an internationally renowned restaurateur. Over the next decade all her children would do well for themselves, able to afford to return to China. But our timing was dismally out of joint. While our fortunes rose, our parents' doom was sealed. None of us, who could so easily afford to do so, would be given a chance to care for them in their old age, a filial duty Chinese have taken pride in since time immemorial.

My last picture of my mother was of her back as she walked away from me into passport control at Heathrow. Her hair was tied back into a chignon. She was a plump figure with soft round shoulders looking like a lovable Chinese mother I remember seeing in picture books as a child. I did not know that at that precise moment she was walking out of my life forever.

Grandmother's aquiline
nose was at odds with her
tiny bound feet.

Grand Master of Peking
Opera, the legendary Qi
Lintong (Father's stage
name).

(*left to right*) Irene (Tsai), Susan, Michael,
Cecilia, William.

My parents' wedding – I wasn't invited!

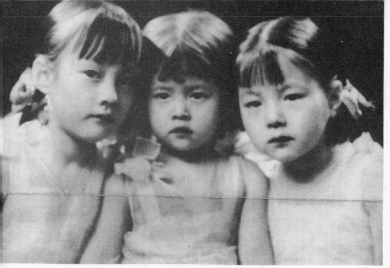

Father with our
Alsatian, Helen.

Father's favourite photo: his 'three little kittens'.

Tsai, a typical Chinese
bobby-soxer.

All six siblings before Elder
Sister's departure to the USA,
(*left to right*) Michael, William,
Cecilia, Irene (Tsai);
(*centre*) Susan holding Vivian.

The last family picture (*left to right*) Michael, William, Mother, little Vivian, Father, Irene (Tsai), Cecilia.

The day I left home for ever.

Father, happy in his study, which was to become his prison.

At home, celebrations for Bruce's 'two-month birthday'.

My son and I in London.

Playing Suzie Wong, with Gary Raymond.

With my namesake.

With Bruce in Singapore, en route to Hong Kong.

Mother in London
– last reunion.

Playing Juicy Lucy on the wrong side of 30, with Hywel Bennett.

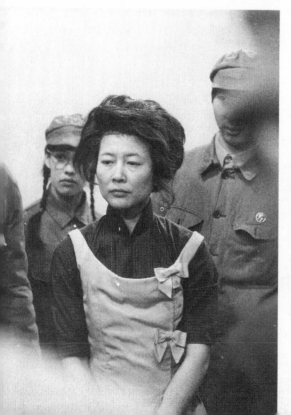

A year later, I skipped 3 decades to play the wife of Mao Zedong's chief rival. (*Right*, meeting the real Wang Kwanmei much later.)

Premier Zhou Enlai backstage congratulates Father as Hai Rui, the role that caused his downfall.

Last family picture from Shanghai: my parents with William, Jane and their daughters, Bingo and Maple.

Zhou Xinfang's posthumous reinstatement, 16th August 1978. William, with his wife and daughters, and Vivian (*right*) were there. Deng Xiaoping's wreath is far right.

Talking with Uncle Jiang Chunfang about my father.

Fu Sheng, our former chauffeur, gives a party for the family at his house.
(*Inset*) Our former servant, Mao Sheng, in 1981.

1985 Festival of Qi style plays. William (Zhou Shaoling) plays Guan Yu; (*left to right*) Tsai, Susan, Tina, William, Jane and Michael.

16

Cabaret and Ken

With two failed marriages behind me I was beginning to realise that I was not cut out to be a family woman. Since I had some success with my career I could afford to be independent and hope to enjoy it. With the savings from *Suzie Wong* – my first real money – I bought my first house, a twelve-room Edwardian terraced house on the wrong side of the river, on Albert Bridge Road. Although I was proud of it, I found that some people thought the address lacked status. My hairdresser, for example, simply could not bring himself to utter the word Battersea, and called the district South Chelsea.

From the day of my second divorce, I would be a free agent, give or take the interregnum periods of falling feverishly in and out of love. So I thought, at least. Life is never that simple, and I would slowly learn that a person's real freedom came from inner and deeper resources.

I cannot deny that I was a flirt, but then I could say that I flirted with women, children and animals as well. Animated beings gave me adrenalin. Sexual games, on the other hand, were only fun when played by mutual consent. Coming from a culture where these games were taboo, or at best terribly refined, I thought a Western man's obsession with proving his maleness in public looked very clumsy.

To this day I still cannot understand why men can be so naive as to think that divorcees should be easy conquests. They assume they are doing the woman a favour. Misunderstandings between the sexes will always be hard to sort out. I suppose women are on the whole incurable romantics about love, while men are perpetual optimists about sex. Apart from my divorce status, small, compact and oriental, it was assumed I must be wonderfully docile and pliable. Added to this, I was an actress, from a profession renowned for its easy virtue. Twinkle, twinkle, I began to recognise the signals. What nerve I had to thwart their expectations!

I felt like honey in the jar, with bluebottles on the rim. Sometimes even women treated me like an object, a quaint piece of chinoiserie. 'Henreee . . .' said an American matron at a cocktail party to her tired executive husband, 'what a cute li'l oriental daaal! I'd jus' love to take her home and put her on the mantelpiece.' Well, inside the China doll was a large person trying to get out, never seen, never addressed. A tiny voice of frustration gradually rose in a crescendo, to a silent scream. Attack was one means of defence and I became increasingly aggressive, particularly towards the men. They would have fared better in their attempts to seduce me if they had heeded Oscar Wilde's advice to compliment a plain girl on her looks and a pretty girl on her intelligence. The late Richard Wattis, that deft and genial actor who so often portrayed civil servants on the silver screen, would warn his straight friends: 'For Gawd's sakes, don't tell her she's pretty or she'll slap you!' Something was clearly not quite right between the sexes but I thought I was alone in what I felt. I had no idea that other women were having the same troubles, until they began voicing their angry protests. Until then I was advised to be grateful for all the attentions showered on me, for I should surely miss it when old age set in. I expected more. I felt a freak.

The 'casting couch syndrome' was a cliché much bandied about in those days. Like most clichés it contained more than a grain of truth. Perhaps because I did not give out the signals, or because I ignored the hints, I was almost never propositioned in my career. Nonetheless, the fear rose in any actress when she went for an interview with a film producer. It would have solaced me to know that pretty boys faced the same risk from their own sex when they went on the same missions.

After Mother left, I found myself out of work. Life styles expand to fit the money available, and I now found myself trying to run a house and deal with an endless stream of bills. For the first time, I realised that I would have to create work for myself.

I toyed with all sorts of possibilities until I saw the answer staring me in the face – that record I'd made, thanks to Lionel Bart. Lionel was rather out of my league, but I put together a cabaret act with the help of Brian Blackburn, a songwriter and performer. Most people felt in some way that *The World of Suzie Wong* had been a musical anyway, so I had few problems getting the bookings. I stuck with cabaret for five years, touring all over Britain and in a few European cities as well, and the experience taught me far more than I could have imagined about performing and people. Working radically different audiences from one night to another was a fascinating challenge.

Appearing before a small group of people in the intimate and smoky atmosphere of a nightclub is in many ways more difficult than working in the conventional theatre, where you perform before a captive audience who have bought tickets specifically for that show. You have other actors to fall back on, unless it's a one man show. In cabaret, on the other hand, your audience has come primarily to wine, dine and play footsie. Unless you're Marlene Dietrich or Lena Horne the audience is often indifferent when your performance begins. You have to prove yourself worthy of their attention, and their respect depends on your material and how you present yourself, both in and out of the spotlight.

When I began my cabaret career – in the foyer of the Royal Festival Hall, of all places – I still worried about the quality of my voice. I'd failed Voice Beautiful, but would I reach Voice Tuneful? I needn't have worried. Very soon I was performing in Clement Freud's little club on top of the Royal Court Theatre, introduced by Clement himself in the spaniel-like manner for which he has become famous. He was not yet a Liberal MP, needless to say. At first, following hard on the heels of his deadpan jokes, I felt as if I were entering a bullring, and I had to persuade myself that I would not be physically gored. The audience was so close. Luckily I could rely on the patient and solicitous David Wykes, who accompanied me on the piano.

As my confidence increased I began to realise that I not only sang in tune but that I could put a song across with the kind of energy that the theatre calls stage presence. Presence is a projection of strength, and it has little or nothing to do with one's physical appearance. With this confidence, I found more good songwriters to help me tailor my act to suit my personality. 'I Went To School In Cheltenham', written by the popular cabaret performer Paddy Roberts, always went down well, telling the story of a Chinese Zuleika Dobson innocently creating minor havoc at a demure ladies' college. My own favourite was the old Harry Champion music hall song 'Any Old Iron', which I sang impishly in English and my own Chinese rendition, sporting a bowler hat, baggy trousers and braces.

I allowed my instincts to feel for what I did best, and how to approach it. Usually I would walk coolly into the room and stand patiently in front of the microphone. I stayed until the audience quietened down, pitting my will against theirs. I had decided to trust the better side of human nature, hoping that if I carried myself with dignity my audience would respond accordingly. And it worked. Women liked me, thank God. Women set the tone in a nightclub, interestingly enough, and introduce an element of the unpredictable. Men together behaved rather like good schoolboys. At one performance for the Singer Sewing Machine Company the very British Jimmy Edwards with his larger than life mutton chop whiskers introduced me by bellowing: 'This is one Singer you can't make!' Perhaps the men behaved well because I was not a blonde with big tits and bum. Perhaps it was because I didn't look like anyone's neighbour that the women accepted me. Being exotic has its advantages. I seemed remote, and therefore no threat to the women. Nonetheless I would like to think that there was an unspoken bond of loyalty between the women and me. I never flirted with their men outside my professional capacity. It was my rule never to be seen before or after performances.

To have food served during a performance distracted the audience and me. I stipulated that no food should be served while I performed, but it was impossible to avoid disturbances altogether. At the Parkside Club in Nottingham I remember a woman sitting just below my rostrum who chattered on non-stop about her holiday in Spain. After a few minutes I found my concentration wandering and finally I had to stop completely. 'Madame,' I heard myself saying, surprised by my own courtesy, 'you have talked incessantly through my act and I have lost my words. Now kindly stop!' She stared upwards in amazement and her mouth fell open. The rest of the audience including, I recall, the group at her own table, cheered. After the show her husband came round to my dressing room, and I received him in some trepidation. Instead, he shook my hand in truly British sportsmanlike fashion and said: 'I've been married to my wife for twenty years, and I've been trying to stop her talking ever since. You're the first person who has ever managed to shut her up. Congratulations!'

In those days I was relieved – now I am proud – that these interruptions were the exception rather than the rule. If a man should make trouble there would always be a gallant in the audience to sort him out. My stratagem was to let the men fight it out amongst themselves. Women performers were at least in less danger of being physically assaulted. One evening I shared the billing with David Frost, at Quaglino's in Jermyn Street, before the television success of 'That Was The Week That Was'. A chinless wonder, incensed by whatever David was saying, hurled a hard bread roll across the room at him. The missile missed its target and hit a perfectly innocent member of the audience squarely between the eyes.

These little mishaps gave me a further insight into the workings of the British class structure. I was especially fond of northern audiences, whom I found more direct and less inscrutable than their southern compatriots. I treated audiences at the Dorchester or the Savoy with arrogance, which they immediately understood and respected (hence a review in *Variety*, which called me a Chinese Eartha Kitt). With a working-class audience, my heart had to go right out to theirs. That said, the only time I died a death was in a northern working men's club. It was a mistaken booking made by accident. I knew something was wrong when I watched the delight with which they greeted the act before mine, in which a fat man guzzled a bag of crisps while trying to sing a song. In fact his partner stood in the wings and sang it for him. They loved it. I was sacked after the first night, though to be fair the club paid me a full week's wages nonetheless. Unemployment was not a problem then and the working men's clubs were doing very well.

Most of all I loved the Cambridge May Balls and the end of term dances held at Oxford. I broke my rule about not being seen before or after a show and turned my engagements into exciting weekends. Pimms on the lawn and a punt on the river on a perfect English summer afternoon led on to a dinner party in my honour and, after my performance, champagne and dancing until dawn. Maria Aitken, the future actress, once gave me dinner in her student digs. We made up an interesting crowd that evening. Maria was still reading English at Oxford but she gave a strong indication of her future talent. Marina Warner, the future historian, was there with her friend Irene Pih, a Shanghainese. I sat next to a stocky man with dark eyes who charmed me by saying in an authoritative guttural accent: 'You must come to visit my country.' I was bubbling over with enthusiasm for a country I had just visited in his part of the world, where I had been very well received. The more I chattered about Israel, the more silent my neighbour became. He was Prince Hassan, advisor to his brother Hussein, King of Jordan.

Ken Tynan, reviewing the first night of John Osborne's play at the Royal Court, wrote: 'I doubt if I could love anyone who did not wish to see *Look Back in Anger*. It is the best young play of its decade.' Well, not only had I wished to see it, but I was in the same audience as Ken that night in 1956. At the time I knew him only by repute.

I liked intellectuals. He liked women looking as young as schoolgirls. We moved in theatrical circles. It was only a matter of course that we should eventually meet. In late 1962 when my divorce from Peter had come through, and I was embarked on my cabaret career, Ken was about to leave his job as drama critic for the *Observer* to become the Literary Manager for the National Theatre (which was about to be installed in its proper and permanent home on the South Bank) under his hero, Laurence Olivier. Ken's public persona seemed the apotheosis of glamour to me. A renowned café society raconteur, he graduated effortlessly from university wit to the most influential postwar drama critic in the country, regarded by some as the greatest since Hazlitt, or Shaw. He could make or break a reputation, while his progressive views on theatre acted as midwife to the new theatrical styles emerging from the polite theatre of inconsequence then in its hoary old age. For a poor little actress like me, who was always looking for work, Ken's power over important people in the theatre – especially directors – loomed large. He was on my highest pedestal.

When I met Ken he was still married to, but separated from, his first wife, Elaine Dundy. Ken and I never lived together – my house in Battersea was far too important a stronghold not to return to, and with two marriages behind me I set a value on my independence – but for a year, whenever I was not working out of town, we saw each other almost every day.

The first thing I discovered about Ken was his vulnerability. Soon after we met he carefully drew out all the photographs in his portfolio to show me, including the programmes of the few productions he had directed and acted in before he became a theatrical critic. I could not help but think that his work behind the footlights had not been altogether successful, and that he would not have pursued his present career otherwise. He also presented me with a copy of his first book, *He That Plays The King*, precociously written at the age of twenty-two while he was still at Oxford. This collection of theatrical reviews so impressed Orson Welles that he had agreed to write the preface. According to Ken, Welles was staying at the Dorchester when Ken sent his manuscript up to his room with a note saying that he would wait in the lobby for as long as it took Welles to finish reading it. Welles had found it irresistible, and invited the young writer up to his room. Ken presented this book to me with a modesty that surprised and touched me. I sensed that he was feeling insecure at the crossroads of his life, between playing the enfant terrible and facing up to the new uncertainties and responsibilities of the National.

In his frequent buoyant moods, Ken delighted in a childlike narciss-ism. Sometimes in the mornings at his Mount Street flat, I could hear him chuckle into the mirror while shaving: 'I'm still the prettiest drama critic in town!' as though he needed reassurance. Not for nothing had he been called 'Peacock' at university – his real surname, actually. Like me, Ken was born illegitimate. His father, Sir Peter Peacock, sometime Mayor of Warrington, threw up the promise of a considerable legacy to live with his mother, Letitia Rose Tynan, and even adopted her surname, but he never married her – unlike my mother and father.

Ken was not at all pretty, in fact. He was tall and lanky and his features were too large for his bony face. But his personality was irresistible. He was never dull, and though he could be irritatingly churlish whenever he was thwarted, on the whole he was good-natured and eager to please – too eager sometimes. When we first met, his slight speech impediment (a stutter which he learned to use to his advantage) endeared him to me at once, reminding me of my strange cousin in the stair cupboard at home.

It was not long before I began to suspect Ken's left-wing credentials, so vigorously professed in public, so invisible in his private life. He did not, it is true, care for owning property. But, for example, when his mother died leaving him a few shares, I overheard him talking stocks and shares over the phone, and thereafter he had to put up with a lot of merciless teasing.

He was extravagant, and an habitué of the most expensive res-taurants. We never once ate at either his home or mine, which suited my dislike of domesticity. He invariably picked up other people's bills when they joined us. When I pointed out that this largesse was not altogether called for he explained that it was a way of insuring against hunger in the future. He had a fear of this, claiming that his mother had never fed him properly as a child – one of Ken's many exaggerations. Like many men he got restless left to himself outside working hours. At a loose end during the day, he would try to bribe me with gifts to have lunch with him. As I needed time to myself, I often refused.

Ken was a bullfight enthusiast, eloquently describing the cruel sport in his famous book *Bull Fever*. His frequent trips to Spain were not exactly third-class package tours. And yet, when we were once in Madrid together and I bought ten hand-painted plates, he accused me of supporting Franco's fascist régime. Maybe it was revenge for being made to carry the heavy parcel – he told me that the most he would ever hold for me was a pencil. I finally said, 'Ken, you think left but live right.' 'Ah,'

TELEGRAMA
VIA TRANSRADIO

London 55 22 1255

tsai chin chez michael chow torredemadrid plaza espana madrid

dearest chin essential you call me soonest stop
am joining you in madrid next weekend stop
cancel all other engagements all my love
ken

Mod. 97

Pueden depositarse despachos para todo el mundo   "VIA TRANSRADIO"   en nuestras oficinas y en todas las de Telégrafos del Estado.
                                                    "VIA IMPERIAL"

arriving madrid airport 11.15 am saturday
tall and divinely handsome in blue stop be there
stop staying till tuesday all love
    ken

Mod. 97

Pueden depos···   ···pachos para todo el mundo   "VIA TRANSRADIO"   en nuestras oficinas y en todas las de Telégrafos del Estado.
                                                    "VIA···   ···RIAL"

    tsai chin cnez michael chow torre de madrid plaza espana
    madrid

    dear brat understand your qualms but fully intend to marry
    you stop please telephone me saturday morning belgravia 4709.
    stop the going may be good but the coming back will be better
    stop love
        ken

Pueden depositarse apachos para todo el mundo   "VIA TRANSRADIO"   en nuestras oficinas y en todas las de Telégrafos del Estado.
                                                  "VIA IMPERIAL"

he replied, 'in an ideal socialist society I would expect everyone to live like me.' He was a self-professed libertarian Marxist. Unrepentant hedonist was more like it, I thought.

I may have been something of an intellectual snob, but Ken was completely taken in by celebrities. He was a friend to the rich and famous on both sides of the Atlantic. In the words of the late literary agent Clive Goodwin, the guests at Ken's parties were 'cast not invited'. Through Ken I rubbed shoulders with the giants of the artistic world – literally so in the case of Helene Weigel, Bertolt Brecht's widow, at a London party given for the Berliner Ensemble. There I found myself squashed on a sofa against this powerful actress, a surprisingly small-boned woman with a lived-in face. When our eyes met she scrutinised me for a second and simply said: 'I was never beautiful'. Thereafter I was dismissed. I fared better with James Baldwin, the black American author of *Another Country* and *Giovanni's Room*. In a restaurant where I had remained silent all through dinner, he suddenly turned to me and said: 'You are beautiful.' I accepted his words gladly and have cherished them since, for I so much wanted to believe that he had described what he saw within me.

Ken and I went to Paris for a week in Spring 1963. At the Tour d'Argent, the three star restaurant, we waited for the legendary Marlene Dietrich to join us. I was not disappointed. She wore a deceptively simple dark blue suit, not all that new but exquisitely coutured, and a beret to match. Her famous cheek-bones were so perfect that I felt God must have chiselled them with his own hands. I noticed that her make-up was not immaculate – presumably she had been in a hurry that morning – but that made her all the more interesting, for it made her human. I barely spoke, but luxuriated in the sound of her rich, dark voice as she spoke to Ken.

Elizabeth Taylor and Richard Burton were in Paris that week, taking a break from the shooting of *Cleopatra* away from the Roman paparazzi. Burton was devastatingly attractive, both intellectual and virile, and Taylor, though not so elegantly turned out, confirmed her screen beauty in the flesh. I found her a woman of tremendous warmth, and we talked about our erudite lovers. Richard had given her a booklist and, by coincidence, I had recently had a similar list from Ken. Hers I cannot remember. All that remains of mine appears over the page.

"The Great Hunger" by Cecil
                Woodham Smith

"Homage to Catalonia"
*   by George Orwell

"Life of Johnson"
(cheap Edition)·   by James Boswell

"Brief Lives"
(cheap Edition)   by John Aubrey

"Maxims" of
(cheap Edition)   La Rochefoucauld

"Island" by
            Aldous Huxley

* "Howard's End" by
            E. M. Forster

    "Urn Burial" by
(cheap Edn.) Sir Thomas Browne

* "The Outsider" by
            Albert Camus (not Colin Wilson)

    "Aneurin Bevan" by
            Michael Foot

Occasionally I got cross with Ken for being so easily impressed by celebrity; it was so very demeaning, I thought, for a man of talent. When Ken was hoping to mark the opening of the National Theatre by commissioning a new production of *Hamlet* with Peter O'Toole in the title role, we spotted the actor with Sian Phillips across the floor of the White Elephant Restaurant. I offered to act as messenger and invite them to our table. Afterwards, the four of us walked back to Ken's flat in Mount Street for a nightcap, where, ever eager to please, Ken began playing records of Irish fiddlers, one after another, until his guests were bored to tears. I could no longer restrain myself. 'For Christ's sake, Ken', I blurted out, 'if you've heard one fiddle playing you've heard them all. Besides, Peter comes from Liverpool!'

Compared to Ken's illustrious world, my modest career seemed too mediocre to discuss, yet when we were alone Ken had the endearing gift of making me feel clever and interesting. I attribute that to his generosity of spirit. Stories of my childhood delighted him. He especially liked my cousin, the one who stuttered like himself. His love for words was infectious and he encouraged me to use them with originality. I learned to be more articulate. It was he who first suggested I write a book, even going so far as to negotiate a contract with André Deutsch. I got nowhere with it, because I was not yet ready. Yet it sowed seeds for the future. Ken widened my horizons.

Our one year old affair ended amicably when Ken became interested in Kathleen Halton, whom he would marry, a beauty second only to Frances Nuyan. I was happy for him, for I recognised that our association was beginning to have a destructive effect upon me as an actress. To live in the constant shadow of a man who judged the great and blasted the mediocre in my profession shook my confidence. I watched him savage performances better than my own, and I felt despair creep over me. I had a powerful sense of my limitations, and for the first time I questioned my even being in the profession.

I was also becoming increasingly aware that I projected the image of a dumb brunette. I was Ken's exotic mascot. I felt that the only significance to my life was as a great actor's daughter, a talented director's ex-wife and now a brilliant theatre critic's girl friend. They were dubious honours. If I were not careful, I told myself a little facetiously, I would end up being nothing but an intellectual's moll. It was time to move on.

ᴇ

How a girl from Hong Kong rose to stardom.

TSAI CHIN

Growing Up

Tsai Chin was born in Hong Kong in 1937, the daughter of one of the most famous actors in the Chinese Classical Theatre. Much of her early life was spent travelling with her father from place to place as his theatrical company carried out their tours.

Tsai's early memories are all connected with the sorrows of departures and saying farewells.

As she grew up, Tsai showed a great love for animals. At one time she had five cats, two Alsatian dogs and twenty chickens.

When Tsai was 10, one of her dogs died. Chinese families are not allowed to bury dogs, as it is against their religion. Tsai was so distressed that she sang her own funeral songs for the dead animal.

The Chins travelled to many of the big cities in China and eventually returned to Hong Kong, where Tsai was sent to the King George V School.

A favourite pastime of Tsai's was the Chinese version of hop-scotch. It is much more complicated than the British game.

Tsai was light on her feet — and very patient. She excelled at this game.

Another talent of Tsai's was acting and she took part in many of the school plays. She even wrote one at the age of 13 and helped to produce it at school.

AT THIS POINT, WONG, YOU WALK ACROSS TO THE TABLE.

This is how they pictured me in *Judy*, a comic for girls.

17

We are Never Real People

In the coming years, apart from appearing briefly once more in the West End in a commercially and artistically unsuccessful play with Dave King, Ursula Howells and the then unknown Donald Sutherland, I was frequently cast as the guest lead in various television drama series whenever there was an episode set in the Far East. I had diversified into cabaret, which took me to many parts of Great Britain and Europe. With this added string, I made many more records (two LPs and seven singles in all). With each launch of a record I sang on television with such frequency that I was beginning to be known as a singer, instead of an actress, which was not exactly what I had in mind.

In 1963 Ned Sherrin's satirical programme, 'That Was The Week That Was', made television history, and at the same time made its regular stars household names. Ned was one of those lovely producers who uses the actors he has worked with over and over again. The first time I met him, I had been called in to BBC's 'Tonight' at short notice to sing a Cilla Black hit (in her key, too) called 'Anyone Who Had A Heart'. The point of the skit I no longer remember, only that I sang it in front of the camera to a large photograph of Chairman Mao. So because I had worked for Ned I was asked many times to appear on TW3, and had great fun doing it. Once Cleo Laine, Millicent Martin and I sang a song called 'We All Look Alike', then there was a skit called 'The World of Suzie Smith', where the Chinese had colonised Britain, in which I played a Chinese general and Jacqui Chan was my colonel posted to London. Jacqui and I were given the rare chance to pitch in with time-worn clichés about our race – only in reverse. I got my brother Michael to appear in it too, when I pretended to be a Millicent Martin complete with blonde wig and a low cut black dress, singing her signature tune in Chinese. The camera panned across the deadpan faces of David Frost, Willie Rushton, David Kernan and others until it got to Michael, who was killing himself with laughter. The joke was that he was the only one who could understand what I was singing.

With a small name to myself, I was welcome on chat and game shows – important showcases to keep me in the public eye. On 'Call My Bluff' I had to bluff the word 'acupuncture', a medical term then unknown except of course to the doctor on the show, the multi-talented and extremely attractive Jonathan Miller. And on the Eamonn Andrews Show I was the Chinese rose between two thorns. While macho Richard Harris, my friend Elizabeth's ex-husband, showed off his charisma, macho Michael Caine kept his Cockney cool. As for me, I just left my brains on the shelf at home and stuck a smile on my face.

So I was busy and worked constantly. Of course my career had the frustrations and disappointments which every actor knows. My chosen line of work was precarious at the best of times, but the insecurity was more acute for a foreigner in the theatre, where language plays such a vital part; for an Asian, it could be still worse. People were always curious to know whether I could get enough work as an actress to make a living from it. After a time this question would put me on the defensive, partly because it was asked so often and partly because of the implied slight. It was as much as I could do to hold back the retort: Look mate, I've worked more than most English actors have had hot dinners (which wasn't saying much considering the number of out-of-work actors about). I did in fact chalk up a long list of performance credits as I went along and managed to support myself in the manner I was by now accustomed to, and I had some advantageous early breaks which gave me access to other venues.

What were the options left to me, anyway? Would I have fared better if I had remained in my native country? The range of roles available to me amongst my own kind would have been incomparably greater, of course. But I am a nonconformist at heart, and I wonder how I would have coped in a strictly puritanical society. As the restrictions on artistic freedom mounted, would I have been stifled by another, and more terrible form of creative censorship? And when the volcano erupted in 1966, and most artists were persecuted in the Cultural Revolution, would I, I wonder, have survived at all?

A loner by nature, I might as well be an outsider, an exile, and take all the advantages of the situation. Without traditional ties and family pressures, I could be a freewheeling agent to choose how I wanted to live and whom I wanted to be with. Life's obstacles were a challenge. I worked hard, and I played hard, sharing the same life style and social mores with the natives, for better or for worse.

The problem of getting work, on the whole, was not a question of quantity so much as quality. And, believe it or not, it was also a question of ethics.

In 1963, the same year that I was doing 'That Was The Week That Was', I received a letter from the World Peace Brigade for Non-violent Action, of which Bertrand Russell appeared to be one of the sponsors. It followed an episode of a TV series in which I played a nurse to Anthony Quayle's mission doctor. 'I have just seen the ATV presentation of "The Enemy",' began my correspondent, a Mr Barnaby Martin, '. . . the Chinese guerrillas are shown to be generally naive, utterly ruthless and almost inhuman in their attitude to their job. The mission characters are shown to have fine moral quality . . . There seems an implication that the forces opposed to the Chinese are honourable and moral people . . . I do not understand why you would agree to take part in this kind of film. Perhaps you are in agreement with the ideas presented, but if not, why would you help to present them?' And so on.

My answer was defensive: 'An actor enters his profession because he fell in love with the theatre. Hence his compulsion to act. Then, quite soon, he realises that he also has to eat . . . However, if he is sensitive and idealistic, when he speaks lines that he knows are not true, he is not devoid of shame.' And I added: 'A suggestion: why not write to the big fishes in the pond instead of bothering with the tadpoles?'

It was a ticklish subject. Regardless of race, the foreign actor or actress is in general deprived of certain invaluable experiences. Firstly, there is little chance of working on a long-term basis with the same group of actors and directors in a theatre company. Barred from playing classical roles which stretch and improve his talents, he has little opportunity to attract those innovative directors who encourage an actor to grow.

The foreigner also encounters the limiting problem of typecasting rather more often than his native colleagues. For Asian or black actors, there are particular disadvantages, now as then. Certainly in my day there was a problem with stereotyped roles. A typecast role may be unchallenging after a while but still demand the portrayal of a real person. Stereotypes, however, are one-dimensional characters, demanding little creative energy or artistic truth from those who play them. This further arrests the actor's development – and every time we accept such a role, we must bear the guilt of presenting our own race in a poor or ludicrous light.

In early cinema, black men were only niggers who rolled their eyes. Chinky chinky Chinamen wore pigtails and shuffled their feet when they walked. If they were not actively evil, they were invariably seen serving white masters. Such images have changed to an extent, but often to be replaced with subtler forms of racial stereotyping. In the sixties, black men might be regarded as studs. Yellow men suggested the violent activities of the secret societies. Even today, I watch TV advertisements that rely on racial cliché to make their point. One way or another, we are not presented as real people.

As actors, the danger for us is that we begin to perform according to the stereotype even when we land a good part. Then the stereotype may begin insinuating itself into real life behaviour: there are professional chinks and niggers as there are professional virgins. As I found out myself, when this happens we become de-personalised. Reality becomes divorced from truth and we lose our collective and individual identity, and with it our self-respect.

I myself have had to live down the disquieting feeling that at one point in my career I let my race down. For my sins, I was Fu Manchu's daughter five times, with Christopher Lee as my father.

Sax Rohmer invented this arch villain in a series of popular twenties' thrillers, which have been filmed three times, each time perpetuating the 'yellow peril' myth in Western minds. Lon Chaney and Jean Arthur played the first father and daughter; Boris Karloff and Myrna Loy picked up the roles, and between 1963 and 1968 Christopher Lee and I made up the last pair. At least, I hope so. Like many B-movies, these films have generated something of a minor cult with their own devoted audiences, a fact which never fails to astound me.

Harry Alan Towers was the producer. Apart from name changes, the plots were all identical: perhaps that explains why I did not bother to read the script when I came to do the fifth film. Fu wants to conquer the world, forcing a Western scientist to assist him. The white and noble scientist always refuses to co-operate until Fu abducts his beautiful daughter. Then the scientist pretends to relent before destroying his evil opponent. End of picture – though as the credits roll, the menacing voice of Fu Manchu is heard warning his Western cinema audience that worse is yet to come.

Every time we made these films, Christopher would complain about his eye make-up and vow never to appear in one again. The poor man had to have a piece of putty stuck onto each eyelid to make him suitably slit eyed and sinister. I didn't have to bother, I was born that way. Actually my eyes are not all that slanted, on account of my drop of Western blood, perhaps – but what the hell, we all look alike. After each film, I too vowed never to do another. But I signed the contracts though I searched my conscience. In those days I saw a lot of Penelope Mortimer, the novelist, and Clive Donner the film director, who patiently listened to my deliberations. Both Christopher and I always came back. We needed the money.

Few actors are in the enviable position of being able to refuse jobs offered. Financial considerations apart, acting, unlike writing or painting, cannot be practised alone: experience comes from what is available. Out of fourteen films in which I appeared, the five Fu Manchu films taught me at least the art of how to look better on camera. There was nothing else for me to learn from them. Looking good on film is an art in itself, far more crucial to successful film acting than stage experience. In films, lighting, not diamonds, is a girl's best friend, and I always obeyed the cameramen who took the patience to light me well for close-ups. They are the ones who control how you look.

To be honest, had it not been for my sense of guilt I would have unreservedly enjoyed making those films. For low budget movies, they took us to some pretty exotic locations. Only one was made in England, and thereafter we gratified my wanderlust in Ireland, Brazil, Turkey, Spain and later Hong Kong. Christopher and I prudently had our fees paid in advance. It was impossible to take things seriously on set, and there was a lot of tomfoolery about. Christopher was a generous actor though overbearing at times; he was also rather parsimonious. In the years we worked together, he bought me one solitary drink, on location in Brazil. I seized on his largesse and ordered the largest glass of Napoleon brandy. Whenever he and I had a close up together, either he had to stand in a hole or I had to be raised on a platform. We speculated how small Mrs Fu must be to produce me when my daddy was so tall, concluding that she must be a midget. All I had to do in these films was to follow my father around and say a few banal lines while trying to look evil. How I envied Myrna Loy in her series. She was allowed to pepper up her part by being a nymphomaniac, while I was just plain wicked.

A few years later, when I was financially solvent, I did make the decision no longer to accept roles that portrayed Chinese in an adverse light. It was a tough decision which lost me work immediately. One day I bumped into Benny Hill on Bond Street, and he greeted me with an enormous hug – though we had never actually met before. He mentioned then that he would like to work with me, and I agreed. Months later, when I read the skit he had devised, I had to refuse. It was the old 'chinky chinky Chinaman and his wife' routine, in which they both talk pidgin English, with every conceivable racial cliché thrown in. I was sorry not to work with him, for though his comedy is largely based on sexism and racism, he remains a clever comedian. Such, however, was my lot.

In spite of my dissatisfaction with the prevailing climate of stereotyping I realise now, from a position that time has softened, how fortunate I was under the circumstances to have gone this far with my career. Viewed as a whole, the roles I played were not entirely without variety and included choice parts any actress would have coveted. Suzie Wong was one of them. All things considered, I was extremely lucky.

If I sometimes doubted the integrity of my roles and questioned my decision to be an actress, there was still one decision I could never regret. London was a grey city of fog and overcoats and the detritus of war when I first arrived, but it had regained its confidence by now. At the beginning of the sixties, from my flat opposite Chelsea Town Hall, I had been perfectly placed to watch the day to day transformation of King's Road, which was to become a sort of mecca for the young generation, as well as providing visible evidence of their new-found power to change their world. In the side streets, genteel upper-crust ladies and stockbroker wives watched from the windows of their pieds-à-terre with bewilderment as Chelsea was transformed into a kind of international village for the young. Youth from different classes and diverse races, in all manner of dress and undress invaded their preserve of respectable tranquillity. Down the road from me towards Sloane Square, Mary Quant had set up a tiny 'boutique' and began to design the kind of clothes that made pretty girls look intelligent and plain ones interesting. In the other direction, in World's End, Vidal Sassoon developed the straight haircut which liberated women from the lacquered artifice of beehive hair-dos. The cut suited the full and strong quality of my hair to a T.

Caution was thrown to the winds. We were out to shock and have a good time. Hemlines rose till they could go no higher, presenting a feast for male eyes. When the Savoy Grill turned away women in trouser suits, the women simply took off their trousers. You could be nouveau riche and proud of it. Italian restaurants like Alvaro's Aretusa Club were all the rage, and kissing Italian waiters was de rigueur. Between antipasti and spaghetti vongole, while gulping down our verdiccio and waving cigarettes, the 'beautiful people' held out mirrors to one another and stroked insatiable egos. We dolly birds, with our long sleek hair, batted thick false eyelashes and crackled our Rita Hayworth laughs, head thrown back, lips parted, teeth showing. Men looked macho, angelic and revolutionary all at the same time, with their long hair and Zapata moustaches. And casting aside the traditions of British men's clothing they unashamedly showed off every contour of their lithe (or not so lithe) bodies with low cut shirts and skintight pants.

We ate out every night and the men paid for the meals, even queuing for the privilege. Some spent their entire salaries taking us out but we didn't care because a man's gotta do what a man's gotta do. Sexual liberation was made reality with the pill, and I relished the sense of controlling my body, and the power it brought. I thought I was completely free – but I took time to learn that controlling my body was not necessarily the same as changing old attitudes. Soon after I separated from Peter during the run of *Suzie Wong*, I put myself on Albert Finney's long list of one-night stands. What a blow to my inflated ego! Albert, a R A D A classmate, had just achieved fame with his portrayal of Billy Liar, and he was much in demand in every way. My dresser, Daisy, a big and jolly woman with typical Cockney humour put me straight: 'You don't want to be killed in the rush, dear.' This motherly advice struck home. Thereafter I would accept dinner invitations from the likes of Marlon Brando or Cary Grant but when it came to the crunch I would decline their favours. Daisy's lesson was that any such movie giant would drop me like a hot potato sooner or later. So it might as well be sooner, while I still had a say in the matter. Two can play that game.

Dealing with drugs was easier for me than coping with sex. I simply didn't bother with them, which surprised a lot of my trendy friends. Jean Cocteau explained why when he wrote: 'Young Asia no longer smokes because grandfather smoked. Young Europe smokes because grandfather did not smoke.' Though he added, 'Since, alas, young Asia imitates young Europe, it is through us that opium will return to its starting point.' In fact the prejudice against opium was stronger in my generation than Cocteau imagined. From our childhood it had been drummed into us that our race's addiction had brought the greatest evil upon us, when it was pushed by the British. Wars had been fought and lost, marking the beginning of China's humiliation. There was a more prosaic reason for avoiding drugs, too: I had a middle-class squeamishness about lawbreaking, and I dreaded the hassle of getting caught. It would surely get into the papers and my parents, if they heard about it, would be shocked and hurt.

Towards the greater world we were innocent idealists, and we had hope to spare for everything, big or small, serious or trite. It was easy for us: the Vietnam war was far away. We were confused, but optimistic. Our world leaders were genuine giants with boundless charisma. De Gaulle was France personified. Krushchev's crude peasant tantrums titillated our ultra-sophisticated sensibilities, amusing us no end. The Kennedys belonged to us all and Martin Luther King had a dream we shared. In China, Mao was changing humanity, with Zhou Enlai beside him, the statesman's statesman, who made me proud.

An Asian nation was stepping out of the Third World to join the club hitherto reserved for the Western nations: Japan. I felt proud there, too – if they had been China's enemy that was something for my parents' generation to begrudge. For younger Chinese abroad, so eager for good art to emerge from their native country, the Japanese substitute was a godsend and I worshipped the great film-makers like Kurosawa and Mizoguchi from afar. In Hong Kong so many of my peers whom I had left flat broke but struggling, had become dollar millionaires, and were contributing to the British colony's economic miracle.

I travelled frequently in those days, mostly because of work but sometimes for pleasure and almost always alone. One year I went to Israel to escape Christmas in London: a happier Israel then. I was most probably one of the very first Chinese to visit the country, and I was given the VIP treatment. Everywhere I went people showered me with friendly attention. A few years later, when I met Topol, the internationally known Israeli actor for the first time in London, he greeted me with: 'You were in the foyer of the Dan Hotel at noon on 24th December, 1965.' Correct, of course: that's how conspicuous I was. Alas, in the souks and jammed market places in Arab countries, the attention I received was not so easily acceptable. I solved the problem by dressing *à l'arabe* with a yashmak covering my face. Like magic, I melted into the crowd, and disappeared. Perhaps the worst was in Sicily, where my appearance caused quite a stir in the most negative way. Those were the days before tourism had become a thriving industry there. Women in the streets greeted me with fear and hostility and fled from me as though they had seen a ghost when I approached them to ask directions. It was my turn to be the 'foreign devil', and I could imagine how Westerners visiting the remote Chinese interior must feel when they are confronted with the same situation.

I was often in the newspapers, and the continued attention I received helped nurse along my acting career. The press, let's face it, needs lively personalities to make interesting copy. (Long before I was anyone, Shirley Conran, bless her heart, writing for the *Observer*, gave me full-page cover.) An actress needs to remind the public constantly of her existence unless she is so grand as to be able to get along without it. I did not have that advantage, so I only took care that my PR was conducted with as much dignity as possible, discussing what I was up to professionally, or revealing how I made up my face or chose my clothes or furnished a house or threw a dinner party. I pontificated, in fact, on just about every subject under the sun when called upon to do so. Except on my personal life.

It has to be admitted that it is always nice to read flattering accounts of yourself in the press. It feeds your ego and people think you are important. That helps them to accept you instantly when they meet you – your reputation has preceded you, and made the introductions already. Good tables in restaurants become available; the bank manager and the policeman treat you with deference; doors open and sometimes the red carpet is unrolled. To find that I had a known identity, however superficial, was not only pleasant but convenient. And in some ways a minor celebrity, in her butterfly lifespan, can enjoy the same advantages as the truly famous without the disadvantages of being hounded and spied on. I may have taken my good fortune for granted, but I didn't knock it.

There were lovely surprises in store. One morning, for example, I opened the paper to learn that a Chinese leopard cub, born the day before in London Zoo, had been named after me. I knew of a kitten and a canary who bore my name, but they belonged to friends. I was only mildly miffed to discover that the leopard was later sold to Canada for a measly £200.

There were dozens of functions and parties to attend, and frequent invitations to weekends in the country where I hobnobbed with the rich and mighty. Since *Suzy Wong*, I had been attending the Woman of the Year luncheon at the Savoy for the Greater London Fund for the Blind, and had become a member of the committee. In 1964 Marchioness Lothian, the Chairwoman, asked me to make the final toast speech on the subject of 'My Favourite Man'. Edna O'Brien, the writer, spoke before me and opted for Robert Mitchum. Uncharacteristically, I chose from quite a different breed of man. It was the election year with Sir Alec Douglas-Home, Harold Wilson and Jo Grimond contending, so I picked the Liberal leader, Mr Grimond, as my favourite man because I said he would be the only one among the three who would certainly have the time to take me out to dinner for the next five years. My short speech brought the house down. The credit for its success must go to William Rushton, who helped me to write it.

There were dinners of my own to give, and I took pride in filling my parties with people I liked and admired and who made good dinner guests. Scintillating conversation around the table made me feel like the 'hostess with the mostest'. Some of these guests were Bernard Levin, producer David Deutsch and his wife Clare, the publisher Anthony Blond, Ned Sherrin, David Frost, actress and future fashion designer Edina Ronay, the impresario Michael White, director Clive Donner, writer Penelope Mortimer, and the Queen's then private secretary, Sir Michael Adeane and his lively wife, Helen. Francis Wyndham, another writer, was a dependable regular, not to mention my ex-husband and his new wife Susie Fuller, and the Tynans. And of course my close friend Elizabeth – only when she was in between marriages. Once I snared The Champ himself for a big party I was giving. As soon as I confirmed that Cassius Clay was arriving with his entourage I phoned Ken and Kathleen and got them round immediately. The next morning Ken phoned to say that now Chairman Mao was the only man alive he still wanted to meet.

So, in the middle of the Swinging Sixties and living in the West, life for me was a bowl of cherries, and I thought it would last forever.

18

Catastrophe

ℯ

On 26th August 1966, I woke up early. It was a beautiful summer morning, and I was to catch the midday flight to New York, and as there might be photographers wanting my picture at the airport, I gave myself ample time to look presentable. Friends drove me to Heathrow. I recognised the passport controller from my frequent trips abroad, and he was jovial as ever. I was right about the photographers and I got onto the plane feeling a little bit famous, and looking forward to the flight. To my restless nature the thrust of the plane at take-off is always thrilling, humming with expectation. That noon it seemed that I didn't have a care in the world.

Back on the ground the first editions of the evening papers were just arriving on the newsstands. The banner headlines read: TSAI CHIN'S FATHER DIES IN PURGE.

I enjoyed the flight meanwhile, and I was amazed by the VIP reception I got at New York. My ex-husband Peter and new wife Susie were supposed to be meeting my plane, but I was astonished when they whisked me to a side exit, bypassing immigration altogether. The Coes must be doing really well to have such clout, I thought. Tired from the journey and punch drunk on the excitement of arrival, I did not bother to analyse the reasons for my extraordinary welcome. In the taxi to Manhattan I laughed and chatted all the way, only vaguely noticing that Peter and Susie seemed somewhat subdued. I shall always be grateful to them, and to the US Immigration Authorities, for making such a considerate arrangement. I did not know that reporters were crowding the barrier, waiting to get my reaction to the terrible news.

I am glad it was Susie, and not some journalist, who finally broke the

EXTRACT FROM
SUN

27 AUG 1966

Tsai Chin's father 'victim of the purge'

TSAI CHIN yesterday — leaving for New York just before the news of her father reached London.

ONE OF Peking's most famous opera singers, Chou Hsin-fang, the father of London actress Tsai Chin, is reported to have killed himself after being criticised in China's "cultural revolution" —official phrase for purge.

Chou, says the Hong Kong newspaper Star, was criticised for appearing in the opera 'Minister Hai Jui Sends A Pro-

EXTRACT FROM
DAILY MIRROR

27 AUG 1966

Tsai's father in death riddle

CHINESE actress Tsai Chin flew from London for an American holiday yesterday — not knowing her father was reported to have killed himself in Communist China.

A Hong Kong newspaper said that her father, 70-year-old opera singer Hsin Fang, committed suicide during the recent Peking purge.

He had been criticised for his part in an opera said to have been a veiled attack on Mao Tse-tung.

EXTRACT FROM
DAILY TELEGRAPH

27 AUG 1966

CHINESE OPERA STAR'S 'SUICIDE'

Daily Telegraph Communist Affairs Staff

The Hongkong Star yesterday published a report from Shanghai that Chou Hsin-fang, a star singer at the Peking Opera, and father of the London actress and singer Tsai Chin, had committed suicide after coming under pressure in the "cultural revolution."

He was said to have been criticised for appearing in an opera which criticised Mao Tse-tung. Tsai Chin starred in the film and stage version of "The World of Suzie Wong" and broadcasts regularly to China on the BBC Overseas Service.

Nurses dragged from hospital —Back Page

EXTRACT FROM
26 AUG 1966
EVENING STANDARD
West End Final

'Tsai Chin's father takes own life'

HONGKONG, Friday.—The Hongkong newspaper the Star reported today that one of China's most famous Peking opera singers, Chou Hsin-Fang, had committed suicide after coming under fire in China's current "cultural revolution."

One of Chou's daughters is the London actress and singer Tsai Chin, well known for her singing of The Ding Dong Song in the film "The World of Suzie Wong." She starred in the London stage version.

The star said Chou had been criticised for appearing in the opera, Minister Hai Jui Sends a Protest to the Emperor, which had been condemned as a veiled attack on Chinese Communist Party chairman Mao Tse-Tung.

Over 70

The paper said its information came from Shanghai and coincided with reports of increasing revolutionary activities by young Red Guard demonstrators.

The newspaper said Chou had been a good friend of Hu Ti-wei and Chin Su-wen, a husband-and-wife Peking opera team earlier reported by Hongkong Chinese newspapers to have committed suicide in protest against persecution in China. News of the three deaths could not be confirmed in Hongkong.

Though over 70, Chou was still active on the stage until very recently. —Reuter.

TSAI CHIN

WS, Friday, August 26, 1966 5

TSAI CHIN'S FATHER 'IS PURGE VICTIM'

Tsai Chin

HONGKONG, Friday.

THE Hongkong newspaper Star to-day reported that one of China's most famous Peking Opera singers, Chou Hsin-Fang, had committed suicide after coming under fire in China's current "cultural revolution."

One of Chou's daughters is the London actress and singer Tsai Chin, well known for her singing of "The Ding Dong Song" in the film "The World of Suzie Wong." She starred in the London stage version. At present she is on holiday in New York.

The Star said Chou had been criticised for appearing in the opera, "Minister Hai Jui Sends a Protest to the Emperor," which had been condemned as a veiled attack on Mao Tse-Tung.

The newspaper said Chou, who was over 70, had been a good friend of Hu Ti-Wei and Chin Su-Wen, a husband-and-wife Peking Opera team earlier reported to have committed suicide in protest against persecution in China.

EXTRACT FROM
EVENING NEWS (London)
Night Special Ed
26 AUG 1966

news in my room at the Algonquin. I was treated for shock and fell asleep after a doctor had administered an injection. When I woke up the next day, frantic five-way discussions ensued between me and my two elder sisters in Maryland and San Francisco, Michael in London and Vivian in Hong Kong. But there was nothing any of us could do, either then or ever. China was sealed against the outside world.

Through the newspapers we would later discover that although Father's position in China was desperate, he was still alive. But we were not able to communicate with anyone in our homeland, and for eight years we lived in agonising suspense over the fate of our parents. How could I know what was happening? Only the previous year I had received a photo of the family celebrating the tenth birthday of my niece Bingo, William and Jane's eldest daughter. Bingo and Maple, her younger sister, stood between their seated grandparents with their parents standing behind them. I remember thinking it was a sad photograph really, for Father was wearing dark glasses due to a cataract and Mother looked strained. With a pang I noticed that she had suddenly grown really old. A few months later, had I been looking, I would have found reports in the American press that criticisms of Zhou Xinfang as a counter-revolutionary were being aired in the Chinese media – a classic technique to undermine public figures due for 'purging'. But I would not have understood that at the time, and in all probability I would still have underestimated the seriousness of his position. I was paying scant attention to complex political events in China.

Indeed, all that I understood suggested that Father was still in favour with the régime, and I saw no reason why that should change. Did I not possess a photo of him shaking hands with Zhou Enlai (cover photo), the revered elder statesman who attended Father's sixtieth anniversary on stage? There were articles about him in *China Reconstructs*, a PR magazine published in a number of foreign languages for distribution worldwide. I could not know that the pressure upon him and his fellow artists to abandon all theatrical traditions and to surrender their artistic integrity to the service of the proletariat was already rising. And above all, I was unaware of the ominous presence of Jiang Qing.

Jiang Qing in the thirties was a modern actress in films and Spoken Drama in Shanghai who had entered the Communist stronghold in Yenan during the Civil War and captured the heart of Mao, becoming his fourth wife. She had no power until Mao was old, when in 1964 she convened a National Peking Opera Symposium in the capital as the launching pad for her radical campaign to reform the theatre. There were three members of the presiding committee: Zhou Xinfang, leader of the theatre committee, Kang Sheng, a radical left-wing politician who would achieve a fleeting glory as the standard bearer of the Cultural Revolution, and Jiang Qing herself. Apart from my father, the other two had little to do with traditional theatre.

An actor, an intellectual, and a man of innocent integrity, it was Zhou Xinfang's duty to lead the symposium. He could scarcely have imagined what he was getting himself into. By presiding on the same committee as these ruthless adversaries he had entered the lion's den. For Jiang Qing's ultimate aim would be to destroy every recognised form of performing art in China, and by extension to destroy every innovative artist who resisted her. Her ambition was to replace all theatrical genres with a single type of her own devising.

China Reconstructs, in an article entitled 'Peking Opera Enters New Era', quoted Father as saying: 'We should not deal with just any contemporary theme, but must put on dramas with socialist revolutionary content.' But he added: 'This does not mean that we no longer want traditional operas.' Jiang Qing thought otherwise.

It is not surprising that at the beginning of the campaign, Jiang Qing found few people to take her seriously. She could be accused of occupying a position by marriage rather than by talent, and there was something ludicrous about a minor actress attempting to teach the nation's greatest their trade. Jiang herself, whose ability to hold a grudge at the best of times was astonishing, felt slighted, even scorned. When the time was right, she took revenge.

By 1966 the power struggle between two opposing wings of the Communist Party had reached a head. On one side there was Liu Shaoqi, the President, a pragmatist and a brilliant administrator. Against him stood Mao Zedong, Chairman of the Communist Party, the idealist who was increasingly disillusioned with the revolution that he had led to victory. The personnel of the new régime had become a privileged class themselves. He felt, moreover, that a whole generation of young people born after the Communist takeover had little idea of what a revolution really meant. Revolution had to be absolute and perpetual. It must obliterate all the old ways of thought that had condoned the greed and selfishness of traditional society, and reject all models, native or foreign. Only out of a complete revolution in cultural attitudes would society change fundamentally, and this must involve everyone. At grassroots level, he would appeal to the nation's youth to lead a class war upon the icons of the past. There must be mass mobilisation. There must be a Great Proletarian Cultural Revolution.

Certainly the 'narrow élitism' of the intelligentsia had to be assaulted: Mao had never trusted them, and felt that they must be radically 're-educated'. Their attitudes were bourgeois and one-sided; they encouraged ways of thinking that did not adequately take into account the needs of the common people. What use was expertise if it did not apply itself to revolution?

Theatre, the most influential art form, must be assaulted. So Father, as the leader of his community, became a prime target for the general purge that clinched Mao's victory over his moderate rival. His crimes hinged upon his play, *Hai Rui's Memorial to the Emperor*, about a Ming dynasty minister renowned for his courage in criticising his superiors. Mao himself was supposed to have encouraged him to write the play in the fifties, at the time of the Hundred Flowers Movement. When it played Shanghai seven years before the purge it had been approved by the Ministry of Culture. But on 26th May 1966 the press accused its author of shooting 'poisoned arrows' at the party leadership.

Zhou Xinfang became the first Shanghai artist to be publicly denounced at the start of the Cultural Revolution, but the ultra-left campaign had been set in motion in Beijing much earlier. The issue was once again a play about Hai Rui, a version written by the distinguished historian and deputy mayor of Beijing, Wu Han, a key political figure in Liu Shaoqi's camp. In attacking Wu Han, the Maoists made their first thinly veiled assault in the war of words that preceded the Cultural Revolution. Hai Rui had become a dangerous subject, and Father had unwittingly become involved in a power struggle he was destined to lose. When the ultra-left got the upper hand, Father found himself accused of the unpardonable crime of subversion against Chairman Mao himself.

We in the West had begun to piece together a picture of the whirlwind that engulfed China. We heard about the young Red Guards waving their Little Red Books and chanting quotations from the *Thoughts of Chairman Mao*. We understood that perhaps for the first time in history, Chinese youth were given official permission, even encouragement, to overturn the traditions of Confucius by openly defying authority and criticising their elders. A century of change seemed to have rushed China from the most rigid feudalism to this explosion of total revolution, where old ideas, old customs were being swept away by the generation born since Liberation. Boys and girls who might never have dreamed of stepping outside the confines of their family or their towns and cities found themselves banding together to travel the country, free of charge, to carry out their exciting mission. They believed they had been charged with the responsibility of running things their way, Chairman Mao's way, and they thought they were free. I could not blame them for their euphoria.

Gradually, inexorably, the euphoria had turned to anarchy; freedom became lack of direction. While leaders vied with one another for control, students and workers split into myriad factions claiming to represent the true party line. In the confusion the Red Guards mindlessly rampaged through towns and cities, and burned books, destroyed homes, museums, ancient temples and monuments.

Ironically, that autumn I found myself in Hong Kong, where I was to shoot another of the Fu Manchu movies in the Shaw Studio. It was my first trip back to the East. To be so near my parents and yet so impotent, unable to help, was a wrench. Yet in Hong Kong, amongst my own race, I could not feel alone: my suffering was shared by thousands who trembled for the fate of family and friends. The sense of shared misfortune gave me strength.

Back in London, work became the keel to my mental equilibrium. There were more films, including brief appearances in a Bond film, *You Only Live Twice*, and Antonioni's *Blow Up*. In both films, if the audience had blinked, they would have missed me. By the late sixties I was making a conscious effort to take non-Asian roles in the hope of extending my range and broadening my skills. Kate O'Mara and I played the female leads in Congreve's *Love for Love* to full capacity at the Watford Palace Theatre. Paul Massie and I toured a revival of *The Two Mrs Carrolls*, the Martin Vale thriller that had been a smash hit in the early forties and made a successful film with Humphrey Bogart and Barbara Stanwyck. I played the second Mrs Carroll, whose husband murdered his first wife for money. Naturally he intends to engineer a repeat performance, and he administers a little dose of arsenic every day. Ever keen, I went so far as to visit my GP to find out what it would be like to be slowly poisoned, omitting to mention that I was researching a role. Dr Higgs, a painfully shy man, for once lost his inhibitions and remonstrated: 'Oh Miss Chin, don't be so dramatic!'

Two years went by without any news of my family in China. But life goes on.

1968 saw Michael, the family's younger son, establish himself in the West at last. For a number of years he had been working as an artist, even exhibiting in the I C A gallery, but he was shy of promoting his own work, and, worse still, at getting paid for it. Yet he had a talent for money, and a nose for the coming thing. Before he reached thirty, he made a conscious decision to become a rich man. He realised instinctively, I think, that success meant media exposure and that exposure was most easily found by associating himself with the glamorous world that newspapers and magazines depended on for copy: the world of theatre, film, society, pop and such, where I belonged. But Michael saw its potential more clearly than I, and directed his energies into exploiting the hyped-up world of fashion.

Chow was our family name (now written 'Zhou'), spelled according to the old system. As the name of a Chinese restaurant, it made a good pun on 'chow', for food, and maybe even Italian 'ciao'. Everyone was into Italians then, after all. And he called his brainchild 'Mr Chow', another brilliant stroke, for people would now address him unconsciously with respect. After him, 'Mr . . .' restaurants and shops sprang up everywhere. Michael, like my mother, was not afraid to be original, which is the secret of his success. It was his sense of the moment that really made Mr Chow the first fashionable Chinese restaurant outside Asia. Michael, who had experience of working as a waiter in inexpensive Chinese restaurants, began by banishing all the clichés. There were to be no dragons or hanging lanterns; as an art student he had a keen eye for the visual, and he designed his restaurants himself as architectural creations. And because he moved amongst young painters, he was able to display their works in his restaurant. Among them were up and coming stars like David Hockney, Jim Dine, Rauschenberg, Richard Smith and Peter Blake. He also decided that Chinese waiters created the wrong atmosphere: he wanted something more relaxed and lively, so he employed Italians. Everyone laughed of course, but the idea was no more absurd than English waiters serving in famous French restaurants.

He researched the menu with enormous care, travelling to Hong Kong for the best recipes from all over China, introducing great Chinese classics like sesame prawns and seaweed, and had a chef to demonstrate making noodles in front of the amazed diners. Michael in fact was a frustrated showman: it was in the blood, after all. Naturally he employed only the best chefs trained and proved in the Far East. Completely dedicated himself, he inspired the utmost dedication in his staff.

Every evening was a production. He really treated his restaurant like a theatre. The lighting was indirect and flattering, to the women especially. The tables were spacious and spotless; the presentation of each dish was imaginative and had to be immaculate. The prices were fairly high: very high indeed for a Chinese restaurant, but that only reinforced the image he wished to project. Mr Chow became the place to be seen; it was trendy, upmarket and avant-garde.

I had my own contribution to make. While he knew the visual artists, I knew 'tout Londres', so between us the first night was a glittering occasion. I brought Sam Spiegel and Danny Kaye for supper before Michael had officially opened for business. I was at the time running a system whereby my admirers could take me out for dinner only once a fortnight; that way, neither of us became bored. So, for three months after the first night I had myself taken out for dinner every night at Mr Chow's. And these friends came back later on their own.

Michael worked incredibly hard to capitalise on the initial success of his restaurant with his partner Robin Sutherland, and before long he had taken up the invitation of Gerry Moss of A M Records to open in Los Angeles. East Coast followed West when he started up on his own another Mr Chow in New York in East 57th Street, and eventually Kyoto, Japan, as well. The same principles of superb food and snobbish service and attractive, novel presentation were applied everywhere.

Michael would become an internationally renowned restaurateur. He started the hard way. He had had to learn English from scratch at the age of twelve in the occasionally hostile environment of an English public school. He had taken menial work to finance his artistic ambitions. He had lived wherever he could, in poverty. He had struggled all his life, and now he broke through. I often contrast his experience with mine: being a pretty girl, success came early and comparatively easily for me. I never learned to play the hustling game because I didn't need to. Now Michael, of course, is deservedly very, very rich.

A few years later, Cecilia in San Francisco opened her successful restaurant, China House, where her regular clients included John Haldeman at the peak of Watergate. So it seems that both siblings had opted for the traditionally lucrative business of the Chinese exile, after all.

ℰ

The year after the opening of Mr Chow I played Juicy Lucy, another tart with a heart, in the film *The Virgin Soldiers*, starring Lynn Redgrave and

Nigel Davenport among others and based on Leslie Thomas's comic bestseller about gauche British national servicemen in Malaya in the fifties. My role was to initiate Hywel Bennett into the mysteries of sex. I was not the first choice for the role, and for good reason: Juicy Lucy was supposed to be Sweet Sixteen and I was now on the wrong side of thirty. I was approached for the part after Ned Sherrin, the producer, had failed to find a young actress who could deliver the funny lines. I put it down to a triumph for the professionals. John Dexter made his debut as director with the film, which had a screenplay by John Hopkins and John Macgrath and starred a host of good British actors.

It was well received by the British critics and early the following year Ned and I flew off to New York to publicise it on 'The David Frost Show'. Ned was not quite at his ease. It was, after all, the first time he and David had worked together since T W 3 and the roles were reversed. David was the host now, and Ned the guest.

It didn't help that *M.A.S.H.* was released a month or two earlier, and stole *The Virgin Soldiers*'s thunder. All the same, I went on alone to publicise the film in Boston and then to the West Coast. In my Hollywood hotel room I was welcomed with a basket of tempting fruits wrapped tightly in cellophane. Before I could lay hands upon it, it was whisked away. The publicist whom Columbia had appointed to look after me had an insanely jealous wife who provided the only amusement on an otherwise routine tour. Her husband was a tired, nondescript little man in his mid-forties, hardly an Adonis, and it was most touching to see the trouble she went through to show how much she treasured him. She followed us everywhere we went, lurking in the corridors of radio and television stations. Eventually I invited her to ride in the car with us and save everyone a lot of bother.

I went on to San Francisco and took part in the annual China Town parade for Chinese New Year, again as part of the promotion for *The Virgin Soldiers*. Though I am generally nervous of crowds, I jumped at the chance of seeing this elaborate and famous parade from the inside. I invited Cecilia to be with me on this occasion, but she came down with flu. Alone, I was made to sit on top of an enormous limousine driven by a Chinese karate expert and wave enthusiastically to the crowds like any self-respecting carnival queen.

By now I was winding up my cabaret career. On the whole, loneliness was a cabaret artist's lot. When normal people were about to retire for the evening, I was preparing to go to work. The energies of an entire day were geared towards 11 p.m., when I performed. Winding down afterwards entailed going to bed in the wee hours. I was having trouble sleeping. Working frequently on tour, I would arrive with a suitcase like a travelling salesman for a week's engagement in some strange town. Since I had a policy of not fraternising with my audience, days were spent in lonely hotel rooms where I certainly put in my fair share of serious reading. In this, I was in great company: Tolstoy, Dostoievsky, Cervantes, Mann and others. Returning each time to London I had little opportunity to arrange to meet friends. I was becoming more and more tense; I suffered from back ache. Only yoga saved me.

<p>

It was impossible to ignore events in China. Certain facts had become clearer with time, such as the idea that from now on all training was to be despised as a continuation of feudal traditions. My father, whose training had nurtured his genius, had become Public Enemy Number One in Shanghai. To know this terrible truth was at least to know that he was still alive.

After three years of anarchy the army was called out to restore order, but they served a new régime. The Cultural Revolution had enabled the militants to purge the Party of moderates. Vacant posts were filled by new cadres loyal to the ultra-left, who became a new élite in almost no time, infinitely more oppressive than their predecessors. The ageing and enfeebled Chairman Mao whose face stared from every wall had defeated his rivals only to come under the influence of the so-called Gang of Four headed by Jiang Qing, his wife. The anarchic excesses of the Cultural Revolution were replaced by the decrees of the draconian Party leadership. The Red Guards, disillusioned and betrayed, were conscripted to work in the countryside with the peasants, followed soon after by younger academics, artists and scientists with all those who could be shown to possess a bourgeois intellectual heritage. The fabric of Chinese family life was torn apart. Husbands and wives were separated, sent to different camps, leaving children to fend for themselves in the cities. The urban conscripts were instructed to learn from the peasants. The sensible peasants found their new assistants rather a nuisance and nicknamed them the Three Too-Manies: too many spectacles, too many watches and too many patches. The Great Cultural Revolution was theoretically accomplished.

The days of persecution, however, were far from over. Compared with the random assaults of the Red Guard, Jiang Qing's attacks were carefully orchestrated for maximum public effect. Shanghai, the city that always aimed to lead in the country whether in fashion or politics, had launched the Cultural Revolution; it was Jiang Qing's headquarters, her power base, and whenever a class enemy was needed to parade before the masses, my father was on hand. He became Jiang Qing's pet purge whenever the mood took her.

It seems almost inconceivable how ruthlessly the Gang of Four carried out their aim to 'reform' drama. Henceforward, by decree, only those actors personally approved by Mao's wife would be permitted to work; the remainder would be sent into the countryside. Their elderly mentors were imprisoned. She laid down rules for writing plays around a few approved revolutionary themes composed of a random mixture of Peking Opera, ballet and an occasional piano score. All Western instruments were banned as decadent, but Jiang loved the piano herself and she could break the rules. The theatrical repertoire was thereby reduced to a mere eight plays. These eight plays comprised the sole entertainment available to the Chinese for almost a decade. Thus, single handed, she almost succeeded in destroying Chinese theatre which has perhaps the richest and longest continuous history in the world.

On 19th October 1969 I read in the *New York Times*: 'The militant mood of the Cultural Revolution in China has largely waned but in Shanghai it flared again recently in a rally held "to criticise and repudiate Zhou Xinfang" . . . The 74-year-old Mr Zhou was accused of "towering crimes in undermining the revolution of Peking Opera personally led by Comrade Jiang Qing."' I was later to learn that at the beginning of the next decade a courageous appeal on his behalf from fellow artists and actors whose hardships had been eased with the suppression of the Red Guards was personally rejected in an episode that has come to be known as 'Comrade Zhang Chunqiao's reply to petition'. The petition had asked for lenient treatment for the old man. Comrade Zhang, a Shanghainese himself, was a member of Jiang's Gang of Four, and he publicly stated that 'for the likes of Zhou Xinfang, not to execute him is lenient treatment. If he is not a counter-revolutionary, then we are!'

19

Collapse

e

It was in the last year of the sixties that I had an affair with a grand master of film-making from a Communist country. I had long admired Andrzej Wajda since seeing his early films, *Canal* and *Ashes and Diamonds*. At the time, Jeff Selznick was hoping that the Polish director would work with him on his film project, and direct Conrad's *Heart of Darkness*. Jeff was a friend, and when he asked me if I could give a party for Andrzej, I was more than delighted to oblige.

I eventually went to Poland to watch him shoot a film. He never seemed to carry a script with him, but scribbled everything on a postcard. This was my first visit to the Eastern Bloc, and I was surprised by the drabness of the people's lives. But Andrzej was irresistible, gentle, childlike and totally absent-minded outside his work. Other people naturally were in awe of him, but he made me laugh a lot. Door keys were invariably misplaced, and once he had to climb through windows to get into his flat. And during long-distance travel we could be stuck in remote places in the dead of night because he forgot to put petrol in the car. Andrzej took me to see the concentration camp in Dachau, now a monument. The disturbing images I carried away with me could not but add to my anxiety over the fate of my parents in China.

Affairs with people who lived in a different city were my favourite, because they could end by mutual consent as soon as anything so much like hard work as a relationship began.

One way or another I did not pause to regret the passing of the sixties, nor – with the exception of events in China – to regard the coming decade with trepidation. It began so well for me. I thought I had been really astute in financial terms by turning my ability and pleasure in renovating old houses into a lucrative sideline. It was a fairly common standby for people in my precarious profession. I got enough financial backing to renovate properties which I then either let or sold, which gave me the freedom to reject the stereotyped roles I was ashamed of. I waited instead for more challenging offers.

So in 1972 I was delighted to be offered the role of Wang Kwanmei in a Granada TV production called *The Subject of Struggle*, produced by the award winning Leslie Woodhead. Madame Wang was the wife of Mao's arch-rival Liu Shaoqi, and the most important woman in China before the Cultural Revolution. On 10th April 1967, Red Guards from Qinghua University captured her and subjected her to a sixteen-hour ordeal of interrogation and 'self-criticism'. A practised politician, Madame Wang proved a tough nut to crack. It was a great coup for the young zealots to have purged such a prominent political figure, and they taped the whole event to be a model for other Red Guards setting up struggle sessions. Five years later the tapes had reached the West, and the Granada play – one of the earliest television 'docu-dramas' – was based on a transcript, interspersed with actual newsreel footage of rallying students. Eric Young, Pik Sen Lim and Rex Wei played my persecutors.

The Subject of Struggle won critical acclaim at every level. *The Times* called it 'a triumph for director/producer Leslie Woodhead'. Elizabeth Cowley of the *Evening Standard* observed that I 'had left The World of Suzie Wong a long way behind with this brave and haggard perform-ance'. Sheridan Morley interviewed me for the rival channel and the interview prompted Clive James to remark in *The Observer* that I was 'no slouch at politics'. There were other unexpected bonuses in store. Jill Tweedie, who interviewed me for *The Guardian*, became a lifelong friend. And to my delight I was told that many members of B A F T A had nominated me for Best Television Actress of the year. At last I was being taken seriously.

The role was significant to me in other ways as well. I was profoundly affected by the extraordinary experience of being subjected, albeit only on set, to the same sort of ordeal I suspected my father of undergoing. My normally clear skin became blotchy during shooting. And once, for a few seconds, I confused art with reality. I forgot that the 'tranquillisers' Wang Kwanmei is offered would be only stage sweets, and I refused them for fear of getting befuddled. It was a cathartic role, for it helped me feel closer to my father. Equally, if not more importantly to me, was that this was the first role I felt able to identify with. Portraying a woman ten years my senior, intelligent and educated with a strong sense of her own identity, I felt a long way from the Juicy Lucy roles I had been offered, with their cute little oriental doll manners and their pidgin English. The artist and the woman within me met at last.

Much to the surprise of the make-up artist I insisted on having myself made up far too old for the part, for I recognised that I had reached that transitional stage in every actor's career between playing ingenue and mature roles. Indeed, in the two years between Juicy Lucy and Wang Kwanmei my screen persona aged some forty years! Although I recognised and accepted the change with enthusiasm, and had seemingly relaunched myself with acclaim as an older, more serious actress, I found that more prestigious work failed to materialise.

Unknown to me, my life would take a disastrous turn. Before that happened I made one more film, *Rentadick*, again produced by my good friend Ned Sherrin. It was great fun to make, because in the *Carry On* tradition the film starred all the British comic talents of its day: Spike Milligan, Frankie Howerd, and Donald Sinden, to name a few, and included the dancer David Toguri, who would later become the most sought-after choreographer in Britain.

In the meantime I struggled against the reflection that in leaving my own culture I had only partly embraced another, and that like a bridge over a widening gulf my grip on both was weakening. I grew afraid that I would tear apart, fall into the abyss. My once firm reach to China and the culture of my homeland was crumbling slowly, like a dream that seems real and solid and unforgettable but which slips away like quicksilver upon waking. The Chinese world I remembered and understood seemed like that quicksilver, slipping away with the collapse of my parents' world. I no longer understood. Naively, like my father, perhaps, I had thought that revolution fought social injustice in the name of human dignity. But what was happening to Father was unjust, and what was done to him was undignified. Both victim and victimisers were debased.

I could not understand how the revolution could turn upon him. He who might have rested on his laurels at an early age became far more than a mere entertainer, motivated by a passionate concern for his country. He had stepped beyond known limits to issue a rallying cry to the generation upon whom the responsibility for making revolution rested. As Ken Tynan wrote: 'There is an umbilical connection between what is happening on the stage and what is happening in the world.' Zhou Xinfang was not only a great artist but also a man unafraid to be before his time. Did not Professor Colin Mackerras, in his book *The Chinese Theatre in Modern Times*, write that 'he made no secret of his view that sometimes theatre should propagate a certain viewpoint. At the time of the May Fourth Movement, a drama in which he performed was immediately suspended by the authorities on the grounds that it was subversive. During the war he was active in reinforcing optimism, patriotism, and anti-Japanese feelings through art. He became an active supporter of the communists . . .' Why then should such a man be destroyed?

Eight years had passed without a single word from my family. My uncertainty as to their fate imposed a terrible strain, compounded by a feeling of utter helplessness. China might have been the moon – except that the Americans were about to demonstrate that it was easier to reach the moon than Beijing. At first, there was comfort in the sympathy of friends, in touching letters from acquaintances and strangers. At first I could cry. Yet although I kept up the façade of being an outgoing, lively person, my interior landscape had changed.

Fear took over, when with the suddenness of a revelation I realised that the world was a dangerous place. Losing my belief in life, I started to lose belief in myself. Depression paralysed me. I sensed a panic within me, and found it hard to sleep. When my eyes closed I saw my mother with sunken eyes and gaping mouth, like the girl in Edvard Munch's painting 'The Shriek'. In one dream I handed her a glass of iced water by way of comfort, but as soon as she began to drink the ice turned to broken glass and choked her. When I woke up in the darkness I felt a hole at the centre of my being. All I could do was to hold my stomach to stop my guts falling out.

Though I knew Father was alive I had never heard word of my mother. I refused to acknowledge her ghost in the night, clinging to the hope that with her courage she would always find a way to grasp life.

Outwardly my life style remained the same. I had moved up-market from Battersea to a lovely five-storeyed Georgian terraced house in S W 1, where I reserved three floors to myself and made the other two floors into self-contained flats. One of the decorators turned out to be a lovely man called Simon Perry, who in later years metamorphosed into a major film producer of such films as *1984* and *White Mischief*. My tenants and I became good friends and I was far from lonely. I could hire a daily woman to clean and a part-time secretary. But my capacity for enjoyment had diminished. I was merely watching myself go through the motions of living. My boredom threshold sank lower every day. Both pills and wine were ready to hand and the doses increased as I tried to ward off insomnia or the fear of terror creeping upon me while I slept. I had B movie affairs with men. Meanwhile I travelled more and more frequently, to Africa, Scandinavia and the Americas, until a friend at the airport observed that one day soon I would run out of countries to go to. And I was running.

In public I was a dizzy marionette spinning faster and faster. Left alone to myself in my tall house in Pimlico, after throwing some big party, I was the solitary figure sitting in my double drawing room sipping brandy all through dawn. I wondered who I was and why I was there at all. Hell, the worst showbiz clichés had come true, for I wanted to stop the world and get off. But I didn't know how or where to get off. I found the answer in another catastrophe.

In 1974 I was ruined.

Ironically, I had gone into the property business to seek financial security. Now the best I could say was that I was not officially bankrupt. The reasons for the financial crash are not only foolish but boring, too, but they affected a number of other people along with me and they stemmed directly from a combination of not paying attention to the property market and taking poor advice by over-extending my credit at the exact moment the great seventies recession set in. As an isolated set-back I could have dealt with it, but now it was the last straw. My will snapped.

I took an overdose in a desperate cry for help. It was a selfish act, as I now see it, for I only gave my friends the runaround. So many people helped me, so many people bore the brunt of what I had done in a desperate moment of despair. Brother Michael and sister Vivian, who was in London at the time, my men friends Ron Worral and Dr Simon Farrel, who lived in the basement, and my girl friends Jeanne La Chard, B B C producer and journalist, and Jill Tweedie. Last but not least, Daniel Topolski and his girl friend who actually found me because I had made a date to see them.

I did not want to die. As I lay prostrate on the hospital bed after my stomach had been pumped out, my lawyer and old friend Carlo Colombotti was at my side. I opened crimson eyes for a moment. 'How are you?' asked Carlo gently, leaning down. 'Fit as a fiddle,' I replied with force, and conked out. It was an expression I had never used before. I can only conclude that my vocabulary had rebounded in defiance to what I had done to myself. Soon after I received a card from Susan. 'I didn't know you're a quitter' it read. The sentence has stuck in my mind ever since.

After I came out of hospital, life speeded up. Michael came to the rescue by offering me a job in Los Angeles at the Mr Chow restaurant he had so successfully started up. I clutched at the offer gratefully, and began to make preparations for leaving.

A month before departure I saw Bruce, my son. He had been sent by his father to look into the possibility of furthering his education in England. Although I had seen my son many times over the years, it seemed unfair that he should be coming to settle in England just when I planned to leave. I sought out my good friends Bernard Levin and David Howell, MP, to advise me on the procedure for applying to British universities. They were generous with their time, but their efforts were wasted: just when we seemed to be making some headway, Bruce was called back home. His father had changed his mind, and decided to send him to Canada for his education instead. In the end this turned out to be an unexpected stroke of good fortune for Bruce and me.

I saw Ken for the last time when I visited him and Kathleen who were surrounded by their children in a lovely house in South Kensington. Ken had been earning a reputation for being more and more outrageous— the enfant terrible streak that he never really outgrew. For some, he was the man who had pronounced the word 'fuck' on television for the first time (the switchboards jammed with the calls expressing support or threatening brimstone; questions were asked in the Commons). Others remembered him as the producer of a semi-pornographic show, *Oh, Calcutta!*. I saw now that he had given up smoking, but I had no idea that he was suffering from emphysema, the disease that killed him in 1980, aged fifty-three. Looking back, I see not his outrageous behaviour but the critic, perhaps the greatest theatre critic of our century, whose views helped shape the direction of theatrical history. I can't help wondering if that would have been enough for Ken, or if indeed he ever really cared at all. I had no premonition of the fact that I would never see him again.

I made an effort to extract some news of my parents from the Chinese embassy before leaving, but the wall of silence was solid.

I felt little emotion at the upheaval surrounding my departure. I informed almost no one, not even my agent Patricia MacNaughton, as if I wanted to seal my life in England, flash-freeze it just as it was. I took nothing of it with me. If I felt anything it was guilt, the most destructive emotion of all. My mind was numb. I felt I had failed at everything, as a daughter, as a mother, as an actress. Like a character in a Victorian melo- drama when the heroine's fortunes are reversed, I donned my sackcloth and set out on a pilgrimage to do penance. China and Europe lay behind me. The future stretched before me like a forbidding, empty desert, and I scarcely dared to hope that I would find my salvation in the New World.

20

Penance in LA

e

They say that life runs in seven-year cycles, and I was in fact to spend seven years in the USA searching for some sense of my own worth. I arrived in LA on 30th July 1974. Michael had kindly paid for the trip. Los Angeles might seem an unlikely starting point for spiritual rejuvenation: but America, land of opportunity, was an energetic place to be. From the start the persistent sunshine in the city seemed to refute my sense of despair, and gradually I began to respond to its life-giving force. I was forced to face my physical well-being, and I was helped by the fact that in my haste to leave England I had left behind my bottle of barbiturates, supplied on the National Health. With no money of my own, I couldn't afford the cost of medicines in America, and I had to do without sleeping pills once and for all. In such a climate it was easy to get caught up in the Californian mania for physical fitness; I did my yoga faithfully, and even jogged. Within six months of my arrival, for the first time in my life I became a 'morning person'. I tuned my body but I had to go further to reorder my mind.

Dripping smooth silk jersey by Missoni, or elegantly turned out in a St Laurent outfit, I walked the marble floors of Mr Chow's Restaurant on Rodeo Drive, the classiest shopping street in Beverly Hills. I had brought some of these designer outfits with me, but others were provided by my boss, Michael. I was under no illusions that as a hostess I was at best a glorified waitress to most of the star-studded clientele. Work in the restaurant was hard – my feet always hurt – but being compulsive by nature I tackled the job with total commitment. After all, I was starting a new job and learning a new trade, and my anonymity served as a shield. I did not want reminders of my recent past. Sometimes, that was

unavoidable, for this was an actor's restaurant. Seeing Donald Suther-
land recalled the years that had passed since we worked together when
he was an unknown, and I was tempted to reminisce about old times.
One evening Coral Browne came into Mr Chow's with her husband,
Vincent Price. She introduced us, and praised me for my performance in
A Subject of Struggle. Such reminders of that other life were hard to bear.

It was also painful to realise that I was no longer in a position to
answer back, merely one of those who only serve. I recall only a few of
the diners at Mr Chow unfavourably; most I remember with affection.
John Lennon and Peter Sellers were lovely, Leslie Caron was a friend.
Steve McQueen's unassuming manner impressed me most. He and his
wife, Ali MacGraw, would turn up early for dinner and leave unobtru-
sively before most people had arrived. They often asked me to sit down
for a chat. Steve once offered me a drink but I declined, confessing that
drink was apt to make me aggressive. 'How many glasses do you need
before you beat me up?' he asked, deadpan.

I didn't need the wine, though, to become a fury. Michael was good
enough for that. By that time, Michael had loved and parted with his
former wife, Grace Coddington, fashion editor of *Vogue*, and had married
the exquisite Tina Lutz – half Japanese, half American. She and her
sister Bonnie were Japan's top models. I had always got on well with the
women in Michael's life – Michael himself was another matter. Our
relationship had never been smooth but now I was having to adjust
to my kid brother being my boss. No ordinary boss, either, for Michael
had worked extremely hard for his success and was under enormous
pressure. He ran a tight ship and expected absolute obedience from his
staff, which he always got. With me he acted the tyrannical patriarch,
and even outside working hours he wanted utter control over my life.
The male chauvinist pig was stuck with a female one.

'Why can't you agree when I tell you this book is black?' he shouted
out of sheer frustration one day.

'Because anyone can see that it's white!' I roared back. A Jewish
friend was present at the time. 'Even Hitler never decreed so much,' she
muttered under her breath.

The fault was probably mine. Michael was generous when he felt
secure, and no doubt he would have taken care of me had I let him. But
we had been cut from the same cloth. Like everyone else in our family
we responded to gentle persuasion but not to aggression. There were
moments when I knew I couldn't continue like this.

In some respects the gods had smiled upon me. I had got myself into good physical shape and I found somewhere to live. By sheer luck, Anchka Brando, Marlon's widowed step-mother, had a small two-room house to let, the annex to her own bungalow on Coldwater Canyon, Beverly Hills' choicest location. She lived here with her father Eugene Frankel, the veteran producer. For all that, it was inexpensive and I could use the pool and the tennis court. And in my sitting room there was a tall cast iron lamp which had been given to Mr Frankel by Greta Garbo to provide a touch of the glamour of Hollywood's golden days.

It is all but impossible to work or live in the States without a 'green card', and here I had an bizarre stroke of good fortune. Since my sisters had become naturalised American citizens the procedure for applying seemed relatively straightforward, but I soon realised that a good lawyer could expedite matters. Twice at Mr Chow's I met a young man with flowing hair, who booked his table under an assumed name and ate alone. I never learned his real name. We got chatting about life in general, and the day after I told him that I was applying for residential status I received a call from a John E. Mason, Jr., of Kaplan, Goodwin, Berkowitz and Selvin, a top law firm. Mr Mason had been instructed to handle my case and I was to consider all the bills as settled. I was never given the chance to thank my benefactor personally because I never saw him again. He wanted to remain anonymous and after all he had done for me, it was his privilege. I didn't try to find out, which would somehow have been looking a gift horse in the mouth. I was much in need of the kindness of strangers.

A trickle of letters had arrived from William and Jane, informing us that the family had finally been permitted to write letters abroad. They mentioned that Father was at last permitted a stove during the winter months, and suddenly I glimpsed some of the horror of their lives, even deprived of any warmth through the bitter cold of Shanghai in winter. There was no mention of Mother. How long I had waited in hope for news of her. Now I did not have to read hard between the lines to know what the omission meant. I finally had to accept the reality that my mother was dead. It felt as if the one thing I had lived for had been taken from me.

Immediately, I sank into a depression. I quit my job after only six months, never expecting that Susan, out of the goodness of her heart, would send me some money to live on. 'We shall not feel depressed because of small amounts of money,' she wrote. 'We will all survive.' Survive I would: I was not going to attempt suicide again. But I was at a loss. I went into retreat and let nature take its course. For seventeen days and nights I lay on my bed in the dark and waited. I don't remember feeding myself. I only remember the sound of Anchka pottering about outside my bedroom window; we had become friends and I think this was her way of letting me know I was not abandoned, that she would be around if I needed her.

I did not ask for help, though. I had to go through this ordeal alone. The determination to survive, to emerge whole, had to be mine alone. But the inspiration did not come. One afternoon I suddenly noticed that my tiny Omega watch was missing from my bedside table. It was the watch that Mother had given me before I left Hong Kong, and on which I had had to pay the £10 duty when I arrived to begin life in England. It no longer worked and had lost its strap, but I carried it with me wherever I went. I combed the room, but when I couldn't find it I stepped out of doors. The sunlight bathed my face for the first time in a fortnight. Beside the house stood a huge rubbish bin, full to overflowing. Without really believing I would succeed I began calmly and systematically to pick my way through each and every sordid plastic bag. It took hours but I found the watch.

When I held it in the palm of my hand in the sunlight, and saw the tiny face trimmed with sparkling gold, I was convinced that my dead mother was looking upon me. It was her voice that spoke from within. I must not waste the life she had created and so lovingly nurtured. The bole was slashed but the tree must not die.

A fever washed over me, but a few days later, at five in the morning, I suddenly got out of bed without effort and went straight to my type-writer. Step by step I recorded the experience of the previous seventeen days. 'Depression is like dancing with the devil,' I began, 'five steps forward, four steps back. But you must be satisfied with the single step gained . . . Step 3, the only thing you are capable of feeling is *fear* – fear of what? Everything. Step 4, all is blackness. Step 5, I think at this point the best thing to do is to let yourself sink and try not to feel guilty. Relax, for it is the turning point . . . You have to come to nothing . . .' I ended it with: 'Remember it will happen again. When it does, read this.'

I did not know it but I was writing fourteen days before my father died, on 8th March, 1975. A letter arrived from William and Jane simply informing me of his death. With his passing, one of my last links to China was severed.

I did not quite know what to expect of myself when I emerged from my depression. The last thing I wanted to do was to traipse between studios in the hope of starting my acting career again in Hollywood. For a while I waited and did nothing. Again my calm and compassionate sister sustained me through this difficult period. Long before, she had become concerned, without saying so, that my unruly life might one day come unstuck. Later she described it as a life of too much spice and not enough starch. 'In your loneliest moments,' she had written to me when I first arrived in LA, 'you must never forget that I love you.' During the years ahead her wisdom would be my guide, and her love and support, both moral and practical, would sustain my spirit. Her husband, ever understanding and generous, made it all the more possible for her to help me. It would be hard to imagine how I would have pulled through without their stable influence and encouragement.

As I began to review life at my own pace I did not get a job, but I was not idle. In the mornings I attended a quarter-dollar school for Mexican immigrants, and polished up on my maths while the Mexicans learned English. I volunteered to clerk every afternoon at the Free Clinic, which provided free medical care for the poor. Once a week I 'womanned' the office of the LA chapter of the National Organisation For Women, where I took down messages left on the answering machine and answered calls. In other words, I made myself feel useful without putting myself under pressure. At the end of the year I left LA to join Susan and her family for Christmas. I would not live in LA again.

Susan had always wanted me to feel that I had a home with them, but until now I had not taken much notice. The day had arrived. Visiting her home regularly over the years, I had become closer to her children than to my own son. Serena was a bright and gentle young lady who lived up to her name, and my teenage nephew Lloyd was brainy like his physicist father. So protected by the warmth of family life in a tranquil suburb I was able to lick my wounds. I enjoyed simple pleasures, like the museums of Washington DC which I visited with Serena, who was studying art history at the time. Most of my days were spent in my room, reading.

Soon after my arrival I came across two books in the local library which would influence my decision to return to the theatre. Antonin Artaud's *The Theatre and its Double* and Jerzy Grotowski's *Towards a Poor Theatre*, both books whose existence I knew of but which I had never read. Previously I had always found books on theatre too commercial or too esoteric for my liking, but what I read now excited me. My enthusiasm revived and I ravenously devoured more information until I had read fifty two books on the subject by the end of my two month stay. Without knowing it, I had rediscovered my world in a different way and on another level. Before, I had worked in theatre on a hand to mouth basis that suited my youthful desire for activity and experience; now I mused on wider questions, on the very nature of acting itself.

A year had passed since I had left Mr Chow's, and it was time to face the world again. Once more Susan pushed me in the right direction when she turned to me one day and said: 'You know I'm not your mother.' I did not at first understand her. 'I'm not your mother. I am your sister, but you are relying on me as a child relies on its mother.'

Two weeks later I decided to go to my American friends Sharon Dunn and her then husband Richard Diperna, who lived in Boston. Susan came to the station to see me off. I was reluctant to leave her side and there were tears in my eyes. Calm as always, she waited until the train was about to leave, and as she stepped onto the platform she turned and said: 'You forget you have a profession.'

21

Second Spring

ℓ

Richard and Sharon had been my tenants in London. Now they offered to put me up for nothing in their comfortable apartment in Cambridge, across the Charles River from Boston. Although I was virtually penniless I was not exactly slumming it. I had a room to myself. Sharon, as editor of her small but prestigious literary magazine *The Agni* (now jointly edited by Askold Melnyczuk) was financially independent from her husband Richard, a successful business consultant. My clothes presented something of a problem, however. It was winter and I needed a coat. With no skills to offer other than acting the only work I could hope to find would be as a receptionist, the lowest office job – and the first job I had had when I was a young girl. Now, at my age, I had to begin again.

But I had only a mink coat with me and I could scarcely go to interviews in that get-up. No one would believe I was in earnest. So I went to the thrift shop and bought a 1950s coat for three dollars. I spent a dollar and a half on a pair of plastic boots, indispensable for trudging through the deep snow. Through wind, rain and ice I set out to search for a job as a receptionist, taking public transport – which I had always loathed. No one wanted to hire me. I was told that I looked too intelligent to stick to a receptionist's job for long!

This was in spite of the résumé I had constructed with Richard's help. The pitch was calculated: I sounded averagely intelligent, but not too flighty: receptionist at Butterfield and Swire, Hong Kong (true); Receptionist at Carlo's law firm Colombotti and Partners, London (false); secretary to Mrs Coe in her property company, London (Mrs Coe and I were one and the same person); Receptionist at Mr Chow's, LA. I still found myself temping while I searched for a steady job. I stuffed envelopes at the Harvard Co-Op, pretending to be Charlie Chaplin in *Modern Times*, stuffing as many envelopes in one day as possible, like a machine. Once I worked as a typist in the pool at an insurance company. While the girls chattered on about boy friends and movie stars I sat and wondered how they would react if I told them that I knew some of the people they mentioned. They would think I was insane. Meanwhile I got tired of typing the company's tediously long name in full, and I began abbreviating it to initials only. At the day's end my supervisor called me in to her office, where the deceptive lighting enabled me to look a mere slip of a girl. She addressed me accordingly. 'I have to break it to you,' she said, with the hesitancy of one about to blight a youthful career, 'you'll never make a professional typist.' As a matter of fact I was rather put out at the time, but I remembered a poster that hung in the NOW office in LA. It showed Golda Meir, the Israeli Prime Minister, with the legend: 'And She Can't Type'.

Trekking from one end of town to the other was a wet, cold and exhausting business in winter, in freezing cheap boots. Facing the underground railway tracks I often recalled Garbo as Anna Karenina. The gloomy atmosphere was perfect for the last tragic scene in the film. But if the temptation to throw myself onto the line ever flashed through my mind I was able to dismiss it with another image: Madame Curie, played by Greer Garson, fainting from cold and hunger in Walter Pidgeon's arms. And even better by extension, Madame Curie, the respected scientist, walking onto the stage, a tiny, white-haired old lady amid thunderous applause. The actress within me could never quite escape the lure of public adulation. Whenever I felt weak, I opted to be Madame Curie.

Finally I was directed to Donna Martin at Harvard's School for Arts and Sciences. Ms Martin, who was assistant to the Dean, had a reputation for employing unusual people. At my first interview she seemed pretty unusual herself. She asked me which job in the whole department I would aspire to, given the chance. Christ, I thought, I don't even know how to refill a stencil yet! Donna took her time hiring me. She wanted me to promise that I would stay with her for a year at least. I do not give promises lightly, and I was unable to satisfy her, but she hired me in the end.

I set about my new job with enthusiasm and threw all my energy into overhauling the entire filing system at the School for Arts and Sciences. I had a wonderful time digging into the archives a few blocks away in an effort to find missing files. I became a regular little martinet. Everyone had to sign for files. I was soon offered promotion but I had to decline. My heart was elsewhere. While still working at Harvard during the day, I had begun to rehearse for David Hare's play, *Fanshen*, based on William Hinton's study of village life in Communist China. The play was to be performed at the People's Theater, the venue for fringe theatre in Cambridge. I auditioned for a part, and got it. Just as Donna had feared, I left my job and returned full-time to the theatre.

The people of Boston and Cambridge take great pride in their city being one of the cultural centres of America. Fringe theatre is taken seriously by the local critics. After my performance in *Fanshen* I was invited to join the prestigious Cambridge Ensemble, a multi-racial company then in its fourth season. My work in the theatre began to change direction. No one knew or cared who I was, or where I came from. We were a small ensemble under the innovative direction of Joanne Green, a small intellectual woman in her forties. It was her ambition to direct Aeschylus' trilogy, *The Oresteia*. When Joanne and I first met she was looking for an actress to play Clytemnestra, who murders her husband Agamemnon for sacrificing their daughter to the gods in order to win the Trojan War. Orestes, their son, then murders her to avenge his father's death. I was stunned to be offered the role, and even more so when she explained: 'Strong actresses who do not revert to playing little girls when they encounter difficulties are hard to find.'

I was elated. The lessons I had learned from my recent years of trauma had been salutary. Indeed my voice gave me an indication of my progress: for the first time on stage I felt it connect with my acting, and I found resonance in it that had eluded me in the past. It appeared that having met in the performance of Wang Kwanmei, the woman and the artist in me were loath to part. Nor did this go unnoticed by others.

Joanne's adaptation of *The Oresteia* became part of the Ensemble's repertoire. Five actors, three white, one black and a Chinese, created a civilisation. The presentation was minimalist, reflecting the ideas of Grotowski's *Poor Theatre*, with a single prop – a roll of crimson velvet – no masks, nor make-up and only a suggestion of costume. *The Oresteia* was well received by the critics and I enjoyed the *Boston Globe*'s description of my performance as 'ice-wonderful'. In the same review, though, Kevin Kelly suggested that I sounded like a Bette Davis parody, because of my British accent. Carolyn Clay of the *Boston Phoenix* described my performance as 'a magnificent, positively mythic Clytemnestra'. And to act in a Western classic was its own reward.

For any role the depth and richness of an actor's interpretation depend not only upon his grasp of craft, but upon his ability to bring to a portrait fresh resources from his own experience. He might, for example, seek a private image to trigger off certain emotions required of him at moments in the play. Thereby he combines his craft with his private sensibility. Sometimes I would search for days to come up with a strong image. Often I returned to my own culture. Thus in recreating the role of Hester Prynne, an eighteenth-century American, I became conscious of tapping into my own cultural roots, and this realisation was to sow the first seeds of harmony within me.

Hester Prynne, the heroine of Hawthorne's classic, *The Scarlet Letter*, has an illegitimate daughter and by refusing to identify her lover is ostracised by Puritanical New England society. Outwardly, she was a million miles from me; inwardly, we shared a great deal. We were both survivors.

She wears two faces, the public aspect of meek humility; pride and vulnerability in private. Did I not once act a Janus, oscillating between gaiety in public and secret despair? 'If I be all tenderness, I will die.' This I understood. Still, I must define my own concept of humility in order to make Hester's feelings convincing on stage. It was the tiny solitary figure in most Chinese landscape paintings that came to mind. The nature painters put this man there to remind us of our insignificance in relation to Nature, suggesting to me therefore that humility is not submission but an acknowledgement that we are not the centre, but an intrinsic part of a universal order. However, much as I tried, I could find no sympathy with Hester's desire to shield her lover. In the first rehearsals I wanted to spit at poor Tim McDonagh who played him. Only when I thought of the unfailing love of my mother for my father did I resolve the problem, for I felt sure that she would have acted as Hester did. So I resolved the difficulties of the role.

Instead of a cast of thousands, as in the book, Joanne's production was a chamber play for two, taking the minimalist theory even further than her *Oresteia*. *The Scarlet Letter* was a great artistic success in its modest surroundings, and Arthur Friedman in Boston's leading journal, *The Real Paper*, listed it as one of the best productions of the year, and mentioned me with others as having given the best performances in Boston.

More importantly, perhaps, a critic from out of town, Joel Clemons, begged the question: should a Chinese woman portray the first heroine in American literature? And answered it himself in the affirmative. His reaction was important to me because it confirmed my belief that a multi-racial company could work, given the right material and the right director to guide the actors, in finding the essence of their characters instead of grasping at superficialities.

So on this modest scale, being allowed to stretch in challenging

Western roles, and succeeding, restored much of the trust I badly needed in my artistic ability.

My three years with the Cambridge was a rewarding and happy time. Like Hester Prynne I was leading an ascetic existence. Work was the centre of my life, rehearsals by day and performances at night. We had to tour schools to make ends meet, even giving a performance for lifers in Norfolk County Prison. The actors got $90 in a good week; it seemed a fortune to an actor working in fringe. In the summer recess I supplemented my income by teaching drama. The mysteries and theories of acting fascinated me; I began to attend lectures on Shakespeare and other dramatic literature at Harvard and found that the discipline of going back to school appealed to me enormously. I might have continued happily as a poor actress working in the poor theatre, had I not awoken to another life-long aspiration: I wanted to go to university.

⊘

'Must an actor feel every time he is on stage?'

'Yes.'

'Can he never succeed on technique alone?' There was no reply.

'Do you know that in the West, as well as in China, there are those who believe that acting is just a craft?' There was a pause.

'It is more than a craft,' he said.

My father was as laconic as ever, but this was the longest conversation I ever had with him. He had come to me in a dream when I began to take what I was doing in the theatre seriously. I had been trying to reach him since childhood, but he had been so elusive that I had constructed a romantic image of him. He had become an abstract ideal rather than a real person. I saw him as a 'practical idealist', a man who combined success with a refusal to compromise his ideals. All my life I had been attracted to men whom I wanted to believe resembled him. I had been merely chasing rainbows.

One day, as I was walking up the steps to my evening class at Harvard University, I had a revelation. It was so simple that I was surprised that I had never considered it before. I need never seek my father's substitute in other men. He could be within myself, I could emulate the ideal myself if I tried. This was the moment of my true independence.

⊘

LA and Boston were chalk and cheese. Around Rodeo Drive in Hollywood the fleeting snippets of conversation I might overhear were invariably about wheeling and dealing. But in Boston, a city justly proud of its world-famous educational institutions – Harvard, MIT, Radcliffe, Tufts – the conversations on the subway or in cafés around Harvard Square dealt with teaching or taking courses, with writing a thesis or completing a dissertation, challenges I envied, really music to my ears. My mother's old ambition for me to study in higher education revived.

In January 1978 I wrote to my friend Jules Feiffer, the New York cartoonist and playwright, to lay out my reasons for applying to university and to ask for a reference. 'I want to go to university because it's about time!' I wrote. 'I have always wanted to know things and have read much in the waiting hours between performances. I enjoyed these hours, but I felt that there were so many links missing. Like a half-blind person I got to the other side of the pavement, but I missed a lot in between. A new kind of discipline is needed. This is my personal reason.

'I want and need to teach acting, the only thing I know something about. (I still want to act from time to time, but I am beyond the career game). In order to be in a better position to do so, I need papers: degrees. This is my practical reason.

'I am at the age when I can look back on my past and say it was fine and look forward to the future and ask how shall I live the next and last quarter of this century? The answer is to be active in the areas that will satisfy me. The rest is a bonus. That is the real reason.'

And I added a credo, a scholastic ambition that sounded grandiose, but which anchored my desires and expressed my hopes: 'I am probably one of the few Chinese with a Chinese theatre background who has acquired an extensive experience of Western theatre. Now I must get into the academic world to find new tools, so that I may one day fashion something between the two dramatic forms. What that may be I don't yet know.'

I only knew that my exploration need be bounded only by my own limitations, not by the area of discovery. And then I knew that I would never be bored again.

My timing was perfect because America had a shopping list to revitalise the intake of her universities: she wanted more mature students, women and minorities to return to higher education. I happened to fit each category. Jules wrote to the head of Drama at Tufts, Professor Karl Burnim, and said: 'She has never been satisfied with the easy or commercial and has moved further and further into the discipline, both emotional and physical, that is requisite for serious performance . . . It seems to me that it would be foolish not to take full advantage of the gift she presents herself.' Professor Burnim, whose department ran one of the few PhD drama courses in the country, later told me that it was a challenge he could not refuse. In return for a salary and a scholarship, I was to share my practical experience with the students. It was a very fair exchange. Both Lord Olivier and Irene Worth have collected honorary doctorates from Tufts. I only wish I could have been as lucky with my MA degree!

Anyone who has volunteered to be educated at a mature age must know the absolute joy and elation I felt. For me it was like awakening to a second spring – as prophesied in the best selling record of the same title I made in my salad days. On the one hand, studying alongside bright youngsters revealed my comparative lack of mental agility and intellectual prowess. On the other hand, I brought to my studies a depth of experience that enabled me to comprehend the subject at an emotional level. So, too, I found that teaching acting, the business of helping others to develop a sense of their own identity through self-expression, meant a giving and sharing in my relationship that had unexpected rewards for my personal growth. Life seemed to be working out, and I saw my confidence rebuilt step by step from those days of blank depression when I had no awareness of my real needs.

To cap it all, my son re-entered my life when he finished his degree in Canada and came to set up house with me in Cambridge. Our relationship, of course, could hardly be an easy one for we had both constructed images of each other to compensate for the strangeness of separation. I hoped guiltily for his friendship, while he angrily insisted that I behave like a mother to him. I had forfeited that role, and I found it hard to play it now. It was the one area of my life in which I felt confused and helpless; but time was on our side.

My newfound strength was moral and intellectual; I confused it with physical power. I had been working all day and most of the evenings, teaching as well as studying; some of the courses involved a great deal of hard manual labour. I was supposed to take a certain number of undergraduate courses as well as the MA degree course, such as Technical Theatre to give us a general knowledge of how a stage actually worked – lighting, set design, costume and their operation. Working six hours a week in set and costume workshops, most of our time was spent building and carrying huge platforms for a forthcoming production. It was the right experience, and one that would give me the confidence to become a director. But I began to feel unwell. I ignored the strain and went at it with a will – goaded on, no doubt, by pride and vanity before these strapping male American freshmen. The result was appalling: I began to haemorrhage. The doctors suspected cancer.

I was advised to have an exploratory hysterectomy in order to establish whether there was any malignancy. My initial reaction under-scored my precarious state. I wanted to scream: Leave me alone! My mind refused to register what was happening. I evaded my fears and my anger by turning to drink again. Only hours and hours of calls from Susan persuaded me to calm myself and think clearly.

By the time I entered my second term, getting up in the mornings to go to school had become very difficult. I had become a workaholic, but although my spirit was willing my legs felt like lead. The idea of missing classes never entered my head. It was Susan who persuaded me to take this choice. I resisted at first. What about my students? I asked. I didn't want to let them down.

I was damned if this inconvenience was going to stop me enjoying my new life. I made intelligent plans. I booked my operation for the end of term, until when I gave bi-weekly classes at Tufts, which was about as much as I could manage. My fellow graduate, Daina Robins, taped classes for me to study in bed at home. Before going into hospital I took all the exams and completed all the term papers, for Professor Laurence Senelick warned that it would be impossible to catch up otherwise. I was referred to an excellent surgeon, a gentle southerner called Mr Hunt, whom I trusted implicitly. The operation was a success and I was told to my relief that I did not have cancer. With Bruce's support, and the facilities of the New England Baptist Hospital (in a room once occupied by Rosemary Kennedy) I felt no discomfort during my week's stay. Back home, with the whole of the Long Vacation ahead of me, I found that a committee had been organised (very American) taking turns to cook and keep house for me. It was run by three friends all involved with the fringe theatre, woman director Bobbi Ausubel, actress Joanna Hefferen, and young Tia Kimberk who looked after me like a devoted daughter, and of course my son, Bruce.

By August my recovery seemed complete and I indulged a craving that had mounted all summer: to visit England again. I stayed with my wonderful and loyal friend Carlo Colombotti. I found a more troubled and less gentle land, but reviving old friendships had a tonic effect on my spirits, and I revelled in all the familiar landmarks. This trip was the start of a long journey of return, in which I would retrieve much that I had lost in the past.

Free from my fear of the operation and rejuvenated by my holiday in London, I returned to finish my degree with peace of mind. Of course I knew that I was approaching things in reverse, and that after so many years as a practitioner I was now learning the theories, studying the forms and ideas that had shaped all the plays in which I had ever performed.

Over two years I achieved an over-view of Western theatre, as exciting to me as discovering the source of the Nile, as something that had always been there to nourish the world I knew, but which had been hidden from me until now. As I came to understand theories of drama, and to connect them with practical and technical skills, I developed the confidence to take another step in my artistic development. Although lazy directors had frustrated me in the past, the idea of doing their job myself had strangely never entered my head. Gradually I felt that I was ready to take up the responsibility of stage direction. The facilities existed in Tufts' Arena Theatre, and the pool of talent was found amongst the students at large.

With my directorial debut I discovered that I had the ability to generate a kind of professional energy and excitement in university theatre. Perhaps by instinct and certainly by habit, I treated my cast and crew like professionals and they rose superbly to the challenge. After a production of Pinter's *The Lover*, which met with approval, I directed Ugo Betti's *Crime On Goat Island* as Tufts' contribution to the annual American College Theatre Festival. It was a great honour for me.

Looking back, I feel that my university experience allowed me to exchange part of my body for nourishment of the mind, so that the pain of ageing was redeemed. For pain it must be. Perhaps elsewhere, in other times, when old age was venerated, growing old was something to look forward to. A Chinese woman would traditionally be treated as the least significant member of a household, a daughter and a daughter-in-law under the rule of men and the matriarch, until she herself became the matriarch and enjoyed an identity and authority by virtue of her age. That might have been something to look forward to, but those days are over, and I am glad of it. Domestic power is not something I particularly relish; and it was too late for me, anyway. I had not earned it.

At Tufts I had found a discipline that liberated me. Spartan, structured and secure from worldly temptations, I no longer needed to make myself feel alive by tearing about the globe, or throwing myself into jaded romantic escapades. These were the futile pursuits of another person. I was following the paths of my heart, and in my heart I knew that the cloisters of the university were but a temporary sanctuary, a place in time to ponder and revive. With my degree completed, I must return to the world, a world less serene, more complex and often unpredictably cruel. My real world. Once there, would I be able to hold on to the values I had forged in peace, and retain the inner strength I had gained? I would be tested, and I was not a little afraid.

I had yet to teach myself to believe in destiny.

22

A Tale More Strange Than Real

ℓ

My breakdown coincided with the outrages that were being committed upon the Chinese people in their name by the notorious Gang of Four, led by Jiang Qing. My recovery coincided with the restoration of sanity. While Chairman Mao lived, his moral authority had protected Jiang from retribution at the hands of those she had tried to destroy. In 1976, on 5th April, the month of mourning, hundreds upon thousands of Chinese had assembled in the great square, Tiananmen, before the gates of the Forbidden City in Beijing, to commemorate the death of Zhou Enlai, the statesman who alone had managed to curb some of the excesses of the Cultural Revolution, and some of the insanities of Jiang Qing's rule. The demonstrations in Beijing were suppressed, but barely five months later, Mao Zedong died.

His named successor, Hua Guofeng, was a faceless bureaucrat, but he was not entirely toothless. In October, Jiang Qing and her ruling group were arrested. Her trial allowed a reappraisal of the past, an exorcising of the horrors; China's sealed windows on the world were cautiously pushed ajar, and under a new leader, Deng Xiaoping, installed in 1978, the Chinese were beginning to breathe in the fresh winds of change.

Deng had suffered himself at the hands of fanatics in the Cultural Revolution and after, like so many with him who emerged now from disgrace, from their menial positions in villages, from house arrest or the prisons. They began to restore the official reputation of many who had died in disgrace. My father was among them. On 16th August 1978, Zhou Xinfang was given a state funeral in Shanghai when his ashes were placed in the Revolutionary Cemetery, attended by eight hundred people. Ba Jin, China's most distinguished novelist, delivered the oration. William and Jane sent me a photograph of the countless wreaths that had come from all over China, including one from the leader, Deng Xiaoping.

Two years later I learned with wild excitement that my brother and his family had been given permission to leave China. Leaving their two daughters, now grown up, in Hong Kong, William and Jane travelled to America. For the first time in thirty years, the siblings would be reunited.

After so many years I wondered what it would be like to meet my childhood companion. In my mind's eye I saw a film sequence in which we ran towards each other with outflung arms through a field of corn while, tugging at our hearts, a thousand violins began to play. In reality our emotions were contained lest they should burst to drown us. Tears had been shed long ago. We were now shy, perhaps giggled a bit, reaching to touch each other. The look of wonder was always in our eyes. William looked as distinguished as ever, but aged before his time. Jane, whom I had never met, looked as pretty as her photographs, but her appearance and manners were strained. They had suffered so much.

The truth of the family's long ordeal, and of our parents' tragic end could be revealed at last. They spoke for a long time, while we, the exiles, heard a tale more strange than real. The awful incidents that had occurred, the barbarous acts committed upon them were often unintelligible to us and remained illogical to them. While they relived their nightmares, we were revisited by our feelings of guilt and helplessness. Sitting close together, the vacant air created by their silences was filled with our troubled thoughts. Each of us was stranded on a separate island of grief.

There was just so much that William and Jane wanted to recall: this was their first opportunity to speak openly to people who loved them, and whom they could trust. There was only so much that we could take in. I remember only a few dates, some facts, in no particular order; the rest of what was said is merely a tangled web of disturbing impressions. To unravel them would surely bring on a kind of madness. The time has not yet come.

Father had been incarcerated for a year, followed by house arrest for the remainder of his life; William had served as much as five years in prison, followed by hard labour. Why our brother's sentence was such a long one is anybody's guess. He was certainly guilty of some of the crimes of which he was accused: he was fond of nice clothes, of dancing to Western music, and he even played cards from time to time. But he paid the heavy price for being his father's son, and the natural successor to his father's innovative work in theatre, which was part of the tradition that had to be destroyed.

Prison, paradoxically, was the safest place for them to be, despite the privations. Within its walls they were shielded from mob rule. The violent assault on our family began on 23rd August 1966, two days after we in the West had learned of Father's rumoured death in the newspapers. Previously for several months under Jiang's direction, Father had been the victim of countless 'struggling sessions' at the hands of the militants within his own theatre community. But once the Red Guard entered his own home where Mother and William's family lived, the household was open to attack by any mob roaming the streets, who cared to make them their sport.

This was scoundrel time. Small men became kings. The basest human urges were given official sanction. The first vile act committed by the Red Guard was to beat our dog to death, while the whole family was forced to stand and helplessly watch the animal's suffering. The tone was set, and what my family had to suffer at the hands of these omnipotent intruders can only be imagined.

I shudder as I write. Horrendous scenes go through my head. Father, an aged man, pulled from his home by brutal youths and paraded through the streets with a dunce's cap and a placard around his head, dubbed a 'counter-revolutionary' by people too young to understand, brutal enough to enjoy the excuse. While William and my father were taken away at any hour of the day or night to be worked over in struggling sessions, for the women at home all sorts of torments, varied and imaginative, were devised. They were made to stand bent forward with their arms outstretched behind them for hours on end. They called this 'airplaning'. Pins were stuck into them for sport. Being slapped around became part of their lives. Compared to these petty and cruel tortures it was a relief when they were ordered to sweep the streets in the neighbourhood while onlookers gawped and some jeered.

Not all, it has to be said. Many in the crowds cried in their hearts. Some of the Red Guards were not in the least happy or proud of what they did. It was imperative that they participated for their own safety. Some even tried to help whenever possible. Mother, in her weak state, was once ordered to demolish the dog kennel with a hatchet. While cursing and abusing her in a show of contempt, one Red Guard, the daughter of a friend, took the hatchet and demolished it for her. Another Red Guard, a complete stranger, took advantage of the confusion during an assault to throw them a bundle of warm clothes.

A revolution had been fought and won for the Chinese people to march into the modern age, and yet such primitive persecution was still practised as in the early feudal era. What was it but tradition that made William the object of persecution, only because he was his father's son? Just as in ancient times the emperor might order the massacre of an entire clan because one member of it had displeased him: so had China advanced beyond the feudal age?

Our house, like others in Shanghai, was ransacked, the crockery smashed, Father's wonderful collection of books burned. His magnificent stage costume, and Mother's beautifully designed furniture were carted away to be sold cheaply. The family was confined to two back rooms. My parents lived in Father's old study, with newspapers on the windows as substitute for the broken glass and with only a few sticks of furniture. William, Jane and their two teenage children lived in the room below, formerly occupied by Ah Zhu, the cook, who was obliged to leave them.

In 1969, a few days after William began his five-year sentence, Father was released from prison. As he and Jane entered the dimly lit room that had once been his study, his weak eyes sought for my mother. She was not there. He said nothing: what was there to say? Jane knew that from this moment he no longer wished to live. For his remaining years he did not once mention Mother; he lived only to see his son emerge from prison. A month later, at the age of eighty, he died.

Mother had died on 27th March 1968, the second year of their torment and the same year that Michael began to be successful. I was surprised how early on she had died, until I realised with bitterness the irony that during the fanatic hysteria, the fever of anarchy, the excesses of violence, Father, the target of the purge, was in fact in a safer position than his wife. He was a public figure, whose disgrace was choreographed by organisations under Jiang Qing's direct command. No one would therefore dare destroy him unofficially. Mother had no such protection. She could be used, killed, to get at her husband; of no interest to the state, she was a prey in the chaos to any group of hooligans calling themselves Red Guards.

Mother was taken away four times to be 'interrogated'. To this day, no one knows who her inquisitors were, but she was known to them. They knew that she had been her husband's helper, that she had sent her children to the West, that she had herself gone there to visit them. She must therefore be a spy. In this season of intimidation, betrayal and perjury, they wanted names, including the name of the official who signed her document for travel to the West. She never gave them satisfaction, and the person concerned lives today to tell of it. I learned from Jane that Mother thought of my father to the end. Each time they came for her she had overcome her dread and gone with them willingly, in the vain hope that her good behaviour would bring him less maltreatment in struggling sessions. The Red Guards used her like a football. Her whole body was puffed and swollen from repeated beatings, and her skin was suffused with purple bruises from head to foot. On 24th March they took Father away to prison. Mother was bedridden and they were not given time to say their goodbyes to each other. I think this was when she knew that she would never see her husband again. Three days later she died. She who had always believed that where there's a will, there's a way, could at last see none. She was just sixty-three.

℘

Seeing our brother William again was one of the first, tentative steps in the process of facing and coming to terms with our loss. The next step, organised some time later by Michael, was a glorious tribute to Father's memory. For ten days in August 1981, at the Lincoln Center in New York, my father's plays were performed by actors from China, led by his son and artistic successor, William. This season of Peking Opera, Qi style, was produced by Michael and the Chinese Theatre Association, and Chinese people came from the four corners of the world to watch.

China had re-entered my life. I could only dimly comprehend the cataclysm, the years of violent change that had reshaped the country of my birth. Or had it? Was it all a temporary insanity, a reaction like my own to upheaval, in which China had advanced too fast for its own good, and run on recklessly, without understanding, to a breakdown? I had rebuilt my life; could China rebuild herself? I had to find out. I wondered, too, whether there was a role for me in the process.

It was Susan, again, who had pointed me in the right direction. At the beginning of 1980, when I had completed my M A degree, she had called from Washington D C and suggested that I go to New York in March to see Cao Yu, the leading playwright and president of the Chinese Theatre Association. With the actor and director Ying Ruocheng, he was making a cultural tour, the first exchange programme between Chinese and American theatre groups, sponsored by Columbia University. I was slow to respond to Susan's suggestion, for I was still trying to put off the inevitable moment when I should confront the world again. But in my heart I knew I had to go. Susan insisted further: had I forgotten the reason I so convincingly gave to Jules Feiffer for going to university in the first place?

In New York the Altschul Auditorium at the School of International Affairs of Columbia University was packed when I arrived, mostly with young Chinese. Arthur Miller welcomed Cao Yu on stage. Cao had acted as host to Arthur and his wife, the photographer Inge Morath, when they visited China in 1978. Cao Yu delivered his speech in Chinese although he spoke perfect English (he had studied play-writing under George Pierce Baker in America); Ying Ruocheng, with his complete command of the language, acted as his interpreter. For us, the audience, it was a moving sight: the tall, lean American and the small energetic Chinese standing side by side, each a legend in their own country. What they said mattered less than the event, the meeting itself.

When the lecture was over I found it impossible to push my way through the enthusiastic crowd to reach Cao Yu. He was almost mobbed, and I saw my visit to New York turning into a wasted effort. Lucky, then, that I had brought along Elzbieta Chezevska, and lucky that the Polish actress had known the Millers when she was married to the writer David Halberstam. Lucky, too, that Inge Morath was so clued up about the Chinese and even spoke the language. For in the confusion, Elzbieta thought on her feet: she dragged me to Inge Morath and introduced us. I spoke the name of my father and for the first time in the West it found a real echo. It was open sesame time. I sailed through the throng, clinging to the back of Inge's waistband.

I had never previously met Cao Yu, so it was something of a surprise when he greeted me like a long-lost friend. Not only because of my father, as it turned out, but because he knew of me. He told me later that he used to have my records, but that the Red Guards had smashed them. I also learned that he had tried to contact me through RADA without success a year before, when he had made a cultural tour of England.

My meeting Cao Yu was crucial. The timing could not have been better. In 1980, not only China's windows but also her doors were beginning to open. No longer was she aloof and indifferent to the outside world. She needed 'foreign experts' – needed them urgently to repair the ravages of the past decade and more, when learning and ideas had been jettisoned and the passage of knowledge from one generation to another had been blocked. A few months later, I received a letter from the Ministry of Culture, inviting me to work in China. So I became the first 'foreigner' to teach drama since the Moscow Arts Theatre withdrew during the Sino-Soviet rift.

Between 30th July 1974, when I had arrived in Los Angeles, and 5th September 1981 when I arrived in Beijing, give or take a month, it was exactly seven years.

Another phase of my life had begun.

Part 3

East

First day with my students at the Central Academy
of Drama, Beijing, September 1981.

Caliban stood on the rock like a man.

Big Big Sister, 1981.

23

A Reckoning

Once I had thought that I should never see China again, yet here I was returning after an absence of three decades. So much had happened to us both.

When I thought back to my last moments with my father, facing him awkwardly in his study, taking a leave that I could not know would be forever, I wondered whether I had ever betrayed his last wish. No, I had not forgotten to be Chinese. How could I? To be Chinese is like a religion, as I've come to realise: China holds you from birth. In spite of my efforts to assimilate the West, my heritage ruled out apostasy.

And yet I had adapted almost entirely to Western ways. What was more, I had found in the West a chance to follow an fiercely independent way of life, even by Western standards. Could I now hope to readjust to a rigid social order where conformity was the rule? Would I feel a stranger in the country of my birth?

And then I wondered apprehensively whether I could cope emotionally with facing my loss. It reflected a conflict within me, articulated as a question by Westerners who knew my private history: should I return to the country that did my family such harm? The answer had to be that my personal misfortune was but a minuscule part of a grand human tragedy. And that China had changed by opening her doors, and that I, like so many of my compatriots, had a role to play, a duty to keep the door ajar. Most importantly of all, I must return to retrieve the fragments of my self left scattered untidily through my past, like the clothes I had once discarded for servants to pick up; now I must collect them up myself.

My trip would be a long journey back in time, but my flight from New

York to Beijing took just twenty-six hours. The last transit stop was Shanghai, my first touch-down on Chinese soil, a significant moment I chose to ignore. I was glad to be heading straight for the capital where for five months I would be immersed in the work I had come to do. I felt that my sojourn there would serve as some sort of emotional quarantine, a much needed period of grace. God alone knew what painful memories awaited me in Shanghai.

I arrived in Beijing on 5th September, 1981. My plane was very late. As I walked into the immigration area I spotted a man holding a cardboard sign with my full name in Chinese characters. From that moment I ceased to be known in China by my stage name, Tsai Chin. My illustrious surname, Zhou, was restored to me. It was China's first gift to me.

My five future colleagues from the Acting Faculty, headed by Dean Ruan Ruoshan, had waited patiently for six hours at the airport to welcome me back to China, passing the time by speculating what I would look like. Later, they told me that they had recognised me instantly: I had my father's eyes and nose, after all. I was indeed my father's daughter.

I greeted them with difficulty in Mandarin, the standard Chinese – quite different from Shanghai dialect – spoken all over China since Liberation. In truth, I had half-forgotten my own dialect. I saw Dean Ruan, a small, plump woman with the sweetest expression, make a quick mental note. Sure enough, soon after I began teaching, she recruited Teacher Wu Guorui from the Foreign Language Institute, who had learned his impeccable English before Liberation, as my translator. A month or so later, talking away rapidly to my class, I was suddenly aware that Teacher Wu had been quiet for a very long time. I turned to him almost accusingly to find a bemused expression on his face. It was then that I realised with enormous joy that I had already begun to speak coherent, if not quite perfect, Mandarin. It was the second gift.

On the first evening, as I installed myself at the Friendship Hotel, I was told by my colleagues that plans had been made for me to rest for a week, in order to take in the glorious sights of Beijing before beginning work. The Chinese are proud of their hospitality and, as I was Zhou Xinfang's daughter, they wanted my homecoming to be special. But the impatient Westerner in me blurted out: 'When can I see my students? I want to start classes right away!' So it was agreed that I would begin work on the following Monday.

The Friendship Hotel, originally built to house Russian advisors during the fifties before the Sino-Russian rift, was a kind of colony situated on the outskirts of Beijing. From the start of China's new Open Door policy in the late seventies, this walled warren of hotel rooms and apartment blocks, served by its own shops and restaurants, accommodated a new group of 'experts', mainly from the West.

As a result the hundreds of foreign nationals served their contracted periods in the capital in virtual isolation from the locals. Whatever limited contacts they had with Chinese ended with their working day. Some of the Western guests in particular may have found their living standards in China higher than they might enjoy at home, but many would have gladly lived closer to the Chinese even if it meant sacrificing some comforts. In the early days of the Open Door policy, such ideas were positively discouraged by the authorities.

I was fortunate to have it both ways. I could associate freely with my own people while enjoying the comforts of Western amenities. An hour by car from my place of work, the Friendship Hotel served well as a base. The transport problem was solved for me, too. Unlike the other 'experts' I did not have to ride in buses or share a taxi into the city centre; nor did I have to ride a bicycle like most of the Chinese. For me, the Institute provided a car and driver, Xiao Wang, a bright Beijing-born youth of nineteen, who helped me improve my Mandarin. I admit I accepted this privilege gratefully. It was just as well. It saved me from collapsing with exhaustion from the gruelling schedule I set myself.

On my first day at the Academy I gave a talk based on a list of questions submitted to me in advance by my large audience of students and professionals. 'Based' – because the list was so long I would have had to be an encyclopaedia to answer every question, such was their thirst for knowledge of the outside world. So I grouped my material under five headings and focused on England and America, the two countries most familiar to me: (1) New methods of training; (2) Audience patronage and subsidies for experimental and commercial theatre; (3) Landmarks of contemporary theatre within the last quarter of a century; (4) Current concepts of theatrical production; and lastly (5) the visionaries and innovators behind the creative impulse. I could not tell how much of all this my audience was able to take in. Brook, Artaud, Grotowski, Beckett, even Pinter, to name a few, were new names to them in these early days of cultural exchange.

The talk lasted a good three hours and was followed by questions. Professor Sun Jiaxiu, head of Dramatic Literature, was a forthright woman in her sixties who had studied in America and was now China's leading Shakespearean scholar. I was taken aback when she read out my entire résumé, which took well over half an hour. I couldn't help smiling when I heard some of the credits rendered in Chinese. The silly title of Ned Sherrin's film *Rentadick* cropped up ludicrously. But the audience got a chance to laugh too. The fact that a leopard had been named after me was greeted with much hilarity, particularly from the men who could not conceive that the ferocious image of a wild cat was something for a woman to boast about.

At 8.30 on Tuesday morning I held my first class in China. After climbing three flights up a concrete staircase in the main building accompanied by Dean Ruan, I walked into a sunlit auditorium with a great sense of occasion. Thirty-seven young Chinese sprang rigidly to attention and greeted me in unison: 'Teacher Zhou, good morning!' I felt very important, like a general inspecting his troops.

To their utter surprise I began by taking off my shoes and sitting on the carpet (something I had specifically asked for), beckoning my students to join me with their shoes off, too. This sort of informality was quite new to my students, and I maintained it throughout our time together. It was not always easy: there were moments in the months ahead when I rather regretted sweeping away all the rituals of respect Chinese students traditionally owe their teacher.

In one part of the room were gathered a large group of observers, drama teachers and stage directors from all over China. It was the first time I had had to conduct a class in public, and I was therefore obliged to tell my students, with the greatest respect to my auditors, that we would have to pretend that one half of the room was invisible.

I ended the first class with a little speech for my students. Touched by their youthfulness, and inspired by the beauty of my own race, I was in an effusive mood. I talked to them about the changing wonders of the four seasons, a recurring theme in Chinese poetry. I told them that as I was in the autumn of my years it was my duty to harvest spring by coming to China to teach them. This sentimental speech did not quite have the intended effect. As Teacher Wu was not yet on the scene, a middle-aged woman from the academy, whose English was rather limited, volunteered to help. She soon got a little lost, and began to content herself with paraphrasing what she understood of the gist. 'Teacher Zhou,' she explained, 'is now lamenting her middle age!'

There was probably some truth in that, but I was reminded that in China, when a woman has reached forty, she forfeits much that is gay and childlike for respect for her age.

It was important for me to understand my students, and their position. For an entire decade they could only have watched eight plays. Eight productions watched for ten years by a quarter of humanity would have made Louis Mayer green with envy. The artistic consequences, however, were devastating. Rescuscitating the theatre would be a slow and arduous business.

The *Yang Pan Shi*, Model Plays, as Jiang Qing called them, were tailored to fit her narrow ideology with simplistic themes and cardboard characters. Without an understanding of the transformative power of true art, Jiang felt that a cardboard character would be more 'universal', more applicable to each member of the audience, and therefore carry her narrow ideology further. Yet one thinks immediately of the truly 'universal' characters like Hamlet or Lear whose complexity and individualism merely deepen their power. In each performance of *Yang Pan Xi*, all across the country, every minute detail of her eight productions had to be meticulously duplicated down to the size and position of the patch on a proletarian jacket. This was Jiang Qing's prescription for artistic perfection. The artists privileged to work in these plays were also hand-picked by her, while the rest of their colleagues were forbidden to practise their profession. (Her preference for certain actors, and athletes too, produced a scurrilous ditty: Heaven and Earth I fear not at all – Only Jiang Qing's midnight telephone call!)

My students, twenty-eight men and nine women between the ages of twenty and twenty eight, were the first group admitted to the Academy when the universities re-opened in 1979, thirteen years after the Cultural Revolution. They had been selected from four thousand applicants from all over the country, and they were now in their final year. After graduation each would be assured of a permanent position in one of the numerous theatre companies in the provinces. There were no unemployed actors in China, and my students were most sceptical when I told them that in the West hundreds of actors chase after one small non-speaking role. But this security within a generally precarious profession was not as ideal as it might appear, because jobs were assigned by the theatrical authorities without the actors themselves having much say in the matter. The lack of control over their future, I later realised, was the cause of much unhappiness and frustration among young people.

The curriculum at the Central Academy is similar to that of a good but conservative school in the West: elocution involves voice, diction and singing; ballet, fencing and Chinese folk dancing come under the heading of deportment. Improvisation and scene work take their model from Stanislavski, as they were taught in the fifties by visiting directors of the Moscow Arts Theatre. This system relied on a methodical approach to acting rather than on intuition, and unfortunately the ten year hiatus had exhausted what creative confidence the teachers possessed. The Stanislavski system was adhered to with a vengeance. The emphasis was cerebral rather than experiential, so the students were accustomed to spending more time discussing the play and writing about their characters than acting.

I asked the students to act out scenes for me. They took them all from Cao Yu's famous plays, written before Liberation and portraying a world that no longer existed. This exercise did more than reveal the extent of their talents, which corresponded to that of any similar group of students of that number: half were naturally gifted and a few exceptionally so, while the rest were average and some would challenge any teacher. It gave me my first real insight into how the Cultural Revolution had affected these young people.

At first I was puzzled by the way so many male students were attracted to a downtrodden role which they played with unabashed melodrama. Later it dawned on me that this sort of character was one of two common stereotypes, the heroic and the pathetic, that were presented without shading in Jiang Qing's model plays. A girl played a prostitute and acted awkwardly, because until recently she had not been allowed to read about such women, let alone encounter one.

Heavy stress on theory had made it hard for the students to be spontaneous. It appeared that the obsessive years of attending political meetings and writing out self-criticisms had encroached upon their artistic endeavours by cheapening the value of personal experience. Furthermore, Chinese traditions of restraint in public held them back from using their imaginations boldly. I came to realise that the formal classical tradition in Chinese theatre had allowed actors to hide behind stylised conventions – a habit my father had tried to break – and this tendency has been carried over into naturalistic acting: they often have problems revealing their inner selves. And yet, when I watched improvisational work done by students from their own experience, I was quite moved. The scenes were real, humorous, something of their own. The students expressed what they saw, and understood.

So in the first two months with them I concentrated on games and voice exercises accompanied by movement, specifically designed to relax the body and to inspire trust in one's own intuitions that would allow it to respond naturally to sound and feeling. The idea of not separating voice and movement was new to them.

Every morning they performed a set of yoga-based exercises. Ironically, Tai Chi, the ancient callisthenics that coordinates breathing and movement, and which Western directors like Peter Brook had adopted so enthusiastically, was regarded by young Chinese as old-fashioned, exercises for old people in parks. There were various problems with voice training, as I should know. In general, voices were admired for their purity of tone rather than for round, resonant qualities. Traditionally a deep, rich voice was not considered feminine, and was therefore undesirable. Therefore I turned texts upside down and back to front in an effort to dispel any self-consciousness and give the students a chance to explore other possibilities while delivering the same lines. Within two months the pitch of their voices, the girls especially, was lowered. Everyone got very excited. It seemed like a small miracle.

My fear of feeling alienated from my own race was soon allayed. I did not feel a stranger amongst them. This was a definite advantage for me over Western teachers in the same situation, who always complained of difficulty in reading Chinese facial expressions. As my Mandarin improved, communication with my students became much freer. If my students laughed at my Shanghai accent, I laughed with them. I regaled them with my stock of theatrical jokes, hoping to establish a bond between my students and actors on the other side of the world. Working with them was a joy.

In the big cities at least, foreigners were no longer a curiosity. I was. I was stared at for my pallid face, paler without make-up, my walk, more strident than the local women's, my up-to-date Western clothes. Most of all I was stared at for something indefinable in the overall impression, what they called 'a certain Western flavour', that made me stand out. The Chinese did not know where to place me. Once in a department store a couple scrutinised me with some concentration before reaching a verdict. 'It is Chinese,' the wife said to her husband, then added, 'I think.'

At first I was downright upset. I would so much have liked to merge into the mass for a change. But I came to the conclusion that I could not have it both ways. Bi-cultural, accepted in both the East and the West, I am never a stranger but always an outsider.

China had changed, and yet not changed. At a glance, China was transformed. Women were no longer second-class citizens. Workers were no longer intimidated, and walked the streets with their heads high. I saw farmers working their fields to the sound of popular music on the radio. I saw no beggars. Common diseases had been eradicated by the national health service and hygiene education. I considered these triumphs for socialism.

To place some sort of control on the spiralling population, official policy stipulates that a couple can only have a single child. Though there are stories of female infanticide in the countryside, responsible citizens, encouraged by the benefits that accrue, willingly co-operate with the authorities. On the whole, daughters have become as precious as sons. In parks I watched with delight – and not without a touch of envy – fathers playing alone with their only daughters, treating them like precious porcelain. However, single children tend to be the focus of attention in their families, with six grown-ups – two parents and two sets of grandparents – doting on a single child. This has led to a new phenomenon of what are called 'filial parents and grandparents'! And these children only learn to share with other children when they go to kindergarten.

But life was still far from easy. Coming from a consumer society it shocked me to see people living without material luxuries that we take for granted. There was a complete lack of colour in their homes, and an almost total loss of aesthetic sensitivity. A poster of Chairman Mao had been the only safe decoration for a room throughout the Cultural Revolution. I watched my friends dig out dog-eared coloured postcards as if they were treasures. To have managed to hang on to them through all the confiscations was a small miracle to them.

Everywhere, shops teemed with people, ten times worse than Oxford Street in the Christmas rush. Demand exceeded supply. Daily food shopping was time-consuming and exhausting: labour-saving devices like refrigerators or washing machines were almost unheard-of luxuries (bearing in mind that things have changed radically since). The former were superfluous, perhaps, because the Chinese, like the French, still prefer to shop on a day to day basis when the food will always be fresh. They thought T V dinners were a joke I had made up, and asked me to describe them many times.

In large cities, two bicycles and one black and white television set per household were the norm. But the housing situation was quite desperate, and high-rises were not going up fast enough. Most people in

Beijing live in *hutongs,* a collection of houses within a compound, connected by a maze of lanes and alleyways. These traditional one-storey *hutongs* with their lovely courtyards dotted with potted plants are truly beautiful to look into, but they have no mod cons and are inconvenient to live in. Many of them had belonged to well-to-do families, but now they are subdivided to accommodate many families who have to share communal cold water taps and lavatories. The earthquake that hit the area in 1976 only made things worse.

Some people do prefer the old houses despite the inconvenience, like the cultured professor I met who could converse easily in dozens of languages, including English. He was very proud of his home, which consisted of only one room (rather large by normal standards) which he and his wife had all to themselves. During the course of our conversation, I discovered that he had been a Mongolian prince and that his family once owned the entire house. 'And what was this room previously?' I asked. 'Oh,' he replied airily, without a trace of bitterness, 'this was the billiard room.'

Many, of course, considered themselves lucky to be allocated a modern apartment in an ugly utility building, where a couple with two adolescent children shared a two-room flat with a kitchen, toilet and basin (but no tub, shower or hot water) and central heating. The rent came to four dollars a month (it has at least doubled since). When I told people that the same space in New York would cost at least five hundred dollars, they were highly amused.

Usually husband and wife both work and divide the household chores between them. There are, I gather, plenty of nurseries for the very young, and older children begin school at seven. Everyone has to belong to a *danwei,* or work unit, without which you are practically a non-person, without wages or ration cards for certain goods like rice or cotton. This paternalistic organisation acts as overseer, protecting, rewarding and chastising as it sees fit. I was of course asked what work unit I belonged to in the West. 'You're looking at it,' I said. 'I am the work unit.'

Family ties are still the strongest force in Chinese society despite the disruptions of the Cultural Revolution. The one child only policy may change this eventually, for there will be no more uncles, aunts and cousins. These ties seem sometimes stifling for a Westernised person like myself, but they have *ren qing*. The first word means man, human, and the second means emotion or affection. Consideration for others radiates out through the family to other bonds beyond. It is a double-sided concept. On the one hand, it breeds nepotism and dynastic selfishness, but on the other it can inspire truly selfless love. As a result they have the patience to endure a hard life and to make the best of disastrous situations, because they feel a connection with their fellow men and the larger scheme of things. I had the strong impression that they do not suffer the kind of alienation that feeds nihilism in the West.

With the arrival of Deng Xiaoping the people have begun to hope for a better life. People have become more fashion-conscious. The permanent wave, forbidden during the Cultural Revolution, has made a big come-back and it is very popular with men, which I found rather a surprise. Now that 'Mao suits' have become optional, people have begun wearing Western clothes – not quite as snappy as the Raymonds and Henrys of my youth in Shanghai, but colourful nonetheless. In spring-time the young women bloom like flowers, particularly in Shanghai. They seldom wear cosmetics, however, though that will come, and it was refreshing to look into unadorned faces for a change.

Because Chinese faces tend not to get lined when they age, Wester-ners often have difficulty judging our age. Conversely I was amused to hear that Chinese have a similar problem with Western women who wear a lot of make-up, which shows at least that the make-up must be effective. And I really roared with laughter when my driver, Xiao Wang, told me that all Westerners looked alike to him!

Young people begin searching for a soulmate after leaving middle school. The relationship with their partner – *dui xiang*, opposite image – is meant to last a lifetime. The course of true love is smoothed if both sets of parents approve, and they marry when they are assigned jobs. Those who go to university wait longer. With the housing situation as it is, the couple are unlikely to start married life on their own, but will live with their in-laws until they have been allocated accommodation. That can take years.

I asked a woman friend how young people cope with sexual tensions before marriage. 'We Chinese are not over-sexed,' she replied defens-ively, as if she were not talking to one. 'People in the West are obsessed with sex.' I cannot argue on that point, but I suspect sexual repression in the young had something to do with the violence of the Red Guards. One of my students had this to say: 'I know people in the West are very free with sex, but they tend to get lost in it. Personally, I want and need a sense of form in my life.' Of course, there's always more than meets the eye. 'Go into the parks in summer and you'll see,' someone else suggested.

In 1981 everyone was talking about the Iron Rice Bowl, the metaphor for the guarantee of a job for life, with which the Chinese have a love and hate relationship. Although they are justly proud that since Liberation their vast population has been fed, clothed and sheltered without foreign aid, they can see the serious drawbacks of the policy. Over the years the contents of the Iron Rice Bowl have been spread further and thinner, and equal distribution of wages with no possibility of upward mobility has bred apathy. People have lost the incentive and habit for hard work.

Since 1981 certain reforms enacted unavoidably have created new problems. Now that the Iron Rice Bowl syndrome has undergone revision, unemployment has unfortunately appeared. But since private enterprises are allowed, young people are starting up small businesses of their own, like bicycle repair shops and small stalls and eating places. At the same time the government has begun to offer retirement benefits to encourage public employees to make way for the younger generations.

In some ways China has not changed. 'Feudalism' had become an entirely abstract concept to me over the years in the West: now it hit me right in the face. I asked questions, hardly expecting an answer. Why did the Cultural Revolution happen? How could four people control a quarter of humanity? Why were people like my father, who loved their country and loved humanity, destroyed? Why were there no constitutional safeguards to protect them? Did that mean that the Cultural Revolution could happen again?

No, China has not become the egalitarian society I had once naively supposed. I know now that utopia does not exist. Privileges taken for granted by citizens in more open societies can often only be obtained through a system of fairly arbitrary bureaucratic sanction or, worse still, through personal connections – the so-called 'backdoor' system.

But the most disappointing aspect for an overseas Chinese like myself was to see petty officials fawning over foreigners while treating their own kind like dirt. History seems to be repeating itself. To find the Chinese who had stayed to build a future for their country, and who had suffered in the process, relegated to second-class citizen status was most heartbreaking for me.

Chinese attitudes to the West veer between xenophobic loathing and blind admiration. Since China was forced to break her isolation last century, crisis has followed crisis and China has never really regained confidence in her sense of national identity. Ordinary people have never really been given a chance to know Westerners as they truly are, neither angels nor demons, but human beings like themselves.

The Open Door was a swing in the mood, from a perception of foreigners as pollution to one of boundless admiration. Foreigners got preferential treatment at all times – the locals felt humiliated but could only express this in private. Publicly they maintained an icy impassiveness. 'Your mother!' I heard one complaining to his friend in the street, 'I was sitting in the restaurant in the middle of my meal, when a waiter ordered me to vacate my seat for some foreigner!' Incidents like these occurred frequently, and overseas Chinese wearing local clothing ran the risk of getting the same treatment. I myself had a few run-ins with petty officials who mistook me for a local because I was wearing locally purchased clothes. At least we could safely protest on behalf of ourselves and our compatriots. It gave me some comfort to know that these incidents were occasionally reported in the newspapers.

24

Father's Comrades in Arts

'I can't imagine how anyone could survive so many years in solitary confinement without going mad,' I said.

'I did callisthenics,' he replied calmly, as though he had lived almost a decade like a hermit in a vale of tranquillity rather than within the four walls of a sordid cell. 'When it was possible to do so, that is. Exercises were forbidden.'

'But how did you feel during that time?' He sidestepped this probing into his emotions and answered matter-of-factly. 'I thought about the day I would be released, and of what I would do then,' he said undramatically, and continued in the same even tone: 'Now I'm doing it, aren't I?'

I was talking to Jiang Chunfang, the man who had translated Stanislavski into Chinese all those years ago, when he had been a Russian scholar, a Communist activist in charge of Shanghai's resistance, and a close associate of my father. Now he was the chief editor of the Great Encyclopaedia of China. I remembered him fleetingly from the old days, a figure mounting the stairs to my father's study at the top of our old house. Now he was sixty-nine years old. Soft-spoken and infinitely patient, he suffered from a form of diabetes obliging him to wear thick spectacles, and the first impression he gave me, of an old man, slow and cautious in his movements, belied a warm personality, a dry wit and a lively mind.

He was a busy man but he made a lot of time for me. Whenever he had a free evening I would go to his house with a tape recorder, and while his grandchildren played around his feet I would record what he had to say about Father, and even Mother. Many of the things I learned from him about them have been written in this book. Uncle Jiang, as I called him, had an extraordinary memory. When I remarked on his gift for total recall, he admitted that he had been born with it, and that this ability had kept him sane during his long imprisonment. He had contrived a mental game for himself. Each day he would pick a friend or acquaintance and meticulously reconstruct his relationship with them from the day, the hour that they first met. His clarity of mind never failed to astound me. Often he would enquire about unfamiliar aspects of life in the West. In my usual volatile fashion I would jump from one thought to another without much attempt at order. Uncle Jiang would listen attentively, sometimes with his eyes closed, and when I had finished my rambling he would, after a short silence, quietly paraphrase what I had just said in a few well-organised sentences. He certainly possessed all the essential qualities for editing China's new encyclopaedia, I thought.

Listening to Uncle Jiang I was constantly amazed and not a little ashamed at how little I knew about my parents. I was curious to know whether they had known that Uncle Jiang had been an underground Communist. 'No,' he replied. 'Your mother was certainly unaware, but I think your father must have had a pretty good idea, especially towards Liberation, when I often had to hide myself backstage.' I am sure that Mother's politics left much to be desired in Uncle Jiang's books; yet in all his stories he invariably revealed more than a touch of admiration for her unconventionality and daring.

I had never known that in 1946, after the Second World War, Father had been close to making an extensive world tour, masterminded of course by Mother, which Uncle Jiang helped organise. Important foreign correspondents in Shanghai were invited to dine at our house to promote the project. 'That evening we all expected a traditional Chinese banquet, but no, your mother's way of doing things was different. She had her chef produce the most extraordinary Western cuisine,' Uncle Jiang recalled. That explained at last why Banana and Mao Sheng from the French Embassy had been hired, and why our Chinese style dining room had suddenly been transformed with Edwardian furniture. These were all part of my mother's gift for planning ahead. In each session with Uncle Jiang, pieces of my jigsaw past fell into place.

My mother, it turned out, had decided to buy a cinema from a White Russian after the war, when inflation was rocketing and people were selling up as quickly as they could to get out of the country before the collapse of the Nationalist Government. Negotiations were conducted at Didi's, the café and nightclub where I had been inducted into Night Life at the age of thirteen. After the first meeting, Uncle Jiang was about to pay the bill when Mother stopped him. She advised him that the seller was a sharp operator and so Jiang was to let him pay all the bills. Uncle Jiang laughed as he recalled the scene. Once a price had been agreed the seller enquired as to the manner of payment proposed, since Chinese currency was worthless. 'Your mother opened her handbag,' recalled Uncle Jiang, 'and I vividly remember her taking out the biggest diamond studded brooch any of us had ever laid eyes on.' The seller's eyes opened wide when he saw the sparkling object, and the three of them trotted off to a friend of his, a German Jew who specialised in gems. 'As it turned out,' continued Uncle Jiang, 'the brooch was worth almost twice as much as the cinema!'

I remember this brooch well, three by two inches, butterfly in shape. Mother had it made from a design of her own. With the loss of all personal property during the Cultural Revolution, I wonder where that brooch is now . . .

Neither scheme, regrettably, came to anything. The political situation was too uncertain. Within three years, after all, China's system of government changed. It saddens me to think that Father never got his chance to tour the West, for even today Westerners tend to think of Peking Opera as a series of acrobatic stunts such as they see in the spectaculars, but which are not the essence of the genre. Unlike Japan's *Noh* and *Kabuki*, China's national drama has yet to be properly represented abroad.

After Liberation Uncle Jiang continued his work in the theatre, but this time his job was to unite the professionals in support of the new Communist régime. In 1952 he was assigned to Beijing, where he has lived ever since. The Great Encyclopaedia was a dream he conjured up in prison. As we spoke together, my respect and affection for him grew, precisely mirroring his feelings for my parents.

Liu Housheng, a younger man, took over from Uncle Jiang in Shanghai. I had no recollection of him from the old days, but when I met him on my return he had become General Secretary of the Theatre Association, a position of considerable power in the decision-making connected with the performing arts. In his book *Salesman in Beijing*, Arthur Miller described Liu as 'a diffident man with short cropped grey hair, wearing a much laundered Mao jacket and a gentle, rather humorous look'. Uncle Liu, as I called him according to custom, was certainly a much more cautious person than Uncle Jiang, and although he was most solicitous for my well-being while I was in China, for which

I was most grateful, he was not easy to get close to. As my father had technically been his boss he still referred to him respectfully as President. His loyalty to my father was apparent, and once in a rare moment of openness he said to me: 'The president contributed much to China, and yet not once did he ask anything of the Party.' I was very touched by his relationship with his wife, who always referred to her husband as the old man. Both of them had been sent away to do hard labour like many others, but few marriages had survived such strain so lovingly intact.

I was much taken with the colourful Jin Shan, Principal of the Academy, whom I jokingly called 'my big boss'. A star of stage and screen since the thirties, he was also a distinguished director of film and the Spoken Drama and a staunch follower of Stanislavski. When we first met his face lit up with pleasure because I looked so like my father, whose methods had been a great influence on him. He exclaimed immediately: 'I am a director and actor of the Qi school!' which pleased me no end. Jin was urbane and sophisticated; Arthur Miller, in *Chinese Encounters*, described him as 'a handsome fellow with a gaunt face and marvellously intelligent eyes.' I could also see how he got his reputation as a ladykiller. To me he appeared like a Scarlet Pimpernel who had led a dangerous double life before Liberation. Unknown to the Nationalists he had for years been an undercover agent for the Communist Party. One story told how Jin had been sent to Manchuria by the Nationalists after the Japanese surrender to take over the Japanese-built film studios. Apparently he stripped the studios of all their valuable film equipment and then managed to convince the Nationalist authorities that he had 'lost' it to the Communists. It was said that when the Nationalists fled to Taiwan he had even offered to follow in pursuit of his clandestine mission, but Premier Zhou Enlai stopped him. When we became friends I made a point of asking him whether either of these stories were true, and he simply gave me a lovely enigmatic smile.

During the Cultural Revolution he had suffered nine years in solitary confinement. Although he displayed enormous energy at his office or before guests, chatting away with ease, he was in fact a very sick man. His wife, Sun Weishi, a famous actress in her own right, had been an orphan brought up by Zhou Enlai, who sent her to be trained as a director at the Moscow Arts Theatre. While Jin was in prison she disappeared, and to this day no one knows what happened to her. It is believed that she was tortured to death. Jin said that this severe purging of him and his wife had been a direct order from Jiang Qing, whom he had once directed in a small part before she became 'empress' of China.

He had, he remembered, considered her to be of little talent. It was he who told me that on the day of the Gang of Four's arrest, before the official announcement, the wineshops were sold out, people were celebrating ecstatically in the street and in their homes, and crabs were sold in bunches of four, one female, three male.

Jin Shan's grief over the loss of his wife and inspiring fellow-worker had been inconsolable. Since his reinstatement, however, he had married her sister, Xinshi, a wonderfully warm-hearted widow with two bright teenage daughters who looked after him. They were a comfort and consolation to one another in their loss.

Before I left Beijing Jin Shan gave me a set of large photographs of the much-praised fifties production of Chekhov's *Uncle Vanya*, in which Jin Shan played the title role under the direction of his wife. He also gave me a book, *Creating a Character*, in which he documented his subtext for the role of Uncle Vanya. From these interesting records it was possible to get an idea of the high quality of Chinese Spoken Drama productions before the Cultural Revolution.

On the day of my departure, in spite of his illness, Jin walked through Beijing's cavernous railway station to say goodbye. He made a very un-Chinese gesture, dramatically taking hold of me and hugging me for a long time. He knew we would never meet again. I heard of his death when I returned to England. He was an artist of integrity, a great man of the theatre. It was a privilege for me to have known him.

On 22nd December at 4 p.m., the Theatre Association, of which Cao Yu was president, honoured me with a reception organised by Liu Housheng at the famous Xin Qiao Restaurant for me to meet the theatre luminaries in the capital. The guests were mostly Peking Opera actors and included my father's former colleagues and disciples. It was a formal occasion and a peculiarly Chinese affair. After refreshment had been served, about thirty people sat around a large room in comfortable red velvet sofas complete with the ubiquitous doilies. Each person took turns to reminisce about the great master of Peking Opera with eloquence and suitably lofty sentiments. Then it was my turn to rise to the occasion in reply to the tribute paid to my father. My unrefined Chinese made me feel quite inadequate so I spoke English. Fortunately, Ying Ruocheng (Arthur Miller's Beijing Willy Loman, one of the stars of *The Last Emperor* and now Deputy Minister of Culture) was present and, flawless in English, he saved the day by acting as interpreter. I was equally lofty in my sentiments. I told the élite group that in the years abroad I had tried to present a good image of the four categories of people within me: a Chinese, a woman, a performer, and the daughter of a great artist. I presented the list in the appropriate order, putting actress and woman last. First was loyalty to my race (without mentioning the Fu Manchu movies, of course), to honour my father's last words to me. Then came filial piety to my parents, the prerequisite of virtue ordained by Confucius, stuff that was guaranteed to pull the heart strings of my distinguished Chinese audience. In making my speech I realised that I was beginning to behave more like a Chinese.

Dean Ruan took me to pay my respects to other of Father's surviving friends, Xia Yan, China's Fellini, a small man surrounded by his cats; and his fellow playwright and film-maker, Yang Hancheng, who greeted me sadly by saying: 'Don't let the tragedy destroy you.' Tragically, Father's greatest friend, Tian Han, the poet, playwright, essayist and critic had died, tortured to death in the Cultural Revolution. What a waste of talent, what squandering of a nation's human resources. With Zhou Yang, whom I would later meet, these men were branded The Four Villains of Literature by Jiang Qing.

Someone I was anxious to meet while I was in Beijing was Wang Kwanmei, now a widow. Her husband, the moderate President Liu Shaoqi, whose clash with Mao Zedong had unleashed the Cultural Revolution, had died in the purge. I wrote to her, assuring her that I had portrayed her with dignity in *The Subject of Struggle*, and I was invited to meet her. Thereafter we saw each other many times, either in her home or on visits to the theatre. She was a handsome woman nearing sixty, with a natural congenial charm, and she seemed to do everything with style. Although I never saw her in anything but a plain Mao suit, her white shirt was always open-necked, and her straight hair, swept back from her calm face, made her look chic. Her sitting room was modestly furnished by Western standards, with ordinary wicker chairs placed in the centre on a floor of light grey lino, and a large scroll painted with bold red flowers between the book-lined walls, which gave the room an air of elegant spaciousness. She attracted great attention at the theatre and in the interval when we withdrew into a special sitting room she was immediately surrounded by people. Unavoidably, many were only sycophants, but although she was the widow of China's former president she no longer had any real political clout and I am inclined to think that her popularity had much to do with her own charisma.

It was not hard to believe the suggestions of the China watchers that the ideological differences between her and Jiang Qing in support of their respective husbands were based on strong personal rivalries. The jealousy, I would guess, came principally from Jiang. The two women had both married, in their twenties, leaders of China who were much older than themselves. In background they were worlds apart. Jiang Qing, a virtual waif in her youth, had to struggle hard to achieve a moderate success as an actress, a dubious reputation to possess, anywhere in the world. And when she became the Chairman's wife she had to fight for recognition as a politician in her own right. In the thirties Jiang played Nora in Ibsen's *A Doll's House*. So now we know what one Nora did after walking out of her front door before the final curtain: she became 'empress' of China. But the suffering she inflicted is hardly a healthy example for the feminist cause. A great pity.

Wang Kwanmei, on the other hand, came from a secure home, with a father who was a Tientsin industrialist. She was sent to the best schools and completed her studies at the American sponsored Yenching University in Beijing. I had never met Jiang Qing, but in photographs taken of her at the peak of her political career, she did not project the image of a happy woman. Her once pretty face looked permanently angry and bitter. Wang Kwanmei had kept her attractiveness despite the terrible ordeals she underwent during the Cultural Revolution. With her background she could easily have pursued a life of luxury in America, but she was idealistic and chose early on to be with the Communists in Yenan. After World War Two, when America briefly acted as conciliator between the Nationalists and the Communists, she was assigned as interpreter to the Foreign Affairs Department of the Party Central Committee, where she met her future husband. To judge by the courageous way she defended him throughout the agonising stages of his demise, theirs was a good marriage. She emerged from it as a woman of strength and dignity.

I suspected Wang Kwanmei's English was excellent but I never got the opportunity to find out. When I asked her a question in English she would invariably answer me in Chinese. I don't know why she did this. Perhaps she thought her English was too rusty, having been forbidden to speak it for a decade. Or perhaps she had a conditioned reflex of self protection from the days of the purge, when even her name, Kwanmei, meaning Bright-beautiful, or America, was picked up on by her tormentors. We never discussed the Cultural Revolution.

As a memento she gave me a photo she had taken of her husband and their youngest daughter, who was then a little girl. It showed them in profile, heads touching, and smiling mischievously at each other. She had managed to avoid the wooden pose so characteristic of Chinese photographs and captured a playful moment in happier days.

25

The Tempest

ᵉ

I visited the theatre at every opportunity. I was starved for Chinese theatre, and I was curious to see how well the professionals were responding to the new climate of openness. In all I took in well over fifty plays during my stay in China, both in traditional and modern genres. The revival of Chinese theatre was little short of miraculous.

Spartan by Western standards, the theatres I sat in took me back to my childhood. After a Cromwellian deprivation of entertainment the audiences were flocking to the theatres. But the young generation were conspicuously absent from traditional theatre. A poor education during the recent upheaval had deprived them of knowledge of their own history and mythology, both of which are central to classical drama. They found the themes unfamiliar and the age-old conventions incomprehensible. They much preferred the Spoken Drama.

As I write, in 1987, Chinese theatre is going through a crisis. The older generation is dying off, or staying at home to watch TV. The younger ones are interested in discos and don't watch even Spoken Drama unless it is something particularly interesting. But I believe that the disco craze is temporary, and that when the young tire of superficial pleasures they will return to the theatre. For that reason it is vital to maintain standards through the lean years.

Yet watching traditional plays again as an adult, I was struck for the first time by their strong reflection of the lives and yearnings of my people. Calamity, injustice and revenge were the frequent themes which figured strongly in recent experience. Many plays ended with a court scene, where the just official – so rare in real life – made his appearance as *deus ex machina* to the absolute delight and relief of the audience. He righted all wrongs and everyone on both sides of the footlights went home contented.

With the pleasure of rediscovering the power of Chinese tragedy came the charm of comedy. But it was hard not to recall with nostalgia the golden days I had known, when great artists demonstrated their mastery of technique. As a professional I also yearned for the appearance of my father, who had a profound understanding of the inner lives of the characters he portrayed.

After a ten-year hiatus, this lack of excellence was understandable. Veteran actors who might have provided a thread of continuity had all but disappeared. The middle-aged actors had suffered ordeals that left them generally in poor health; their performances could lack energy and spirit. Their careers had been curtailed in the crucial years of their artistic development, and they recognised their shortcomings and felt despondent.

By obvious contrast the younger generation looked fresh and vital, but they were unseasoned and as yet ignorant of their proud theatrical heritage. Older actors complained that their lax attitude towards their vocation left much to be desired. It will take time for the dust of anarchy to settle, before professional etiquette and the discipline so vital to classical theatre can be instilled.

Some of the worst Western influences had become entrenched. Perhaps the most damaging of all was the use of microphones which threatened the whole art of projecting operatic voices. It appeared that insensitive and successive attempts to update Chinese traditional theatre, using Western devices without discrimination or attention to artistic truth, were having a diminishing effect on the aesthetics. Sometimes, watching a particularly unsuccessful experiment, it seemed they were throwing the baby out with the bathwater.

I was slightly disappointed, too, by some of the techniques of Spoken Drama. Even in naturalistic plays, Chinese actors tend to hide behind a mask of make-up; especially when playing Westerners, their enthusiasm for powder and blond wigs knows no bounds. It was bizarre to endure the sight of Chinese mimicking Westerners, for I had spent so much of my life unhappily watching Western actors stereotype the Chinese.

Perhaps some of the most unsatisfactory performances were portrayals of great national figures. I sat one evening next to a man who seemed oddly familiar. He was, it transpired, a retired actor, whose glory had been to play Chairman Mao on stage. The resemblance was uncanny. In the fifties, he told me, he had known three other actors who specialised in playing other leaders: Premier Zhou Enlai, President Liu Shaoqi and General Lin Piao. (I shuddered to think what had become of their careers when the two last men were purged). These three men, he told me, had to live with photographs of their subjects in their homes – a constant reminder of their formidable presence. They were instructed to observe them at close hand as well, and would sit mutely nearby during Party conferences. This must have been an overwhelming experience. Perhaps that explained why the performances I saw verged on carica-ture; perceptive observation, it seemed to me, had become confused with slavish imitation.

It is always easy to criticise.

There was an enormous variation in the quality of performances. At the lowest end, the acting was old fashioned, histrionic and cliché-riddled. Male tragic roles frequently reminded me of Donald Wolfit at his worst. Young women in comedy tended to coyness, with evident audience approval. But then this is an easy way out for thespians anywhere: American audiences will always respond to cuteness and sentimentality, while in England, campness on stage invariably gets a laugh.

At the top quality end, truthful and sensitive acting was demonstrated by the cast of *Teahouse*, the famous revival production of a play by Lao She, who drowned himself in the Cultural Revolution. It was a produc-tion with the original 1950s' cast at the Beijing People's Art Theatre, and gave a strong indication of what Chinese actors can really do in modern theatre.

Some of the plays I saw in Beijing's Youth Art Theatre heartened me enormously. Microphones were not used. Both actors and audiences were young, and the plays dealt with problems close to their hearts – mainly career and marriage, a far cry from the dry ideological irrel-evance of the Model Plays. *Gold*, for example, dwelt on the trauma of unemployment and delinquency. Or again, an all-woman cast, directed by a woman, performed a play that addressed itself to the problems of marriage seen from a woman's point of view.

China has encouraged new playwrights, but the difficulties in staging a production – difficulties which in the West are usually economic ones – are still those of politics and censorship. Older writers I spoke to of restrictions smiled and said that if they were prevented from speculating about answers they had still raised the questions. This confirmed to me with some force that through the ages it has really taken tremendous courage to be a true artist in China. In the West, in this century, when an artist becomes controversial, fame and fortune may follow. In China such artists risk losing whatever privileges they were accorded, and sometimes their lives. However, compared to their former lack of artistic control, their present situation represented an improvement. Patience is a virtue even I had begun to acquire in China. This was the country's third gift to me.

The younger writers were not as patient, however. After the ordeals of the Cultural Revolution they were determined to write about things as they really saw them. Many found the criticism and corrections of their work by the authorities so frustrating that they abandoned writing drama and took to writing novels instead. I asked whether this was a freer medium, and they told me that it took an official time and effort to read a long novel while going to see a play only required two hours. A group of very talented young writers have been waging a continuous battle for 'The Freedom To Create': I look on their efforts with admiration, and upon their existence as a encouraging sign of things to come under the present government.

China was first introduced to the works of Shakespeare at the turn of the century in loose adaptations, but by the forties the dedicated but impoverished scholar Zhu Shenghao had faithfully translated his complete oeuvre. Prior to my arrival in Beijing, no fewer than five Shakespearean productions had been staged since the Cultural Revolution, including *Measure For Measure* by the company of the Beijing People's Art Theatre, directed by Britain's Toby Robertson. In Shanghai, a remarkable production of *Romeo and Juliet* had been staged at the Drama Academy by an all-Tibetan class.

Shakespeare is by no means unfamiliar to the educated Chinese. Naturally they believe that most Britons know his poetry by heart and can quote it at length. It seemed a strong reason for choosing *The Tempest* in November as a vehicle to practise everything we had explored during our two-month workshop. It would be the premiere production of *The Tempest* in China. It would also be the students' first public performance.

I invited Teacher Liang Bolong, my worthy assistant in class, to be my assistant director. His command of his own language meant that we could work over Zhu Shenghao's scholarly text, making minor cuts and alterations to make it more accessible. The Academy approved of the play, which they hoped would 'expose the students to more culture'. There were thirty-one students to cast, always a problem for directors in drama school, and there were enough supernumaries in the play to give everyone something to do. Apart from Prospero, the characters could be understood by young actors fairly easily. In some ways the play can be compared to a Peking Opera. Comic and tragic scenes are juxtaposed; Miranda and Ferdinand, the two lovers, conform to Chinese ideals of love: chastity, purity and marriage with parental consent. I hoped, too, that the strong themes of calamity, injustice and revenge would find an echo in a Chinese audience, who could be expected to understand the lesson of forgiveness and redemption which the years after the Cultural Revolution have taught. In that sense, I thought that the play might help me come to terms with personal tragedy.

'You aren't going to make Caliban a monster, are you?' I was asked by the head of Dramatic Literature, the Shakespeare scholar Sun Jiaxiu, at our first faculty meeting to discuss the production. The Chinese like to see Caliban as a victim of colonialism – a theory which I myself respected, having grown up in semi-colonial Shanghai. I have had a soft spot for Caliban since I first read the play when I was young, even though I understood little of it at the time. I assured the Academy that I had no intention of making Caliban an object of opprobrium. The same argument, however, meant that my original idea of putting the cast in Chinese costume was vetoed: it would have implied that the Chinese were colonisers.

It was my turn to have objections at the first production meeting with the set and costume designers. They were eager to see the BBC television production on a tape lent by the British Embassy. I insisted they work without preconceived ideas. I also turned down the Academy's suggestion that we invite well-known composers and choreographers from outside, and requested only the assistance of the academy's own music and dance department. Whatever we would achieve would be a joint effort, created from the resources available.

The only 'resource' we could not afford to be without was an actor of the calibre required to take on the complex role of Prospero. Without Huang Dingyu in the class, I should have chosen another play. Not only was I impressed by his natural talent and intuitive intelligence, but he happened also to be better educated than the rest and had a strong sense of professional discipline. It was attributes like these, I thought, that would enable a young man to take the part of a mature man in a play.

Caliban, the antagonist, was to be played by Du Yuan, a rugged youth who would be sure-fire star material in the West. He was to do not so badly in China, either (he is the star of *Wild Mountains*, which came to the London Film Festival in 1986). I noticed him on the first day of class, because he challenged me a number of times. He was not afraid to think for himself and he made a perfect rebel.

Yang Qing, with her bright eyes, fine teeth and endless legs looked a proper Chinese Farah Fawcett: though I found to my surprise that her kind of looks were not considered particularly attractive in China. I cast her as Ariel, and she proved an intelligent and hardworking actress who possessed the most exciting talent among the women. I was sure she would go far (and she has).

The real beauty, with flawless skin and the ideal 'melon-seed' shaped face, I cast as Miranda, Prospero's fifteen-year-old daughter, but it was really Wu Dan's quality of natural innocence that attracted me. I hated the idea of having a young actor play Prospero as a doddering old man, so I wanted the juvenile leads to be as young as possible. I gave the youngest boy in the class the role of Ferdinand.

Chinese theatre is rich in comic traditions, and the casting of the two clowns, Trinculo and Stephano, played by Zhao Sen and Liu Boming respectively, presented little difficulty. I had only the problem of discipline to contend with, because Trinculo was so inventive he was hard put to repeat the same actions twice!

The unhappy moment came when the cast list was read out. Students who got small parts became incredibly upset because taking a minor role could mean that they would be assigned to a minor theatre company. For life. I too was miserable but powerless to do anything about it. It was a crying shame, for the growth of an actor is unpredictable; a poor assignment could lead to apathy in an actor who feels that he is stuck in the same place whether he improves his craft or not. For what it was worth, I received an assurance from a high ranking cadre that the rigid assignment policy would be changed in the near future.

From the first day of rehearsal the honeymoon was over. A more real and deeper relationship with my students began to develop, shattering many of my preconceptions. I had imagined my students to be docile like sheep, and probably dull, especially in contrast with the extroverted American students I had taught. But the 'Confucian' China of rigidity and conformity is not the whole picture. China has also produced the opposing philosophy of Taoism, which lays a non-conformist stress upon individual action. And the older students, it had to be remembered, may have had experience of being a Red Guard. Whether they actually participated in the disorder I do not know (naturally no one would admit to it now), but their generation had seen much violence against establishment targets, and beating up teachers was a recent memory.

I noticed an air of open defiance amongst young people generally, quite different from my youth. They projected an attitude of not being easily taken in by what authority cared to dish out to them. On the whole I saw this as a healthy phenomenon. My concern with my students was to teach them the value of professional discipline. They were hardly putty in my hands, but they got as good as they gave. I was out to challenge them.

I felt that they had had enough theory and to the surprise of all concerned I did not sit down and endlessly discuss the play. I did not allow anyone to jot down so much as a single word on paper throughout the rehearsal period. I looked for practical improvisational work. We acted out the characters' histories and various off-stage occurrences to familiarise them with the content. They learned their lines gradually rather than by rote. We began working from a Western approach, inside out, so that the actors could experience rather than intellectualise. Ferdinand, for example, was ordered by Prospero to carry chairs up and down the large rehearsal hall, just as he would be made to carry logs in the play. At first he thought it was all a bit of a joke, but after a long while, tired and perspiring, he began to feel real anger. Later the students told me that such emotional recall helped them in performance.

Directing Chinese actors for the first time in a Western classic was a great opportunity for me to experiment with synthesising the two approaches to acting embodied in Eastern and Western traditions respectively. Eastern classical acting had remained very stylised, with emphasis on form, an outside-in approach, while Western tradition now concentrates on motivation and emotional content in characterisation, using a natural free-form style.

Once my students were accustomed to reacting spontaneously and moving freely under impulses arising from the situation, they became frustrated when I began blocking them – arranging and setting their movements around the stage. In this second phase of rehearsal, every vocal expression and physical movement, down to the smallest gesture, had to be specific, and I stopped them each time they slipped into general acting. Their old habits of histrionic self-indulgence died hard, but eventually they came to realise that the restraints forced them to dig further for internal motivation.

For the same reasons I kept the production itself very simple. Set and costume were pared down to a minimum. The set consisted of two rocks, so that the students would not have to compete with the elaborate decorative sets the Chinese are so fond of painting. They wore plain tunics and trousers, except for Miranda, the only mortal woman in the play, who wore a long dress. I borrowed the colour symbolism of Peking Opera to denote status and character – yellow for royalty, red for marriage, and so on. While the spirits wore stylised make-up and the two clowns were tricked out in a mixture of Western and Chinese clown make-up, all the other characters were natural-looking. Since Miranda looked fifteen, her father Prospero could be in his thirties. Therefore, no paraphernalia like wigs, blond, white or brunette, nor even a false moustache for any of the actors.

The worst confrontation came in the dress rehearsal, when the male actors wanted to put on their usual heavy rouge and thick eyebrows, which looked merely grotesque to my Western trained eyes. I eventually made up a man and a woman 'naturally' and challenged them to tell me which make-up, theirs or mine, looked like a human face. It was their will against mine.

In December, by way of a reward for all our hard work, the Dean permitted us to conduct our last rehearsal in the open air. This was another experiment of mine. Inspired by Peking Opera voice training in the open air, I hoped that by stretching their voices to the limit over an open space, my students would rediscover the sensuousness of using their voices in the confined space of the theatre later. Two coach loads, including some of the observers, arrived at Tian Tai, the grand alabaster altar where for centuries China's emperors had worshipped heaven. The weather was bitterly cold, and I wonder how much my students actually enjoyed the experience, but we made 'a happening'. Passers-by stopped and stood in the freezing cold listening with rapt attention to the poetry of Shakespeare in Chinese!

The old Faculty theatre had been burned down in the sixties, and the new one was still under construction, but through the relentless efforts of Dean Ruan we were permitted to perform in the best little theatre in the city. It belonged to the army and seated 500, the perfect size for my students confidently to project their voices without the assistance of the microphone.

ℯ

The first night of *The Tempest* on 12th January 1982 was an unexpectedly grand affair. Sir Percy Cradock, the British Ambassador, attended with Keith Hunter from the British Council. To my great surprise a number of high-ranking Chinese politicians were also present – though I did not know who they were and therefore did not feel nervous or intimidated. The only man I recognised was Zhou Yang, once the head of the Department of Propaganda, a powerful machine controlling the arts. (Jiang Qing had branded him as one of the 'Four Villains of Literature'.) A tall, imposing man in his late sixties, Zhou Yang and I were left alone for a few moments to talk before the performance began. He looked at me with his troubled and piercing dark eyes, coming straight to the point. 'It was I who got your father into trouble,' he said. 'I persuaded him to write the play about Hai Rui.'

I was touched by his remorse. He had suffered horribly himself in those years. 'No,' I replied, 'whatever my father may have written, they would have sought to destroy him.'

Because of my father's prestige, my debut as a director in China became an important occasion attended by my father's peers. If there is a heaven, I hope my parents looked down with a smile.

I kept my promise to the Faculty. The final image seen by the audience was that of Caliban unfolding himself to stand like a proud man on the rock where Prospero had stood at the beginning of the play.

Criticism of my production was not voiced within my hearing. I know some missed the strong story line of a Chinese play. Some appreciated my use of Peking Opera conventions, but some failed to notice. Many commented on the fresh approach, delighted by the naturalness of the voices and make-up, by the economy of acting and movement and the uncluttered set. They called the production *shu fu*, comfortable, and I was gratified by the judgement of Professor Chong Daoming, one of the two critics respected for employing artistic rather than political criteria. He called it *min-zu hua*, which loosely translated means Chinese in spirit, without, he added, sacrificing Shakespeare's intentions. I was delighted to overhear someone say that if only everyone behaved like Prospero there would not have been a Cultural Revolution. Perhaps I was most gratified by my students' reaction to the long-awaited showing of the BBC production. They viewed the film with a new found confidence, and I heard Trinculo remark cheekily that he preferred his own interpretation!

Privately I wondered whether I had lived up to my own expectations and those of the people who had invited me. I did think that I had at least fulfilled my role as a bridge between two cultures in a practical sense. I had managed to bring Keith Hunter of the British Council and Dean Ruan Ruoshan together to pave the way for more British teachers to come to China. A year later, Cicely Berry, Voice Director of the Royal Shakespeare Company, and Kenneth Rea, Movement teacher at the Guildhall Drama School, spent time at the Drama Faculty.

In the final analysis, I think it is for my students to judge what other contributions I made. I could only appraise the merits of my trip through the personal satisfaction I gained on an emotional level. I was not unaware that my qualifications received support from my father's reputation. My father's pre-eminence would have been hard to live down, even had I wanted to. My mother's aspirations for me meant inevitably that I would take him for a model, and I understand the sense of inadequacy that is the curse of all children of successful parents. Father has become the fountain of my inspiration as well as the source of my anxiety and despair – a contradiction that I shall have to reconcile for as long as I live.

I could only take pride in isolated moments. On the last night I watched my students from the wings, as I had watched my father countless times in my childhood. For that moment I was moved by the thought of being my parents' daughter, directing a Western play in China, and in that fleeting moment I felt as never before that my life was complete.

My contacts with students during the term had been on a strictly professional level, conducted before a roomful of observers. For a week after the production I had the chance to know some of them better on a personal level. I visited their homes, and met families from different social strata. We had become closer and I wondered with much sadness whether our paths would ever cross again.

They gave me small mementoes of our time together. One was a scroll of a Tang dynasty poem, copied in beautiful calligraphy, that we had used for voice exercises. I used it because it was the very first poem taught to me by my Classics master seemingly hundreds of years ago, and now it was the only Chinese poem I could remember. One student had rushed up to me in class and said: 'Teacher Zhou, do you know that is you?'

> Leaving home young, returning old,
> My accent unchanged, my hair turning grey;
> Children see me, but do not know me.
> Smiling, they ask: 'Guest, where are you from?'

26

The Return of the Prodigal Daughter

It was the end of January. An overnight sleeper carried me away from the dry yellow plains of the north towards the populous valley of the great Yangtse, speeding me over lush green fields towards my home at last.

During the two-day journey I thought of the living, not of the dead. I thought of Big Big Sister, Teacher Ding, tall Billy, Fu Sheng and Mao Sheng. These five people were the only dear ones from my childhood left here to me now. I mused on the Tang poem. If my hair was grey, theirs would be white by now. I wondered how my two former servants would address me when I saw them: as Third Miss, perhaps, or as Comrade?

I had taken the train instead of the plane because I needed time to collect myself. It was another self-imposed delay, another reprieve from the emotional confrontations ahead. Just as I have forgotten who saw me off from Shanghai station all those years before, so I now cannot recollect who was there to meet me. I know only how, when I first saw Teacher Ding, her open, gentle face unlined, her hair not white but turning grey, I felt that nothing had changed, and a sense of life's continuity thrilled through my body, as though time had not been severed, as though my parents were there behind her, as though life had not been so cruel after all.

I put up at the Jing Jiang Hotel, China's Savoy. A former residence of the rich before Liberation, this was the very place where I chased Japanese children with my rich little friends, doing my bit for the anti-Japanese war effort.

News of my homecoming travelled fast. Before I had unpacked, my former chauffeur was sitting opposite me in my hotel room. His solid and quiet presence, representing all that was simple and permanent before life became so complex and uncertain, renewed my sense of security.

'Do you remember, Fu Sheng,' I began almost immediately, 'how you used to run alongside us children when we were learning to ride bicycles?' He remembered more clearly than I did. We had been better known to him than his own children, and we saw more of him than of our own father.

But had I at that moment expressed my gratitude for his service and sacrifice in words, I knew that this man of humble birth would feel deeply embarrassed. I should not be so demonstrative with my feelings as I once was as a little girl. Such implicit sentiments were best left alone; a grown woman should know better.

Ah Zhu, our cook, had died. She had put herself out to be kind to Mother to the last, at some personal risk. But Mao Sheng, the male cook, soon joined us. He hadn't changed. Always his own man, he had surreptitiously visited my parents during the last desolate years of their house arrest. In the love and loyalty they showed my family Ah Zhu and Mao Sheng went far beyond the call of duty, and their incredible courage restored much of the trust I once had in the simple goodness of people.

Fu Sheng and Mao Sheng were now retired. They had long ceased being private employees, though Mao Sheng had gone to cook for the Theatre Association, of which my father was president, and Fu Sheng still drove my father as an employee of the same organisation. During the Cultural Revolution he had been demoted to doorman.

I found Mao Sheng still expounding on his beloved political theories, to which we listened attentively as usual. He often reminded me not to go out in the world and say bad things about China. Why would I do such a thing, I protested, unless with justification.

No one called me Comrade, a form of address more in fashion with the British Labour Party in the sixties than in China in the liberal eighties. But I was addressed differently by my former servants. I had become 'Third Little Sister', which I found endearing. However, I could not keep from smiling when Fu Sheng slipped into his old habit of calling me 'Third Miss'.

Only a few weeks ago in Beijing, I was asked by Sir Denis Foreman, Chairman of Granada Television, on his first visit to China, with producer Derek Granger, to differentiate between the two great cities of

China. 'Look,' I said with a rather grand sweep of my hand, 'Beijing is Washington and Shanghai is New York.' Sir Denis got the point.

It was January, bleak and cold, the worst month of the year; the city looked awful. In Beijing, the capital city, old and new monuments commanded respect and dignity, symbols of power. In Shanghai, the unwalled houses exposed themselves in all their dilapidation for all to see, obscured only by the washing hanging outside almost every window. To judge by appearances it was hard to credit this city as the commercial and artistic centre of China, processing a third of her exports – the bulk of her foreign revenue. But then, the city had been the headquarters of the Gang of Four and it was obviously recovering from shock.

If my home city looked depressed, I hadn't reckoned on the energetic inhabitants. Behind unsightly façades lived the irrepressible Shanghainese! They were as animated and alert and optimistic as ever. A sense of freedom was in the air and with the recent policy of economic liberalisation, the Shanghainese were fully expecting life's opportunities to come knocking.

My first duty was to sweep my parents' graves. But they had no graves, because of the introduction of cremation. As a patriot, my father's ashes belonged to the nation. His urn has been enshrined in Shanghai's Long Hua Revolutionary cemetery since 1978, when he was posthumously reinstated. My mother's ashes had come out of China with William when he emigrated to the States, and it makes me sad to think of my parents' remains being so far apart. I was given to understand that at the time of my father's death, some kind soul mingled their ashes together. Arrangements were made for me to visit the Long Hua cemetery on the outskirts of the city. Teacher Ding accompanied me with two of my father's friends.

It was a big, silent place. At the entrance stood a huge stone, on which were cut the words of Chairman Mao: 'To die for the benefit of the people carries more weight than Taishan.' (Taishan is China's most sacred mountain). As I passed it I could not help but think of my parents' suffering and death during the Cultural Revolution. Had their sacrifices benefited the Chinese people? Perhaps, if the lessons of the cataclysm had given others a better, freer life.

The four of us walked sombrely down the long concrete pathways lined with tall evergreens that led to the plain buildings where the ashes of hundreds of patriots were interred. Inside one of these halls I saw glass cabinets lining the walls like bookshelves. I was led to my father's shelf, and found a photograph of my father propped up against an urn draped in red. I was comforted by the fact that he had come to rest among friends.

At last I was able to pay my respects to my father in person. It was a public moment to express a very private grief. I did not want to cry but my body began to shake. I had a short poem with me, written in English, telling him that I had come to see him and Mother, a meagre offering from a prodigal daughter. I slid open the glass door and placed it beside his photograph. By this simple action I was able to stop myself trembling. I touched his photograph before sliding back the glass. Then I bowed deeply three times. That was all. Throughout this brief ceremony I could hear a woman crying her heart out for her lost one in the next chamber. She wept for me, too.

Thus I began my small, personal odyssey to people and places remembered from my youth; but the rivers of life had flowed on without me, and much had disappeared. In Beijing I had received a barrage of letters from apparent strangers claiming to be long-lost relations and past friends. They had heard of my homecoming in the newspapers. Apart from an isolated few, I barely knew who they were. It was an awkward situation and the price to pay for abandoning one's roots.

I was really only eager to see the people who had figured large in my childhood, for my stay in Shanghai would be short and I was exhausted from the punishing schedule of work in Beijing. Big Big Sister was the sole survivor of my close relatives to witness the day of my return. Teacher Ding and I visited her in her garret room. She was in her seventies, and looked her age, but her health was good and she seemed contented with her lot. She had relatives living in the same house, and the room she occupied was large by normal standards. And she had it all to herself. She laughed and cried at the same time when she saw me again. 'Never did I dream of seeing this day,' she kept repeating in her strong Shaoxing accent. 'Now I can die happy.' Speaking of death reminded her of her aunt and she began to weep. 'Your mother lived for your father and in the end she died for him . . .' I wiped the tears from her eyes with her handkerchief, but I did not cry myself. I did not want to talk about my mother.

Big Big Sister was still a spinster, but Liberation, I learned, had boosted her self-reliance. For the first time she had been able to go out to work, as a minder in a kindergarten where she had enjoyed independence, and found self respect. Now retired, she spoke proudly of her well-deserved old-age pension.

Teacher Ding, by contrast, had been independent before the revolution and dedicated her work to the New China. She had become a veteran cadre of the Communist Party, and worked as assistant manager in a small hospital. Faithful to her ideals and her hopes for the new China, she had lost her husband in the sixties purges, yet she showed no signs of bitterness. He had died, leaving her two grown-up and loving daughters. Soon she would retire.

Only once did she betray her grief. Chen Yi, head of the Ministry of Propaganda in Shanghai, invited us to a dinner in my honour, and the party of twelve were in good spirits, relaxed, talking of one another's families. Chen explained that William and I, having followed in our father's footsteps, were the prince and princess of China's royal theatrical heritage. The company was charming, and when someone turned pleasantly to Teacher Ding and enquired after her husband, the thought of his death caught her unawares and her eyes sparkled with tears. She immediately suppressed her feelings. Everyone that evening had lost a loved one in the Cultural Revolution; I felt that I, too, must control my emotions.

I was eager to meet Billy Zhou again, my grown-up childhood friend who had taken me to my first nightclub, Didi's. He did not appear at my hotel, and I set out to find him. All private phones had been cut during the Cultural Revolution, so I took a taxi to his old address. I understood why he did not come to see me: he did not want me to think that he had any ulterior motive. When the Open Door policy brought the first friends and relations back from abroad, the excitement was incredible. The overseas Chinese felt guilty about the sufferings of those they had left behind, and they naturally wanted to compensate somehow. So they brought with them television sets and stereos, suitcases of Western clothes and other consumer goods. In many cases this created an uneasiness between the donor and the recipients. The Shanghainese wickedly called it 'stripping the pig', and the pig in question was the eager beaver from abroad who went home uncertain whether he would be welcome for his largesse, or for himself. Some had spent thousands of dollars on presents and were fearful of returning because they could not afford another trip. In these circumstances many real friends like Billy stayed away for fear of being misunderstood. He needn't have worried. I had very little to give away.

'Wow,' I said to Billy when I found him at home with his wife, 'you do look smart.' Although his wife, wearing plain Chinese clothes, looked less like Barbara Stanwyck, Billy looked like a million dollars. He was immaculately dressed in a tailored Western suit. 'We were lucky,' he explained. 'For some reason the Red Guards missed searching our house, so I can wear my old clothes again.' His suit was made in the forties – the style back in fashion today. He looked like a mature model for Armani suits. His full head of hair was snowy white, but apart from a slight stoop he was elegant and tall as ever.

I looked over his flat and saw that his furniture was still intact. 'We were really lucky,' he agreed, sensing my thoughts. 'Because they didn't search the house my property was not confiscated. I only got beaten once, when they took me off to interrogate me about your family.' His tone was so matter-of-fact that I had to smile with bitterness.

Sooner or later I would have to face the house in Changle Road, where I had spent the happiest three years of my youth before leaving China. Unlike Billy's home, our house had been completely ransacked. And I learned that many of the things which had been confiscated, far from having been shared out to the needy as I had once supposed, had in fact been stored haphazardly in vast warehouses for those in a position of privilege to pick over. Technically these belongings were restored to their former owners, but it would be impossible to trace them now.

I was returning to my former home which had been so full of happy memories and was now robbed of all loving people, all familiar objects. It was the visit I most dreaded. Finally Billy accompanied me.

The house was in a sorry state, and full of strangers. An office had occupied it after the outbreak of the Cultural Revolution, though I had no idea whether these were the same people who now greeted me with such politeness. I did not want to find out. Many organisations affiliated with ultra-left militants were being slowly disbanded, and these strangers would soon be moving out.

I went through all the rooms, but I hardly noticed a thing. I was seized by an urge to escape, to run away from all this, from the dirty toilets and peeling walls, from the apathy bred by a repressive régime. I could understand the want of money, but I hated to see that no one could be bothered to keep the toilets clean.

Over the years since leaving home, how many times had I walked through empty houses in my recurring dreams? The houses were never like this house, and somewhere beyond I heard the voices of my parents.

Now the voices were silent. And I was the ghost, wandering through the shell of a house.

When I reached the door to my father's study at the back of the house I stopped. This was where I had last seen him. This was his beloved sanctuary, which later became his prison. For the remainder of their lives, my parents were kept in this room, newspaper pasted over the window-panes to replace the shattered glass, and forbidden a stove in the freezing Shanghai winters. They would wake each morning with frost on their lips. They survived the cold only because of that one good soul, the Red Guard, who had thrown them a bundle of warm clothing.

My brother William had had the room locked before he left for America. When it was opened for me I found the room clean and empty but for a desk and chair. The glass was back in the windows and one enormous photograph of my father on the wall dominated the room. There was nothing of Mother.

I needed desperately to be alone. Privacy being unknown in China, the stranger showing me around solicitously followed me into the room, with Billy trailing behind. I made a special point of excusing myself, before locking them out of the room. Alone at last, I sat on the only chair, facing the photo of my father. I decided that this was the moment to have a good cry. But no tears came. Years of drought cannot release the downpour automatically.

Without fully realising what I was doing, I fell on my knees. I found myself performing the ancient ritual of abasement and respect for my elders, which until then I did not believe in. I thought that they had been right to ban it after Liberation. I kowtowed to my father's portrait, and to his *nei ren*, his inner person, my mother. Three times. Each time my head touched the floor, I felt a sense of absolution.

Unexpectedly, later, an intense but silent rage possessed me. It was at a reception arranged by the Shanghai Theatre Association, of which my father was once president, for me to meet his friends and colleagues in Shanghai. Uncle Liu himself came down from Beijing to officiate. The older actors again sang his praises: this was, I realised by now, also a eulogy for the great days of classical theatre. About fifty people gathered that afternoon in the main hall of the Shanghai Theatre Association, the former mansion of an Englishman. Many people sat with me around a long table. After a short round of cheerful introductory speeches we waited for the first person to talk about his work with the grand master. A veteran actor in his seventies began to speak. Almost immediately I sensed a change of mood in the room.

The speaker was a very fine and renowned actor, one of those who form the backbone of any theatrical institution. I recognised him as Father's regular partner. Their collaboration on stage went back to the late twenties. I was told that during the Cultural Revolution, this colleague and friend of Father's did not behave honourably towards him. But since I had heard so many stories of betrayal from those recent terrible days, often conflicting and hard to take in, I had decided, more for my own emotional equilibrium than anything else, to judge nobody but to treat them as I found them.

The actor began to speak. From the start, everyone in the room could see that he was having difficulty getting his words out. The mood grew increasingly tense, even hostile, as we waited. Finally his feeling of remorse overwhelmed him and he broke down completely, sobbing uncontrollably. It was painful to watch him, and I averted my eyes from the sight of his guilt and humiliation. Looking across to the mirror opposite, I caught sight of a tortured face and was shocked to discover that it was my own. Only then was I conscious that the muscles below my cheekbones felt like stones. But my feeling was compassion, not hatred.

It was rage, too, about life. Suddenly this incident brought home to me the full weight of the millions of large and small cruelties of the Cultural Revolution. I plucked up the courage to look at the actor again, and the anger blazed afresh. Had the Cultural Revolution never happened, my parents, being healthy, might still be alive, and this broken old man could have lived out his life in peace, with grace, as an old man should, in the pride of his artistic achievements and in the joy of friendship with my father whom he obviously loved so deeply.

Perhaps the most forceful rage was directed against myself. For I, too, was consumed by guilt. Neither Father, nor Mother, nor my brother or his wife were ever persuaded to denounce anyone. But one vital question haunts me still. How would I have conducted myself, in their position?

Tears came at last, but elsewhere, at the home of the senator and former actress, Yuan Xuefen, a devotee of my father's art.

'The last time I saw the president was in one of the struggling sessions,' she recalled. 'We were both main targets.'

She paused. 'Your father had become totally blind by this time,' she continued at length. 'Somehow we were left alone at lunchtime . . .' For a second I wanted to laugh: trust the Chinese always to break for lunch.

'I shoved a piece of old bread into your father's hand,' she went on. 'As he could not see, he asked who I was. When he heard my voice, he held my hands tight for a second . . .' My concentration wandered and I could not bear to hear any more. The image of a blind old man being pushed around and manhandled was hard to block out. Tears, uninvited tears began to flow. I made no sound. As the tears continuously flowed down my face, I wiped them away with the palms of my hands.

<p>

Everywhere I went the ordinary people treated me with especial kindness when they learned that Zhou Xinfang's third daughter had returned. My sentimental journey was inevitably filled with bitter-sweet memories. Setting the clock back was like being Alice in Wonderland. The rooms in the house where I lived as a little girl had shrunk, which was to be expected. A nice professor now lived with his family in my old bedroom at the back, from whose window I had once watched with fascination the infamous prostitute across the way. He kindly invited me into his crammed room and gave me tea. Across the street on the main road I saw happy children at play in my former primary school which seemed less bleak than I remembered it. A few miles away, McTyeire High School, now a co-ed, with its imposing buildings and neat lawns, remained as impressive as always. But sadly, in parts of the various theatres where my parents worked, Father's familiar dressing rooms and Mother's offices had changed forever. My pilgrimage to the restaurant where my parents married evoked no special image, because I had not been invited to their wedding. But I could see that it had not changed. The art deco dais where they had stood together to exchange their marriage vows remained miraculously intact, in spite of the recent violence – like my parents' love for each other to the bitter end.

I was eager to visit The Great World, the once notorious sin palace for Chinese men, out of bounds to me during childhood. Sun Chufen, a friend Cecilia had made after my departure, was a writer, and it was he who accompanied me there. This was no longer out of bounds – but then there was very little to see! It was now a youth centre, and while Chufen gave a lecture to hopeful young writers, a very pretty girl showed me around the cavernous interior, up and down zigzag staircases and a maze of corridors leading to rooms on complicated levels. It was hard to imagine the seedy colour of the past. In this respect, times had changed for the better.

'All right, let's go to your homes right now!' I announced to Fu Sheng and Mao Sheng, when our little group were sitting around in my hotel room. They both lived in the countryside of Pudong, and they had wanted me to visit their families across the river. On purpose I gave them no warning, knowing full well that if I had both families would have gone through endless trouble and expense to welcome me.

Big Big Sister did not come with us, but Chufen did. Six of us piled into two taxis for the hour long journey. City-bred, I had almost never been to a Chinese farm. Along the way I saw people working in the fields, mostly women. Once or twice we stopped and I talked to them. They were very cheerful and the rural scene seemed idyllic to me, riding in a taxi.

Farmers, it appeared, were doing well from the abolition of the communes formed in the 1950s. They could keep their surplus after fulfilling the government quota, so they had an incentive to work hard. They were, in fact, China's new rich: the poorest were the ordinary educated people who received only a fixed salary.

Fu Sheng was a good example. With his large family spanning three generations he had hands enough to work the land, and their pooled income was considerable. They would be building not one but two houses, next to one another, similar to the new houses I saw dotted about the countryside, with two storeys and a verandah but no toilet, built out of breeze blocks. Fu Sheng's old house was a traditional single-storey building with sweeping roofs around a courtyard. 'You aren't going to knock that down?' I asked in horror. But Fu Sheng had no time for romantic notions. The old quarters had been dark and inconvenient. When he had amassed enough bricks and building materials the whole village would turn out and help him build the house in no time at all.

Mao Sheng still lived in an old house set around a square courtyard. I waxed ecstatic over his four-poster bed, an heirloom passed down for many generations. I delighted in putting an incongruous Western value on their properties: do you know how much your bed would fetch in antique shops in Chelsea?

The month passed quickly. Often we talked into the small hours, laughing helplessly about some long-forgotten incident. I teased Teacher Ding about being her least favourite pupil and she admitted that I had been a handful, generously adding that she had perhaps been too young herself to appreciate a hyperactive child. They gave me wonderful stories about my parents in the old days, and their love for them warmed and moved me. Sometimes they talked about the bad days of the Cultural Revolution, but as they recounted horrible incidents concerning my parents, particularly my mother, they would sometimes stop in mid sentence. Our sadness spoke for itself. Being together was enough.

A few days before I was to leave Shanghai, I made the rounds with Teacher Ding to pay my respects to people who had been close to my father. Among them was Ba Jin, the distinguished novelist who wrote the celebrated novel, *Home*. He had read the obsequies at my father's memorial service. I was delighted to meet this sprightly old man in his eighties, who had survived the troubled years almost by a miracle, so that I could thank him in person.

'I can give you all parting gifts, but none of you may do the same,' I warned as I prepared to leave. 'What you don't realise is that you are giving me a lot of trouble. I simply don't have room in my suitcases and I can't pay for overweight luggage.' Big Big Sister was having none of it. She showered me with tins of the finest tea.

Not having been on an aeroplane, Big Big Sister's image of air travel dated from her youth, when everyone was given VIP treatment. So she was terribly disappointed to arrive to see me off at Shanghai airport, only to discover that I would have to queue to get on the plane.

Parting was not easy. The oldest were the hardest to take leave of. These were the uncertain days when the fear of another Cultural Revolution ranked uppermost in every mind. Our group huddled together for the comfort of the last few moments. They took my hands in turns, like lovers; we looked into each other's eyes, lost for words. All of us had the same thought. Will we ever meet again?

Epilogue

In March 1985 all my sisters and brothers made a return visit to China, invited to participate in a national commemoration of our father, Zhou Xinfang, on the ninetieth anniversary of his birth. For fifteen days in Shanghai a festival of his plays was performed, starring his son and successor Zhou Shaolin – my brother, William – who had by then become an American resident. (Two years later William made his first film in the West, playing a key role in *Sour Sweet*, the film of Timothy Mo's bestselling novel.)

While Zhou Xinfang's children were together, a public ceremony of remembrance for his wife – who had not yet had a funeral since her tragic death – took place at last on 5th April. For a housewife not belonging to a *danwei*, 'work unit', to be thus honoured was unprecedented. It was the women of the Shanghai Women's Association, led by Ms Zhang Weici, who organised the affair. They wanted to pay tribute to Qiu Lilin for the assistance she had rendered them during the Japanese Occupation and in the years before Liberation. They called her 'the unsung heroine'. Many devoted to Mother helped to organise the ceremony. Teacher Ding, needless to say, and also Mr Ding Jingtang, the man who owed his life to her from so many years ago, when she paid in gold to have his name struck from the Nationalist blacklist. We, her children, also put in our efforts and Cecilia, who felt least loved by her mother, worked the hardest among us.

Before the six of us were once again scattered to the four corners of the world our former chauffeur gave us a banquet in his new twin house in Putong. Three banquet tables were laid in his two living rooms, and his guests – our relatives, friends and Mao Sheng – enjoyed a feast prepared by the best local chef engaged for the occasion. Afterwards, Fu Sheng presented us each with an entire leg of the best cured ham! Unfortunately, health regulations meant that none of us could take our wonderful gifts to the West, so we shared them among our friends in Shanghai.

<p>

Renewed contact with my roots has made me more whole, more complete, but this act of completion is never-ending. Nearly another seven years have passed since my first return to the country of my birth, and in these years, with China's doors opening wider, her people are enjoying more freedom. That must be good. I go back whenever I can now, to work or just visit, and these trips encompass Hong Kong as well.

When my parents died I became conscious of my own mortality. Life has taken on a significance, a new value. I no longer suffer from depressions: they are energies lost in avoiding reality. One day I may relapse. Who knows? For I see that life is change, and the only thing that remains unchanged is change itself.

Work has become the sole purpose of my existence. I do four things which I enjoy enormously: I direct, occasionally teach, and I have begun to do some acting again; the fourth has been writing this book. Perhaps one day I should go beyond, by learning to be as well as to do.

I am often asked where I consider my home to be. I feel myself a Londoner. I feel myself a Shanghainese. Otherwise, home is where I work. I travel now not to escape but to meet the demands of life.

Writing this book has been a cathartic experience. With its completion I'd like to put the past behind me – not forgotten, but acknowledged, so that I can look forward to the future. That, I think, is the way to live with meaning in the present.

Afterword to the 1994 Edition

"Anyway, that's my thinking," says Auntie Lindo in the film *The Joy Luck Club*.

And that was my thinking in *Daughter of Shanghai*, which tells my story up to the early eighties. The book was first published in 1988 in England, where I was then living. Since that time, there have been, as I expected, enormous changes in my life.

One of the most moving themes in *The Joy Luck Club* is that of emotion—painful, clashing, but shared between mother and daughter. In the film, the young Waverly finds her mother Lindo old-fashioned, the embarrassing product of another country, another culture. For Lindo, her daughter's embarrassment is a terrible rejection, a negation of Lindo's very existence. It brings her feelings for her own mother into sharp contrast, and makes their memory all the more bittersweet.

The film has touched millions of hearts. Perhaps it's because we all share an inescapable feeling of regret or even guilt that we've taken our parents for granted. For those of us who have already lost our parents, this feeling of guilt can never be fully redeemed. I began tracing my parents' past after they were no longer living. And yet I have wondered: If my mother had lived and subsequently immigrated to the West, would we, like Lindo and Waverly, have had as many problems in our habitual association with each other? After all, apart from cultural disparities, the generation gap is a tough barrier to cross. I will never know for sure. What I do know is that both our mothers made sacrifices by letting go of their daughters at a very tender age for our own survival. I parted with my mother at sixteen so that I could go abroad to study. Had I remained in China, I now realize, I could easily have perished with her during the Cultural Revolution. As for Lindo, she was given away in marriage in the hope of a better existence. "After today," Lindo's mother tells her before their parting, "I can never give you any more advice." From then on, that advice has to last Lindo a lifetime, as I have had to hold on to my mother's words to me. "Easy to appreciate, memory," as Lindo admits, swallowing her tears.

Ironically, the chance to play Auntie Lindo came at a time when I was not particularly concerned about my acting career. *Daughter of Shanghai* was a critical and commercial success and got a lot of attention from the British press, even making it onto the morning TV news. The following year I found myself acting in the West End again in David Henry Hwang's *M Butterfly*, starring Anthony Hopkins. We were a happy company because of Anthony, and it was a great privilege working with him. He is a great actor and he is also a very good person. His simplicity and honesty reminded me of that other great artist, my father.

This was 1989—a year unforgettable for its darker side. That June, the peaceful demonstrations of the students for social reform in China caught the world's attention. We were all glued to our television sets. My own feeling of euphoria, however, was marred by an overpowering fear. I knew in my bones that if all went wrong, the students' courage would be tested to the full. As indeed it was.

The Tiananmen massacre was not an unprecedented incident. The difference, thanks to technology and mass communication, was that it had been seen on television for the first time. These young demonstrators were so brave and pure in their struggle to change the world. What would they be like, I speculated, should they someday become leaders themselves? The old party officials who sent in the tanks to crush them had once been as heroic as they, fighting for their own just causes.

The Chinese community mourned, and we sat in vigil for the students outside the Chinese Embassy. Lynn Farleigh, a leading cast member of *M Butterfly*, seeing how distraught I was, went to talk to Anthony; the result was that we gave a benefit performance in aid of Chinese students stranded in England because of what happened. Everyone, including the stagehands, gave their services free. It was held on a Sunday, allowing the theatrical community to participate as organizers or as members of the audience. At the end of the show, Anthony gave a short speech before everyone stood for a minute's silence in commemoration of the Tiananmen dead. It was very moving.

My directing work in China halted; I did not return until 1992, when I found China changing by the day. Her economy was booming, and it was good to see the Shanghainese enjoying the pleasures of material comforts for a change after half a century of deprivation—not to mention the more important and sober benefits of increased freedom of speech and better education. Whether one likes it or not, in truth, China has become a capitalist country in all but name. Was the students' demonstration foolhardy or premature, especially given the events in Russia after the demise of communism? Was the Chinese government wise in making economical reforms tentatively and in stages? Did the students' demonstrations make a difference? Had they died in vain? And what about those still incarcerated? These are agonizing questions. Yet I cannot forget their valour.

If power corrupts, then did Jiang Qing turn into a monster after she became the leader of the Cultural Revolution? She was my father's tormentor, the cause of my mother's death, and much more. Yet, in 1991, when her suicide in a Beijing jail was announced to the world, I felt an inexplicable sadness. I guess, in a sense, I had been living with her far too long. That same year, I portrayed her in a one-woman play from America called *Madame Mao's Memories* by Henry Ong. The show, performed in a fringe theater, got full media coverage; people were curious to know why I should want to play the part of the woman who had given me so much pain. For me, it was another natural part of healing, though I must confess I was not oblivious to the fact that such a role was irresistible to any actress. And there was another factor that was impossible to resist: This was my turn to have control over Jiang Qing for a change—on stage, my privilege as an actress. A *tour de force* in a minute scale admittedly, compared to her operational arena; but as an artist, it was the only weapon I had. But I was determined to be a good deal fairer in my representation of her than she ever was of my father, and in bringing her character to life I found in her victim as well as victimizer. Perhaps in a more enlightened society she could have made her position—achieved by only three women in China's history—more a beneficial than an evil thing. But fate had it differently.

It must also have been fate that brought author Amy Tan to my dressing room after a performance of *M Butterfly*, where we first met. When I read her book, I was swept into it immediately; when it came time to audition, I was asked to test for the role of another mother, but I asked to play Lindo instead. At the time, it was instinct. In hindsight, I must have sensed that out of the four mothers in the film, it was Lindo who had an innate sense of who she is, which makes her determined not to see herself as a victim under any circumstances. What's more, because Lindo is insufferable at times, her character in this emotional film provides the only moments of comic relief. Lindo was envisaged as a large woman who has rather let her looks go, which was hardly my style! But I wore many padded costumes, and anything that smacked of chic was out. As for her hairstyle, I thought I looked a bit like a Chinese Queen Elizabeth. After Lindo's visit to the beauty parlor, I looked a bit like a Chinese Margaret Thatcher! All four actresses who played the mothers in the film had to look worse for wear than we really do—all for the sake of art.

And what a fulfilling artistic effort it was too, crowned by critical *and* commercial success. For an Asian actress to act in a mainstream film with a sensitive director like Wayne Wang was a rare treat. He knew better than to let his actors resort to cliché in our interpretation of our race. When the film first came out, the buzz was that it would collect some Oscars; both Caryn James for *The New York Times* and Siskel and Ebert singled me out for a best supporting actress nomination. Alas, the film was ignored by the Academy—even the script, the joint achievement of Amy Tan and Ron Bass that remained true to the spirit of Amy Tan's novel. So there was joy but no luck where Oscars were concerned. Was I disappointed? Not much. I hoped, but I did not expect.

In any case, there have been ample rewards. Since *The Joy Luck Club* I have been offered a lot of work in Hollywood and played many different kinds of women in a variety of professions: A teacher in *Byrds of Paradise*, a cop in *Crowfoot*, a bitchy friend in *The All American Girl*, a doctor in *Chicago Hope* and, at this very moment, a fashion buyer in *Sisters*.

So there's little to complain about, and much to celebrate and enjoy. I just press on, doing my best. . . .

—Tsai Chin
August 29, 1994

Credits

STAGE

UK:
The Final Ace, Charles Fenn (New Lindsey Theatre, London)
Princess & The Swineherd, Nicholas Stuart Gray (Arts Theatre, London)
Ali Baba (Dundee Repertory Theatre, Dundee)
The World of Suzie Wong, Paul Osborn (Prince of Wales Theatre, London)
The Gimmick, Joseph Julians (Criterion Theatre, London)
The Magnolia Tree, H. W. D. Manson (Royal Lyceum, Edinburgh)
Aladdin (Gaumont Theatre, Doncaster)
The Two Mrs Carrolls, Martin Vale (UK tour)
Love for Love, William Congreve (Palace Theatre, Watford)
M. Butterfly, David Henry Hwang (Shaftesbury Theatre, London)
Madame Mao, Therese Radic (Liverpool Playhouse, Liverpool)

USA:
Fenshen, David Hare (People's Theatre, Boston)
The Oresteia, Aeschylus (Cambridge Ensemble, Boston)
The Scarlet Letter, Nathaniel Hawthorne (Cambridge Ensemble, Boston)
Puntila and Matti, Bertolt Brecht (Cambridge Ensemble, Boston)
Br'er Rabbit, Joel Chandler Harris (Cambridge Ensemble, Boston)

FILM

Yangtze Incident, dir. Michael Anderson (Rank)
The Inn of the Sixth Happiness, dir. Mark Robson (20th Century-Fox)
Violent Playground, dir. Basil Dearden (Rank)
Invasion, dir. Alan Bridges (Warner-Pathé)
The Cool Mikado, dir. Michael Winner (H. Baim Production)
Man's Fate, dir. Fred Zinnemann (Unfinished) (MGM)
The Face of Fu Man Chu, dir. Don Sharp (Warner-Pathé)
The Brides of Fu Man Chu, dir. Don Sharp (Warner-Pathé)

The Blood of Fu Man Chu, dir. Jesus Franco (Warner-Pathé)
The Mask of Fu Man Chu, dir. Jesus Franco (Warner-Pathé)
The Vengeance of Fu Man Chu, dir. Jeremy Summers (Warner-Pathé)
Blow Up, dir. Michelangelo Antonioni (MGM)
You Only Live Twice, dir. Lewis Gilbert (MGM)
The Joy Luck Club, dir. Wayne Wang (Hollywood)
The Virgin Soldiers, dir. John Dexter (Columbia)
Rentadick, dir. Jim Clark (Rank)

TELEVISION

Emergency Ward 10 (ITV)
The Man of The World (ITV)
International Detective (ITV)
Tonight (BBC)
The Defenders (CBS)
Spot The Tune (Granada)
Adam Faith Show (BBC)
Juke Box Jury (BBC)
Star Parade (TWW)
Tuesday Rendezvous (ITV)
Blue Peter (BBC)
The Late Late Show (RTE)
The Dick Haynes Show (RTE)
Byrds of Paradise (ABC)
The All American Girl (ABC)
Sisters (NBC)

That Was The Week That Was (BBC)
Five Foot Nine Show (BBC)
Call My Bluff (BBC)
Dixon Of Dock Green (BBC)
The Enemy (ITV)
The Troubleshooters (BBC)
You're On Your Own (BBC)
Late Night Line-Up (BBC)
The Eamonn Andrews Show (ITV)
Juke Box Jury (BBC)
The Subject of Struggle (Granada)
The David Frost Show (New York)
Say Brother (Boston)
Crowfoot (CBS)
Chicago Hope (CBS)
Due South (CBS)

RECORDS for Decca Label

LP: *The World of Tsai Chin*
    The Western World of Tsai Chin

Single: *The Ding Dong Song (Second Spring)*
    School in Cheltenham
    Any Old Iron
    Good Morning, Tokyo
    How Shall I do it
    The Chinese Charleston
    Button's & Bows

DIRECTING

The Lover, Harold Pinter (The Arena Theatre, Tufts University, Boston, USA)
Crime On Goat Island, Ugo Betti (The Arena Theatre, Tufts University, Boston, USA)
The Tempest, William Shakespeare (Central Academy of Drama, Beijing, China)
The Seagull, Anton Chekhov (Hong Kong Repertory Theatre, Hong Kong)
Twelfth Night, William Shakespeare (Hong Kong Repertory Theatre, Hong Kong)

Index